Group Processes

Dynamics within and between Groups

RUPERT BROWN

BLACKWELL
Oxford UK & Cambridge USA

First published 1988
Reprinted 1989, 1990, 1992, 1993

Blackwell Publishers
108 Cowley Road, Oxford, OX4 1JF, UK

238 Main Street, Suite 501,
Cambridge, MA 02142, USA

British Library Cataloguing in Publication Data

A CIP catalogue record for this book is available from the British Library.

Library of Congress Cataloging in Publication Data

Brown, Rupert, 1950–
Group processes: dynamics within and between groups/Rupert Brown.
p. cm.
Bibliography; p.
Includes index.

ISBN 0–631–14439–0 (pbk.)
1. Social groups. 2. Interpersonal relations.
3. Intergroup relations. I. Title.
HM131.B726 1988
302.3–dc19

Typeset in 11 on 12pt Times
by Colset Private Limited, Singapore
Printed in Great Britain by
Page Bros, Norwich

This book is printed on acid-free paper.

Contents

Preface

For some years now, at least in the industrialized West, groups have received rather a bad press. Football hooliganism, inner-city riots and protest demonstrations are frequently attributed to 'mob rule'; governments proclaim the virtues of individual enterprise and choice, and denigrate policies aimed at promoting social welfare and collective responsibility; newspaper editorials regularly blame industrial unrest on small groups of 'militants' coercing ordinary workers to take action against their wishes; collective bargaining is being replaced by private contract between employer and employee; the owner of a small business, battling against government bureaucracy, is championed, while a group of workers occupying a factory due for closure is ridiculed.

Within social psychology the picture is not much different. Even the most cursory survey of currently popular textbooks and the main scientific journals reveals that group processes receive very short shrift indeed compared to phenomena associated with dyadic or interpersonal relationships and – increasingly in recent years – individual cognitive processes (Steiner, 1974, 1986). Where group behaviour is discussed, considerable emphasis is often given to its negative or socially undesirable aspects – deindividuation, prejudice, social loafing and 'groupthink' – rather than the more positive aspects of team spirit, intergroup cooperation, group productivity and collective problem-solving. Indeed, such is the concentration on the allegedly antisocial nature of groups that one commentator has been moved to suggest, only half-jokingly, that 'Humans would do better without groups' (Buys, 1978).

One of my intentions in writing this book is to contribute to a reversal of this cultural and scientific bias against groups. This correction is necessary, I believe, both scientifically and politically. First because, as I hope will become evident, groups are an inescapable part of human existence. Like them or not, they simply are not going to go away. People grow up in groups, sometimes called families; they work in groups, as engine crews, design teams or hunting parties; they learn in groups; they play in groups, in a multitude of team games; they make decisions in groups, whether these be government committees, village councils or courtroom juries; and, of course, they also fight in groups, as street gangs, revolutionary cadres and national armies. In short, human beings are 'group beings'. Thus, a social psychology which ignores or neglects the study of groups is unlikely to be of much assistance in helping to understand many important areas of human endeavour.

The second reason follows from the first. It seems to me that many of today's most pressing social problems involve groups of various kinds. The control of environmental pollution demands not only nationally agreed policies on waste disposal and gas emissions but international collaboration as well; the protection of children from abuse or neglect requires the collective diagnostic skills of medical and social work professionals as well as sensitive intervention work with the families concerned; the growing threat of racism may well need a greater awareness amongst different ethnic minorities of their common oppression and the development by them of political strategies to bring about long overdue social change; and, above all, the persistence of internation conflicts around the world in an age of nuclear weaponry urgently necessitates better methods of resolving or avoiding such conflicts and underlies the importance of finding ways to abandon the arms race. In all these examples we are concerned with people's behaviour as group members, both towards those in their own group and to those belonging to other groups. It follows, then, that if social psychology is to make even the smallest contribution to the resolution of these problems it will come not from the insights derived from a psychology of the isolated individual but from the informed application of our knowledge of group processes.

Now a few words on how I have chosen to present this book. Let me straight away warn any readers looking for the exposition of a single conceptual framework that they will be disappointed. I have been deliberately eclectic in the theoretical approaches I have espoused. This is for both intellectual and pedagogic reasons. Intellectual because I have come to the conclusion, after more than a dozen years of researching into and teaching group processes, that there is no one theory that can do justice to the complexities of intra- and intergroup behaviour. To be sure, some theories are more useful than others – and in this book I have not hesitated to point up the weaknesses of those perspectives which seem theoretically ill-conceived or empirically unfounded – but ultimately it seems to me that for a half-decent explanation of most group phenomena of interest we need to draw on the strengths of two or three *different* theoretical models. This implies that for teaching purposes it is equally inappropriate to present everything from just one point of view. For while there are obvious gains in theoretical continuity and coherence from such a monopolist strategy, these are, to my mind, outweighed by the value of exposing students to a variety of competing explanations. A pluralist approach like this is more likely to encourage them to make the kind of critical choices of their own which, I believe, is a fundamental objective of the educative process.

If I have been eclectic in my choice of theories, I have been equally catholic in the range of empirical sources I have drawn on. In these pages will be found quantitative results from tightly controlled laboratory experiments and large-scale surveys, qualitative material from field interviews and participant observations, anecdotes from contemporary life and even the occasional literary allusion. Again, the pluralism is deliberate and is much influenced by the views of three of the founders of modern group psychology, Kurt Lewin, Muzafer Sherif and Henri Tajfel. Lewin was the originator of the phrase 'action research', a conception of scholarship in which theory and practice are inextricably linked. Theory, for Lewin, only had validity to the extent that it was effective in promoting social change: 'research which produces nothing but books will not suffice' (Lewin, 1948, p. 203). Sherif, too, was acutely conscious of the need to bridge the gap between academic research and social reality. As the creator of group psychology's most artificial – and yet deeply significant – laboratory experiment (Sherif, 1936; see chapter 2), and as the inspiration behind some of its classic naturalistic studies (Sherif, 1966; see chapter 7), he remains the most successful exponent of the coordinated use of field and laboratory methods. Tajfel had slightly different concerns. Ever impatient with methodological orthodoxy (he once remarked to me that an over concern with methodology was like packing your bags for a journey you never make), he was particularly keen to stress the importance of locating individuals, and the research findings they produce, in their social and cultural context. Theory and research which did not take account of the social system in which people lived were, for Tajfel, 'experiments [conducted] in a vacuum' (Tajfel, 1972). It was these dialectical views of theory and practice, laboratory experiment and field study, social research and social context, which dictated my choice of the kind of empirical work to feature most prominently in this book.

The fact that I have chosen to eschew theoretical and methodological singularity does not mean that there are no unifying themes running through the book. The most general of these is an assumption that dynamics *within* groups and dynamics *between* groups are closely related. For three decades after the war the study of 'group dynamics' was synonymous with the analysis of the inner workings of the small group. Indeed, most of the major texts with these two words in their titles confine themselves precisely to that domain (e.g. Cartwright and Zander, 1969; Shaw, 1976). In the past decade there has been a growing recognition of the significance of relations *between* groups in shaping people's behaviour (e.g. Turner and Giles, 1981; Worchel and Austin, 1985). However, as yet, there have been few concerted attempts to integrate these two areas of study (notable exceptions are Sherif and Sherif's, 1969, classic text and the monograph by Turner et al., 1987). Another of my aims, therefore, has been to demonstrate the connections between intra- and intergroup processes. Although in any one chapter there will be more emphasis on one aspect than the other, the close link between them is the dominant message of the book.

Subsumed within this general argument are three other recurring themes. The first is the idea that *groups are a source of social identity* for people. It has long been recognized that our group memberships contribute in a major way to our sense of who we are and of our place in the world. Indeed, this idea was central to the thinking of some of the earliest social psychologists (e.g. Mead, 1934). However, despite its early prominence, the concept of identity featured only sporadically in the work of those interested in groups (e.g. Lewin, 1948) and only recently has it been restored to its proper place at the heart of the study of group process (Tajfel, 1978a, 1982a; Turner et al. 1987). Most of these developments have been concerned with the implications of identity processes for intergroup behaviour in analyses of social conflict and prejudice. However, as I hope to show, several traditional topics in the study of group dynamics – e.g. deindividuation, group structure, social influence – may also be illuminated by an understanding of the role of social identification in group behaviour.

The second theme is the *distinction between task and socio-emotional orientations.* This is a widely held distinction between those aspects of group life which have to do with task performance and the achievement of group goals, and those which concern people's relationships with one another. The distinction originated in the pioneering work of Bales (1950), who believed that these two orientations were fundamental and opposed facets of all group processes. According to Bales, people in groups are basically concerned with achieving some task; to do this successfully they need to be sensitive to other group members' needs and motives; such interpersonal concern detracts from getting on with the job at hand and so there is a resurgence of task activity; and so it goes on. As we shall see, this basic distinction crops up in various different guises in the study of leadership, social influence and group productivity. It is thus a useful second theme with which to integrate research on groups.

The third theme is the *importance of social comparison processes*. Dominating the literature on small groups after the war was Festinger's (1954) theory of social comparisons. In this theory it was proposed that other people serve as vital reference points for the evaluation of our abilities and the validation of our opinions. This simple idea has been used extensively to analyse and understand a wide range of phenomena – for example, group formation and cohesion, status relations within groups, conformity and polarization in group decision-making. In recent years the importance of comparisons at the *inter*group level has also come to be recognized, particularly in relation to the causes of relative deprivation and the maintenance of social identity (Runciman, 1966; Tajfel and Turner, 1979). Thus, the idea of social comparison is one of the crucial links in demonstrating the relatedness of intra- and intergroup behaviour.

In chapter 1, I begin with the concept of the 'group' as it has developed in social psychology, and go on to establish the importance of groups as an aspect of identity and analyse behaviour in the crowd, one of the most elementary forms of group. In chapter 2 some elementary group processes are considered. The most central of these is the tension between task and socio-emotional orientations. Other processes considered in this chapter are the consequences of joining a group, the effects of different forms of interdependence and the acquisition and development of group norms. These group processes take place within an organized framework or group structure. The nature of that structure and its implications for group members are examined in chapter 3. Groups can be structured around roles, communication channels and, above all, by status. The existence of status differences and their origin in and maintenance through social comparisons occupies most of the chapter. High status is sometimes formalized into positions of leadership, and that topic is also treated in chapter 3. In chapter 4, the discussion turns to processes of social influence in groups – the means by which uniformity in the group is attained or, alternatively, changes in group norms are brought about. Both majority and minority influence are examined. In chapter 5, I consider the age-old question of whether it is better to work alone or with others. Several areas of individual versus group productivity are reviewed and the adequacy of current theories of group performance is assessed. A closely related topic, also considered in chapter 5, is group decision-making.

In these four chapters the spotlight is mainly on the interior of the group, although intergroup factors are never completely absent. In chapter 6 the emphasis shifts towards people's behaviour towards members of groups other than their own when the origins of intergroup prejudice and social discontent are discussed. Some of the more individualistic accounts of these phenomena are criticized. An alternative explanation for intergroup conflict and harmony is put forward in chapter 7, one which stresses the importance of objective relationships between groups. The effects of such positive and negative interdependencies on intergroup attitudes and ingroup cohesion are described. Ways of bringing groups into contact with one another, which are likely to reduce prejudice and discrimination, are also assessed. In the final chapter the focus remains on intergroup behaviour as I consider research which suggests that simply belonging to a group is enough to cause intergroup discrimination. One explanation for this finding is in terms of the cognitive process of categorization. From this basic process, the explanation for a number of other judgemental biases emerges. In a final section I return to the notion of social identity with which the book began. A central idea here is the importance for individuals of being able to see their group as positively distinct from other groups. The chapter concludes with a discussion of the implications of the pursuit of distinctiveness for groups in situations of status inequality.

Acknowledgements

This book carries my name only on its cover but, like most intellectual creations, it is really a collective product. I would like here to acknowledge the help of those who have contributed to its completion, especially: Derek Rutter, who painstakingly read the whole manuscript in draft form and who was a vital and constant source of encouragement from the start of the project; all my colleagues, who shared with me the excitement, frustration and fun of conducting the collaborative research which finds its way into these pages – most notably, Dominic Abrams, Susan Condor, Jeremy Holt, Gillian Oaker, Bernd Simon and Jennifer Williams; various students and friends, who read portions of the manuscript and gave me valuable comment on its intelligibility (or otherwise) – particularly Steve Hinkle, Sarah Makowsky, Maria Pennock, Tom Trinder, Pat Warren, Kevin Wilby and Pat Wilson; and the secretarial staff at Keynes College, who did such a good job of turning my appalling scrawl into an immaculate typescript – Diane Graham, Yana Johnson, Kate Ralph, Frances Rhodes, Marilyn Spice and Carol Wilmshurst.

CHAPTER 1

The Reality of Groups

In this book's title and in its preface the existence of human groups is taken for granted: I have assumed both reality of groups and some agreement over what we mean when we use the word 'group'. But in fact both of these assumptions have been the subject of considerable controversy in the history of social psychology. Since the turn of the century, there have been heated debates not just about what groups are but whether, indeed, groups exist at all. This chapter returns to those debates in order to clarify some of the issues that will recur throughout the book. I begin, conventionally enough, with a definition of the group which, while admittedly imprecise, will at least provide us with a few signposts to guide us through the terrain ahead. The discussion then turns to the question of the relationship between the individual and the group: is the latter reducible to the former or can they both be considered as real and inter-related entities? My answer to this question stresses the importance of making a distinction between behaviour in interpersonal settings and behaviour in group settings, and I outline some of the social psychological processes that may underlie this distinction. A key concept here, as indeed it will be throughout the book, is that of *social identity* – a person's sense of who she or he is. Finally, by way of illustration of these issues, I examine social behaviour in that most rudimentary of all groups – the crowd.

Definition

Even the most superficial survey of textbooks on group dynamics quickly reveals a wide diversity of meanings associated with the word 'group' (see Cartwright and Zander, 1969). For some theorists, it is the experience of *common fate* which is the critical factor (e.g. Lewin, 1948; Campbell, 1958). Thus, we can say that the Jews in Nazi Europe constituted a group because of their common (and tragic) fate of stigmatization, imprisonment and extermination. For other thinkers, the existence of some formal or implicit *social structure*, usually in the form of status and role relationships, is the key (e.g. Sherif and Sherif, 1969). The family is a good example here: we can regard the family as a group because its members have very well-defined relationships with one another (as parent, child, sibling etc.) and these relationships usually carry with them clear power and status differences. As we shall see in chapter 3, the emergence of structure is, indeed, a very prevalent feature of a great many groups. However, a third school of thought suggests that these structural relations come about because of a still more elementary feature of groups – the fact that they consist of people in *face-to-face interaction* with one another (e.g. Bales, 1950; Homans, 1950). And, of course, this is true for most of the groups we belong to – our family, our work group and a host of others.

The second and third types of definition only really seem applicable to small groups (say, of twenty members or less) and would seem to exclude large-scale social categories such as ethnic groups (as in the example of the Jews cited above), social class or nationality. And yet, as we shall see in later chapters, these category memberships can influence people's behaviour just as surely as the most cohesive face-to-face group. This problem has led some writers to propose a much more subjective definition of the group in terms of people's *self-categorizations* (Tajfel, 1981; Turner, 1982; Turner et al. 1987). According to this view, a group exists when 'two or more individuals . . . perceive themselves to be members of the same social category' (Turner, 1982, p. 15). Thus, to return to our first example, Jews constitute a group because a significant number of people say to themselves 'I am a Jew'. The value of this characterization is its simplicity and its inclusiveness. It is difficult to imagine a group in which its members did not at some stage mentally classify themselves as actually belonging to it.

Despite its attractive parsimony, Turner's definition is perhaps rather *too* subjectivist; it seems not to capture an important feature of groups – that their existence is typically known to others (Merton, 1957). After all, as social scientists we probably would not be much interested in studying two people who secretly decided that they would define themselves as a group, but whose existence remained hidden to everyone else. A central theme of this book is that we need to consider groups not just as systems in their own right but *in relation to* other groups. For this reason, I propose to extend Turner's (1982) definition and suggest that *a group exists when two or more people define them-*

selves as members of it and when its existence is recognized by at least one other. The 'other' in this context is some person or group of people who do not so define themselves. This could be, for example, the experimenter in a laboratory study or, more generally, others (or other groups) in the social environment.

The individual-group relationship

Before we can begin investigating the properties of groups and their effects, there is an important issue which must be discussed first.[1] This concerns the nature of the relationship of the individual to the group – what Allport (1962) described as social psychology's 'master problem'. To put it at its simplest, the question is this: is there more to groups than the sum of the individuals that comprise them?

Allport himself was in no doubt about the answer to this question. In one of the earliest social psychology texts he wrote: 'There is no psychology of groups which is not essentially and entirely a psychology of individuals' (Allport, 1924, p. 6). The thrust of this often-quoted remark was aimed at some of his contemporaries who held that groups had some mental properties over and above the consciousness of the individuals which make them up. Thus, Le Bon (1896) and McDougall (1920) both talked of a crowd possessing a 'group mind' which led it to perform deeds which would be considered unthinkable by the individual crowd members on their own. We shall return to this theory of crowd behaviour later in the chapter but for the moment let us consider Allport's argument against this 'group mind' thesis. Allport's main point was that a term like the 'group mind' could not be independently verified; it was not possible to touch or observe this entity which was supposed to possess consciousness, *apart from the individuals that comprised it*.

In this he was surely right: to talk of a group having a 'mind of its own' does seem to be an unfortunate lapse into metaphysics. However, in rejecting the idea of a 'group mind', Allport wanted to go further and dispose of the concept of the group altogether. Although in his later writings (e.g. Allport, 1962) he appeared to modify his position somewhat, at heart he was still an individualist, believing that group phenomena could ultimately be reduced to individual psychological processes. One consequence of this has been that much subsequent theory and research on group dynamics has followed his lead and has attempted to show that such phenomena as prejudice and conflict are little more than interpersonal behaviour on a larger scale.

Here is Berkowitz, for example, an influential figure in the social psychology of aggression: 'Dealings between groups ultimately became problems for the psychology of the individual. Individuals decide to go to war; battles are fought by individuals; and peace is established by individuals' (Berkowitz, 1962, p. 167).

This reductionist view has not gone completely unchallenged, however. Others have argued that a rejection of the 'group mind' fallacy does not imply that we should abandon the study of group processes in their own right, separable from but still related to individual functioning. Beginning with Mead (1934), and followed by Sherif (1936), Asch (1952) and Lewin (1952), these thinkers have insisted on the reality and distinctiveness of social groups, believing them to have unique properties which emerged out of the network of relations between the individual members. This idea was nicely expressed by Asch (1952) with a chemical analogy. A substance like water, he argued, is made up of the elements hydrogen and oxygen and yet has very different properties from either constituent. Furthermore, these same molecular constituents when differently organized or structured produce substances with quite different characteristics (e.g. ice, water, steam). Thus, in a real sense the compound H_2O is *not* the simple aggregate of its constituents but is crucially affected by their arrangement. So, too, with human compounds, or groups:

> For an adequate formulation of the individual-group relation, we need a way of describing group action that neither reduces the individual to a mere target of group forces of mystical origin, nor obliterates the organized character of group forces in the welter of individual activities. We need a way of understanding group process that retains the prime reality of individual *and* group, the two permanent poles of all social processes. We need to see group forces arising out of the actions of individuals and individuals whose actions are a function of the group forces that they themselves (or others) have brought into existence. We must see group phenomena as both the *product and condition* of actions of individuals. (Asch, 1952, p. 251)

Or, as Steiner (1986) expressed it, rather more succinctly: 'there are no groups without individuals, and there are very few individuals who are not also functioning parts of groups' (Steiner, 1986, p. 285).

For both Asch and Sherif the reality of groups emerges out of people's common perceptions of themselves as members of the same social unit and in various relations to one another within that unit. Associated with these perceptions are various group products such as slogans, norms and values, and these, too, can become internalized and hence serve to guide people's behaviour. For these reasons it is possible to accept Allport's critique of the 'group mind' and yet disagree with his conclusion that the concept of 'group' has no place in a rigorous social psychology. Endorsing the words of Sherif, that pioneer of group psychology, the view taken in this book is:

> We cannot do justice to events by extrapolating uncritically from man's [sic] feelings, attitudes, and behaviour when he is in a state of isolation to his behaviour when acting as a member of a group. Being a member of a group and behaving as a member of a group have psychological consequences. There are consequences even when the other members are not immediately present. (Sherif, 1966, pp. 8–9)

The interpersonal–group continuum

What does it mean to say a person is 'acting as a member of a group'? Tajfel (1978a), one of the most important theorists of group processes, also stressed the need to distinguish interpersonal behaviour from behaviour in group settings. He suggested three criteria which help us to make the distinction. The *first*, and most crucial, is the presence or absence of at least two clearly identifiable social categories, e.g. black and white, man and woman, worker and employer. The *second* is whether there is low or high variability between persons within each group in their attitudes or behaviour. Intergroup behaviour is typically homogeneous or uniform while interpersonal behaviour shows the normal range of individual differences. The songs and chants of striking miners against the police in the British coal dispute of 1984–5 provide a graphic illustration of behavioural uniformity. And, in another time and place, some of those same miners may have enjoyed a drink in a pub with some of those same police on a completely personal basis. The *third* is whether there is low or high variability in *one person's* attitudes and behaviour towards other group members. Does the same person react similarly to a wide range of different others (as in the case of ethnic or gender stereotyping, see chapter 8), or does she/he show a differentiated response to them? In brief, Tajfel saw all social behaviour as lying on a continuum defined by the polarities of 'intergroup' and 'interpersonal'. In the former case, the interaction is seen as being determined by the membership of various groups and relations between them; in the latter, it is more decided by the individuals, personal characteristics and interpersonal relationships (see Tajfel, 1978a; Brown and Turner, 1981). This distinction is nicely described by Harris (1985), discussing her anthropological study of Balybeg in

Northern Ireland – a town, like so much of that strife-torn area, deeply affected by the religious divide of Catholic versus Protestant. She comments on 'The readiness with which people switched from a view of their neighbours based on a perception of reality in which each was an individual with a mixture of traits, good and bad, to a myth of good and evil, a myth of "our fellow" and "their fellows" ' (Harris, 1985, p. 32). In the first case the people's religions seemed rather insignificant; in the second they had become overwhelmingly important.

What underlies this 'switching' process which Harris describes? Turner (1982) has suggested that it is governed by changes in self-concept functioning – changes, that is, in the way people view themselves. Turner views the self-concept as comprising two components: personal identity and social identity (see also Gergen, 1971). Personal identity, in his view, refers to self-descriptions in terms of personalistic or idiosyncratic characteristics; for example, 'I am a friendly sort of person' or 'I am a lover of blues music'. Social identity, on the other hand, denotes definitions in terms of category memberships; for example, 'I am a woman' or 'I am a Manchester United supporter'. This idea that belonging to a group forms part of people's identity is, as we shall see, a central aspect of the study of group processes. It helps us to make sense of much of people's behaviour towards other groups (see chapter 8), as well as helping us to understand why it is that group members so often show such uniformity in their attitudes and behaviour (see chapters 2 and 4). The reason behind this uniformity, suggests Turner, is that in defining ourselves as a member of a particular group people also typically associate themselves with the various common attributes and norms which they see as being part and parcel of that group. So, not only do individuals see members of *other* groups in stereotyped ways, they also see *themselves* as being relatively interchangeable with others in their own group. Hence their attitudes and actions take on the uniformity which is so characteristic of group settings.

If it is the case that identification with a group has these consequences for *intra*group behaviour, then perhaps it is more appropriate to modify Tajfel's original interpersonal–intergroup continuum so that it becomes the interpersonal-*group* continuum, indicating a distinction between social settings where a group or groups are not salient and those where they are very much in evidence. This is very similar, then, to the suggestion from Asch (1952) quoted earlier in which the 'individual' and the 'group' were described as the 'two permanent poles of all social processes'.

As illustrations of this interpersonal-group distinction, let us consider the findings from two experiments. (These are given here in barest outline only since they are both described in more detail in chapters 4 and 8.) The first comes from Deutsch and Gerard's (1955) study of conformity. This was modelled on Asch's (1951) classic demonstration that people may be influenced to give incorrect answers to a straightforward physical judgement by the presence of a unanimous but incorrect majority (see chapter 4). Deutsch and Gerard showed how this conformity could be dramatically increased simply by defining the collection of subjects taking part in the experiment as a group with a clear-cut goal. In our terms, the introduction of this 'grouping' cue shifted the situation towards the 'group' pole of the behavioural continuum with a corresponding increase in uniformity of behaviour *between* individuals. The second illustration is provided by an experiment by Wilder (1984a). Following an artistic preference task devised by Tajfel et al. (1971) (see chapter 8), subjects were asked to estimate the range of judgements given by others in the experiment. Wilder found that this perceptual range could be reliably reduced by first categorizing the subjects into two groups on the basis of their initial preferences, and then asking them to estimate the variability of the outgroup responses. When no group division was present, each person's judgements of others were more heterogeneous. The shift towards the 'group' pole had this time increased the uniformity *within* individuals in their perception of others.

Before we leave this issue, there are three further points to be made. The first is that what distinguishes interpersonal and group behaviour is not primarily the number of people involved. Thus, in the example of police and strikers, what located that interaction towards the 'group' pole was not the fact that many people were involved or that they acted in particular ways or, indeed, that they belonged to different groups. What indicated it as an instance of group behaviour was the uniformity of their behaviour, which suggested that the participants appeared to be interacting *in terms of* their group memberships rather than their distinctive personal characteristics. This is important because social encounters are frequently rather ambiguous to define. Take, for instance, an interaction between just two people who happen to belong to different social categories (e.g. a man and a woman). Is this encounter an interpersonal one because just two people are involved or is it a group-based interaction because of the category difference? From the barest description I have just given it is not possible to say; what would be needed before we could characterize this situation would be a close study of the content of the interaction between them. If it appeared by word and gesture that the participants were orientating towards each other in a relatively predictable and sex-stereotypic fashion then this would indicate an instance of group behaviour. In the absence of this, the idiosyncratic nature of the interaction would suggest a more interpersonal encounter.

This raises the second point: that the interpersonal–group distinction is based on a continuous dimension and is not an either/or dichotomy. Most social situations will contain elements of both interpersonal and group behaviours. After all, people enter even the most group-based interaction with a unique prehistory and set of personal dispositions and, on the other side of the coin, even the most intimate exchange between two lovers will contain some group-stereotypic features. While this necessarily complicates a complete analysis of any particular situation, since both sorts of processes will be at work, it does not obviate the need for a clear understanding of the difference between these sorts of processes and how they both interact.

The third and most important point is that, if we accept this difference, then it follows that we may need rather different kinds of theories to understand group process than we typically use to explain interpersonal behaviour.[2] Theories about interpersonal behaviour typically invoke either or both of two kinds of process. One is the operation of some factor within the individual – for instance, the person's personality make-up or emotional state. The other is the nature of the relationship between individuals – for instance, relations of attitude similarity, status and power. In other words, variations in people's behaviour are explained either by differences between the people themselves or by differences in the personal relations between them. But once we are dealing with group situations such explanations are less useful because two of the key characteristics of group situations have to do with *uniformities* between individuals rather than their differences. One football fan may taunt another, particularly if they are wearing different coloured scarves, in ignorance of, or in spite of, many similarities of attitude, socioeconomic status, physical appearance and personality. And if there are a thousand such supporters together, the multiplicity of personality types and the complexity of interpersonal relations both within each group and between the groups become enormous, and *yet* their behaviour is often strikingly uniform. The conclusion must be, therefore, as we wrote in an earlier volume: that the direct extrapolation of theories about interpersonal behaviour to group contexts is inherently fraught with difficulties and thus that alternative theories, relating specifically to group behaviour, are necessary (Brown and Turner, 1981, p. 46).

One of the purposes of this book is to examine those other theories and assess their utility and relevance for understanding ourselves and our society.

The crowd as a group

On a spring afternoon in 1980 a working-class area in the centre of Bristol, with little previous history of unrest, suddenly erupted into violence.[3] This 'riot', as it was later dubbed by media commentators, was occasioned by a police raid on a local café, ostensibly to investigate allegations of illegal drinking and drug-taking. Initially the raid provoked little reaction, but within an hour the police and their vehicles began to be pelted with bricks from onlookers. Police reinforcements – around thirty or forty officers – were summoned to the scene but by now the situation had escalated and a large crowd of several hundred people had gathered. Further attempts by still more police to disperse this crowd and to rescue their abandoned vehicles and colleagues were unsuccessful, and later that evening police cars and other vehicles were set on fire and some shop and bank windows were smashed. For much of that night the neighbourhood became a 'no-go' area to the police, although by the next day the crowd had dispersed and the incident was over. In all, forty-nine police were injured in some way, six police vehicles were completely destroyed, and one or two business premises were damaged.

By the standards of what was to happen the following year – most notably the riots in Liverpool and London in the summer of 1981 – or what had occurred in some American cities a decade or so before, this was an insignificant enough event. However, as an example of crowd behaviour with which to begin our discussion it will serve our purposes well. The more so since the events in question have been studied by a social psychologist who was living in Bristol at the time and who has provided a penetrating analysis of the episode (Reicher, 1984a). We will return to Reicher's work later in the chapter but before doing so four further points about this so-called 'riot' must be mentioned. The first is that the violence was not random or uncontrolled but seemed to be aimed at very specific targets. Foremost of these, of course, were the police and their vehicles. Some property was also damaged (e.g. a bank and a pub), but the majority of local shops and private houses were untouched. The second is that the crowd consisted almost entirely of people who lived in the immediate neighbourhood and who were known to one another – many by sight, some very well. Third, the violence was geographically contained. There was no attempt to spread it outside a very well-defined area which constituted the centre of the local community. Finally, spontaneous comments made by crowd participants reflected a strong identification with and pride in that community, a feeling of acting to defend themselves against 'outsiders'. By the same token, the police clearly regarded the 'rioters' as a group, albeit one which had 'taken the law into its own hands'. This last point is particularly important because it satisfies us that we are, indeed, dealing with an instance of group behaviour (see above).

How, then, are we to understand these events in Bristol and others like them? Why do crowds behave as they do? An early attempt to answer these questions suggested that 'by the mere fact that he [sic] forms part of an organised crowd, a man descends several rungs in the ladder of civilisation. Isolated, he may be a cultivated individual; in a crowd, he is a barbarian – that is, a creature acting by instinct' (LeBon, 1896, p. 36). According to LeBon, the anonymity, contagion and suggestibility which he saw as being endemic to crowds caused people to lose their rationality and identity, creating instead a 'group mind'. Under the influence of this collective mentality, and freed from normal social constraints, people's destructive instincts are released, resulting in wanton violence and irrational behaviour. For Le Bon, then, the Bristol 'riot' would be a classic instance of this 'decline into barbarity' similar to those which he claimed to have observed at the time of the Paris Commune in the nineteenth century.

Although, as we have seen, Le Bon's hypothesis of a 'group mind' quickly came under attack and has since largely been rejected, his speculations about the effects of anonymity in the crowd have proved enormously influential for subsequent attempts to explain collective behaviour. Foremost of these has been Zimbardo's (1969) theory of deindividuation published under the title 'The human choice: individuation, reason and order versus deindividuation, impulse and chaos'. Zimbardo has taken up many of Le Bon's ideas and formalized them into a model involving a number of input variables, some intervening psychological changes and the resulting behaviour. For our purposes, the three most important 'inputs' are anonymity, diffused responsibility and the presence and size of a group. According to Zimbardo, being in a large group provides people with a cloak of anonymity and diffuses personal responsibility for the consequences of one's actions. This is thought to lead to a loss of identity and a reduced concern for social evaluation. This is what Zimbardo terms the psychological state of deindividuation. The resulting 'output' behaviour is then 'impulsive', 'irrational' and 'regressive' because it is not under the 'usual' social and personal controls. Although Zimbardo does allow that this disinhibited behaviour might take prosocial forms (e.g. Zimbardo, 1969, p. 300), the main thrust of his theory – as is clear from its title – is to suggest that people's behaviour will degenerate in crowd settings. The violent behaviour of the crowd in Bristol on that April afternoon would, for Zimbardo, represent an example of this. The example would be strengthened still further by the fact that the violence escalated over the evening as darkness fell. According to the theory, the darkness would have increased the anonymity of the crowd members, resulting in still more antisocial behaviour.

To provide evidence for his theory, Zimbardo (1969) conducted a number of laboratory experiments in which groups of participants, under the pretext of a 'learning experiment', were given the opportunity of administering mild, but apparently real, electric shocks to the putative 'learner' in the experiment.[4] In some conditions these participants were deindividuated by being asked to wear a large, shapeless coat and a hood over the head with holes cut out for their eyes and mouth. In other conditions, they retained their individual identity and were given large name tags to reinforce this. In the first experiment, involving students, the results were largely supportive of the theory: the mean duration of 'shock' administered was nearly twice as long in the deindividuated condition as it was in the individuated one. However, in a subsequent experiment, using a very similar procedure with Belgian soldiers, an exactly opposite result was obtained: those in the anonymous conditions delivered consistently *shorter* length 'shocks' than those who were identifiable. In a rather circular explanation for this unexpected finding, Zimbardo suggested that the soldiers, because they were already in uniform, were deindividuated before the experiment began. The effect of donning the coats and hoods for the deindividuation condition of the experiment was, he argued, to re-individuate them (Zimbardo, 1969, p. 276)!

However unsatisfactory this *post hoc* explanation may be, other studies have reported findings consistent with Zimbardo's theory. For instance, Watson (1973), in an archival study of ethnographic records, found a clear correlation between cultures which indulged in highly aggressive practices towards their enemies (e.g. torture or mutilation) and those which also regularly changed their appearance before battle (e.g. by face or body painting or the wearing of masks). Of the twenty-three cultures studied, thirteen were judged to be highly aggressive and, of these, twelve engaged in various rituals to disguise their appearance before battle. On the other hand, of the ten less aggressive societies only three had similar rituals. Although, clearly, deindividuation is only one of a number of possible interpretations of this correlation, Zimbardo's theory has also received support from a more controlled experimental study by Jaffe and Yinon (1979) where they simply compared the mean intensity of 'shock' administered by individuals with that administered by groups of three. As predicted, those participating in groups consistently gave much stronger 'shocks' than those acting on their own. This difference was even evident on the first trial before there had been any discussion in the group.

Despite this supportive evidence, it is becoming increasingly clear that Zimbardo's one-sided emphasis on the negative consequences of group membership (e.g. identity loss and antisocial behaviour) is misplaced. As we have seen from his own experiment with Belgian soldiers, anonymity sometimes *reduces* aggression. Similarly, Diener (1976) found that anonymity had no effect on aggressive behaviour and that group membership actually decreased it. It is also the case that the circumstances which are alleged to cause deindividuation may give rise to other forms of behaviour apart from aggression. In another experiment, Diener (1979) showed that a prior experience of activities designed to create group cohesion (e.g. adoption of a group name, group singing and dancing) subsequently led individuals to engage in more unusual and uninhibited behaviours (e.g. playing with mud, finger painting with their nose, sucking liquids from baby bottles) than those who had had an initial experience which made then feel rather self-aware. Finally, and perhaps most convincing of all, Johnson and Downing (1979), using a very simple modification of Zimbardo's procedure, found that an increase in *pro*social behaviour can result from deindividuation. Like Zimbardo, they compared anonymous and individuating conditions. Although all subjects had to wear special clothing, in the individuating conditions the subjects' names were attached to their costumes and other people's responses could be identified. However, Johnson and Downing also varied the situational norms prevailing in the experiment. In half the conditions, the costume consisted of a robe resembling a Ku Klux Klan outfit, a point remarked on by the experimenter. In the remaining conditions, the participants were asked to wear an equally anonymous looking robe but one which was alleged to have been a nurse's gown borrowed from a hospital recovery room. In the subsequent 'learning' experiment those wearing the nurse's uniform chose to *reduce* the level of 'shocks' administered, and especially in the deindividuated conditions (see figure 1.1). In fact, deindividuation by itself failed to increase aggression significantly, even for those wearing the Ku Klux Klan outfit.

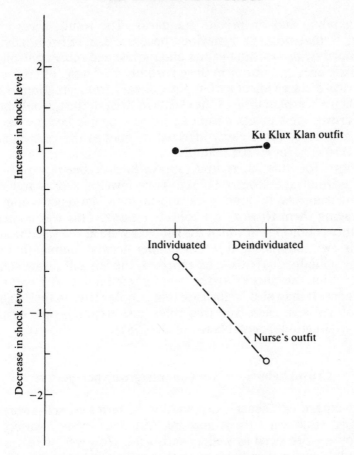

Figure 1.1 Aggression as a consequence of deindividuation and situational norms (adapted from Johnson and Downing 1979, table 1)

The importance of these findings is that they show quite conclusively that being in a group, even a primitive group like a crowd, does not necessarily lead people to act in a wantonly destructive fashion as Zimbardo seems to imply. Quite how they will behave depends very much on which norms are salient in each particular situation (Turner and Killian, 1957). This is the conclusion reached by Diener (1980). He argues that the key factor in crowd behaviour is a loss of self-awareness. Drawing on Duval and Wicklund's (1972) 'theory of objective self-awareness', Diener suggests that factors present in some crowd situations – for example, anonymity, enhanced arousal, cohesion – lead people to direct their attention outwards and correspondingly less on themselves and on private standards. The result, according to Diener, is that people's behaviour becomes *less* self-regulated (i.e. determined by pre-existing values and mores) and *more* controlled by immediate cues and norms in the environment. These, of course, will not always dictate violent action but will vary from situation to situation. Diener's explanation of the events in Bristol, then, would be that as the crowd grew in size and in excitement people became less self-aware and hence more easily affected by cues in the environment – others throwing rocks, for example.

Support for this alternative approach has been provided by Prentice-Dunn and Rogers (1982). They lowered self-awareness by exposing subjects to loud rock music in a darkened room and encouraging them to work on collective tasks. This was contrasted with other conditions in which the subjects were asked to concentrate on their own thoughts and feelings under normal illumination while working on individual tasks. As expected, the less self-aware subjects gave more intense 'shocks' to the 'learner' victim in a later part of the experiment. It may also be the case that people differ in their habitual levels of self-awareness and that this, too, affects people's suscep-tibility to situational cues (Nadler et al., 1982).

Crowd behaviour from an intergroup perspective

The advantage of Diener's explanation in terms of self-awareness, then, is that it can account for a wide variety of behaviours – prosocial as well as antisocial. However, it shares with Zimbardo's earlier deindividuation theory an emphasis on behaviour becoming deregulated in crowd situations. For Diener, as for Zimbardo, being in a crowd still generally implies a *loss* of identity[5] and hence a *loss* of self-control. But do people always lose themselves in a crowd and get out of control? Let us return to that Bristol 'riot' with which we began this discussion. There are a number of features of that event which do not fit easily with such a point of view. Recall, first, that the crowd's behaviour, despite its violent character, was actually rather controlled. It was aimed at specific targets (e.g. the police) and avoided others (e.g. local shops and houses). Further-more, it was geographically confined. If people had been responding simply to stimulus cues, why did they not chase the police far beyond the immediate neighbourhood and spread the violence elsewhere? Secondly, it is important to note that in that event in Bristol, as in other disturbances, the rioters and the police behaved differently.

And, yet, the police constituted a crowd also! If people simply lose self-awareness in a crowd and respond to immediate stimuli we need to know why the police attend to different stimuli from the rioters. Thirdly, it cannot really be said that the crowd was anonymous in that instance. As we have already noted, most of the participants were known to each other, at least by sight. Finally, those taking part in the 'riot', far from losing their identities, seemed quite unanimous in a new sense of pride in their community engendered by their activities.

These points have all been made by Reicher (1982, 1984a) in a important new approach to the study of crowds. Reicher begins by noting two features of many crowd situations. First, they nearly always involve more than one group. In the Bristol example we have the local inhabitants and the police. In other cases it may be rival groups of football supporters (as in the Heysel stadium tragedy in Brussels in 1985), or strikers and strike breakers (as in the British coal dispute of 1984-5). The fact that crowd behaviour is so often *intergroup* behaviour has been virtually ignored in all previous theories of the crowd (Reicher and Potter, 1985). This is important for Reicher's second point which is that people often take on a new identity in a crowd rather than become anonymous. This follows from Turner's (1982) suggestion about the different components of the self-concept – the personal and the social. In a crowd, people may indeed lose some sense of their personal identity but at the same time they will often adopt a stronger sense of their *social* identity, as a member of this or that particular group. Hence the positive comments about their neighbourhood made by the Bristol 'rioters' (Reicher, 1984a), and similar remarks made several years earlier by a participant in the Watts riot in the USA (quoted in Milgram and Toch, 1969, p. 576).

According to Reicher, therefore, crowd behaviour involves a *change* rather than a loss of identity. Alongside this change are changes in what are seen as the appropriate or normative standards of behaviour. These now become determined by the group rather than by private, idiosyncratic or environmental factors. This helps to explain why the behaviour of rioters and police can be so different. Although exposed to the same environmental stimuli, in adopting their respective identities they become influenced by very different goals and social norms (see also Turner and Killian, 1957). This point is nicely illustrated by a recent experiment of Reicher's which adapted Zimbardo's deindividuation paradigm (Reicher, 1984b). Using science and social science students, Reicher capitalized on some existing differences in attitude towards animal rights in the two disciplines. (Science students are generally more in favour of vivisection than

social science students.) In the experimental session half the participants were made especially aware of their faculty affiliation by being
seated together and by being referred to by the experimenter as the
'science group' or the 'social science group'. The remaining subjects
were less aware of this faculty difference since they were all seated
together and referred to by individual code numbers. In addition to
this group salience manipulation Reicher also deindividuated half the
subjects in each condition using a Zimbardo-type procedure: they had
to wear baggy coats and masks. In the 'group' condition these tunics
were of a different colour for each faculty; in the 'individual' condition they were simply all white. The subjects' own attitudes towards
vivisection were then elicited. As can be seen from figure 1.2, these
attitudes were markedly affected by the group salience variable: when
subjects were reminded of their faculty membership their attitudes
came more into line with the group norms – more pro-vivisection for
scientists, more anti-vivisection for the social scientists. Even more
interesting, though, was the fact that this conformity became more
pronounced for the scientists when they were deindividuated (see
figure 1.2)[6]. Far from being deregulated, as Diener might have predicted, their attitudes seem to have become *more* regulated by the
appropriate group norms as their identity as scientists became more
clearly defined. This supports Reicher's contention that in some

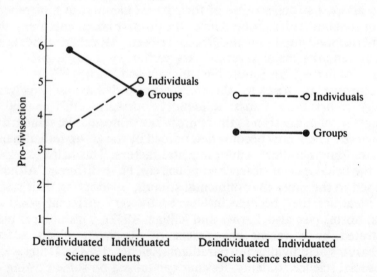

Figure 1.2 Attitudes towards vivisection after deindividuation and heightened group salience (from Reicher 1984b, figure 1)

'deindividuating' circumstances people's identities change rather than simply get lost.

In conclusion, we can note three important points. The first is that Zimbardo's pessimism about crowds, like that of Le Bon's before him, seems unwarranted. Depending on what norms are salient in the situation, both pro- and antisocial behaviour can become more probable in group settings. Where Zimbardo may be right is to suggest that people's behaviour in such settings may become more extreme. (This polarization which is so typical of groups is dealt with more fully in chapter 5.) The second and related point is that people's behaviour in crowds does not always undergo a degradation. Both Zimbardo and Diener suggest that in crowd settings people suffer a loss of identity and a loss of control. However, Reicher's research with both laboratory and natural groups suggests that this is mistaken. His careful studies have shown that people's behaviour is still regulated, albeit by different psychological processes. In particular, it seems that crowds often have particular targets or goals in mind in acting as they do, and also that these actions are often motivated by an identification with certain social categories. Third, these goal and identity-directed aspects of crowd behaviour are particularly evident if crowds are viewed from an intergroup perspective. In nearly every instance of crowd behaviour it is possible to identify an outgroup which may either have served as the stimulus for the crowd's initial actions or have become the focus for its subsequent attentions. This third point is particularly important. As we shall see throughout this book, a group rarely exists in isolation and its relationships with other groups are critical for understanding what goes on within that group itself.

Summary

1 A group has variously been defined as two or more people experiencing some common fate *or* coexisting within some social structure *or* interacting on a face-to-face basis. The simpler and more comprehensive definition adopted here is two or more people possessing a common social identification and whose existence as a group is recognized by a third party.

2 Some writers have argued that groups can be reduced to the simple aggregate of the members that comprise them. However, just as chemical compounds may differ radically from their constitutent elements so, too, people in groups may act very differently from how they behave when they are in isolation.

3 It is possible to conceive of all social behaviour as lying on a continuum

from interpersonal settings to group settings. The key features of the latter are that two or more social categories can be identified, behaviour of group members is typically rather uniform and individuals' treatment of others becomes stereotyped. Underlying this continuum is a transition of psychological functioning from personal to social-identity processes. These different processes may require us to adopt different group-based theories for the study of groups.

4 The crowd can be considered as an elementary form of group. Some have suggested that in crowds people become deindividuated and, as a result, act in an antisocial, unreasoning and uncontrolled fashion. However, a careful study of crowd and crowd-like situations reveals that people's behaviour can sometimes become more prosocial and is often aimed at specific targets (suggesting some goal-directedness).

5 Most instances of crowd behaviour involve more than one group. Once this intergroup aspect is recognized, it is possible to see behaviour in crowds as becoming more and not less regulated, involving a change rather than a loss of identity. In this change people's *social* identities as group members become more important, their *personal* identities as unique individuals less so.

Further reading

Asch, S.E. (1952) *Social Psychology*, ch. 9. New Jersey: Prentice Hall.

Brown, R.J. and Turner, J.C. (1981) Interpersonal and intergroup behaviour, in Turner, J.C. and Giles, H. (eds) *Intergroup Behaviour*. Oxford: Blackwell.

Diener, E. (1980) Deindividuation: the absence of self-awareness and self-regulation in group members, in Paulus, P. (ed.) *The Psychology of Group Influence*. Hillsdale, NJ: Lawrence Erlbaum.

Reicher, S.D. (1982) The determination of collective behaviour, in Tajfel, H. (ed.) *Social Identity and Intergroup Relations*. Cambridge: Cambridge University Press.

CHAPTER 2

Elementary Processes in Groups

In this chapter and the next, I consider some of the fundamental characteristics of life in groups. For convenience of exposition, the emphasis in this chapter is rather on process while in chapter 3 it will shift to more structural aspects, but the distinction between them is not very clear cut. Some of the issues covered here could have been dealt with in later chapters and vice versa.

Four major topics are discussed. I first consider what happens when we become a member of a group – or become aware of that membership, which is not necessarily the same thing. Under this heading, I look at the consequences of group membership for the self-concept and examine what may lie behind the rituals of entry (some of them seemingly bizarre or discomforting) which typify the attainment of group membership. The second section deals with interdependence in groups – how we are linked to others in terms of outcomes and the effects of different kinds of linkages. An important conclusion which emerges here is the significance of the group's goal or task in determining its behaviour. The third topic – the distinction between task behaviours and socio-emotional behaviours – is a key one not just in this chapter but for the book as a whole. Running through the whole field of group dynamics we find again and again the polarity between 'getting on with the job' and 'having regard for others'. Appropriately enough, it is the work of R. F. Bales to whom the credit for first clarifying the distinction should go, which dominates this third section. I begin with his pioneering 'interaction process analysis' and then go on to evaluate SYMLOG, his most recent contribution. In the fourth and final section, the wheel turns full circle as I return to the question of entry into the group, this time in relation to the acquistion and development of social norms. As I shall show, the group's prevailing customs and traditions exert a profound influence in regulating behaviour, not just in the immediate collective situation but also when the individual is alone or has left the group some time previously.

Becoming a member of a group

The process of becoming part of a group can often provoke anxiety. Whether it be a child going to a new school or to a different class within the school, an adult changing jobs or new recruits to a political party attending their first meeting, the experience of entry into the group, while often exciting, may involve a degree of stress. Why should this be? It is tempting, perhaps, simply to label these reactions as 'fear of the unknown' and leave it at that. Indeed, as we shall see later in the chapter, the process of new group members acquiring norms may well be motivated by attempts to reduce uncertainty in a novel situation. But a more detailed study of what happens when people join groups reveals that there are other processes at work too. These have been discussed in some detail by Moreland and Levine (1982), who have proposed a temporal model of group socialization covering the whole sequence from people's initial investigation of the group and recruitment to it to their eventual exit. An important feature of their model is its emphasis on the reciprocity of the individual and the group: it is not just the individual who experiences changes as a result of entering the group; the group also has to accommodate its new members. In this section I deal with two of the many phenomena discussed by Moreland and Levine (1982): changes in people's self-concepts as they join a group, and the actual process of initiation into the group. Although in discussing these I shall mainly be concerned with the effects of the group on the individual, it should be kept in mind that changes are also occurring in the other direction. These are covered in more detail in chapter 4.

Changes in self-concept

As we saw in chapter 1, our social identity – our sense of who we are and what we are worth – is intimately bound up with our group memberships. Thus, one of the first consequences of becoming a member of a group is a change in the way we see ourselves. Joining a group often requires us to redefine who we are which, in turn, may have implications for our self-esteem. This process of redefinition was nicely illustrated during interviews I once conducted with shop stewards in a large aircraft engineering factory (Brown, 1978). One of the questions in the interview asked the respondents what they felt about belonging to their particular section and what they would feel about moving elsewhere. The majority of those interviewed expressed a strong desire to remain where they were and many of them went on to explain why that particular group membership was important to them. As one of them put it:

> I went into the army. I had no visions of any regiment to go in or different kind of preference for tank or artillery. But once I was in the artillery, to me that was the finest regiment. Even now it is and I've left the army twenty years . . . I think it's the same as when you come into a factory. You get an allegiance to a department and you breed that. And you say, 'fair enough I'm a Development worker', and you hate to think of going into Production . . . Once someone gets in a department you've got that allegiance to it. (Brown, 1978, p. 426)

This change in self-definition so graphically described by that shop steward is a very common consequence of joining a group. Kuhn and McPartland (1954) devised a simple instrument to explore these self-definitions. Respondents were simply asked to pose themselves the question 'Who am I?', and to provide up to twenty answers to it. Kuhn and McPartland found that all but a small handful of their respondents gave at least one 'consensual' or group reference and over half gave ten such responses or more. The kinds of consensual responses people gave varied from explicit group references (e.g. 'I am a student', 'I am a Baptist') to those which referred more to societal role positions (e.g. 'I am a husband', 'I am a daughter'). The instrument's validity was supported by the finding that self-professed members of religious groups were much more likely to give religious group references in their answers than were those who did not belong to a religion.

The aspect of self which will be most readily elicited by an instrument such as this is probably affected by the context in which it is administered. Thus, in Northern Ireland the persisting sectarian conflict makes religion a salient category which is reflected in people's self-descriptions. Trew (1981 a, b) reported that some 15–19 per cent of her samples of school children and students spontaneously referred to the categories of Protestant and Catholic in response to the question 'What are you?'. And when actually given the opportunity to choose from a provided list of self-descriptive labels, this figure jumped to over 90 per cent (Cairns, 1982). Another important contextual factor seems to be the numerical size of the ingroup relative to other groups. McGuire et al. (1978) found that Hispanic and black children, who were in small minorities in the North American sample studied (8 and 9 per cent respectively), were much more likely to mention their ethnicity when asked to describe themselves than were the white (majority) group. McGuire et al. suggested that the numerical inferiority of the minority groups makes them psychologically distinctive for their members and hence made them more salient to their self-concepts. Similar results have been reported for the salience of gender in predominantly male or female households (McGuire et al., 1979; see chapter 8).

These studies were not directly concerned with the acquistion of self-definitions associated with new group membership. Indeed, many of the groups investigated were, in any case, socially ascribed categories (e.g. ethnicity) rather than groups which one might voluntarily join. However, an experimental study by Moreland (1985) suggests that new members do go through a process of self-redefinition and that this may also have behavioural consequences. Moreland (1985) suggested that people joining a group often face an initial hurdle of being accepted as fully fledged members. This leads them to categorize themselves – and doubtless be categorized by others in the group – as 'new' members in contrast to existing or 'old' members. In his experiment Moreland led two members of a discussion group to believe that they were new to the group, alleging that the remaining three members had actually met together twice previously. (In fact, all five members of the group were novices, so that the remaining three, who were given no misleading information, acted as 'control' subjects.) Moreland found that initially these 'new' members were more anxious than the 'control' subjects and anticipated that they would enjoy the forthcoming sessions less. Furthermore, it was clear that the categorization of their world into 'old' and 'new' members reliably affected their behaviour: analysis of their verbal utterances revealed that they talked more to their fellow 'novices' and expressed more agreement with them than with those whom they believed had already acquired fully fledged membership status. This behavioural discrimination between 'new' and 'old' members declined over time as the groups met together for further sessions, and was paralleled by a gradual increase in the favourability of the novices' attitudes towards the group as a whole.

So far I have discussed changes in self-concept consequent on group membership simply as changes in the way we define or describe ourselves. But becoming a member of a group may also have consequences for our evaluation of ourselves, for our self-esteem. If we internalize our group memberships as part of our self-concept it follows that any prestige or value associated with those groups will have implications for our feelings of self-worth. This was shown by Zander et al. (1960), who studied the psychological consequences of belonging to cohesive and non-cohesive laboratory groups which then experienced success or failure. Cohesive groups were created by maximizing cues for 'groupness': members were seated close to one another, encouraged to think up a name for their group, and attention was drawn to the members interpersonal similarities. By contrast, in the non-cohesive 'groups' – although it is doubtful whether the word 'group' is really appropriate here – members were allowed to sit anywhere, the group was assigned a number rather than being allowed to generate a name, and the participants were never openly referred to as a group. The groups were set a fashion design task at which half were deemed to have done well relative to other groups, while the remainder were alleged to have done poorly. In measures of self-esteem this group outcome only affected members of cohesive groups: the group's success or failure being reflected in raised or depresse$\dot{}$ levels of self-esteem. For the other groups the outcome of the group task was immaterial. Furthermore, the cohesive group members' anticipation of *personal* competence to carry out some future (and unrelated) task on their own was also reliably affected by their group's perceived achievement. Although, as we shall see, the effects of group success and failure are not always as straightforward as this (see chapter 7), this experiment does show how the positivity of our self-concept can be influenced by the social evaluation of the groups to which we belong.

Initiation into the group

In the last section we concentrated on changes in individuals as they become group members. How does the rest of the group respond to these newcomers? Moreland and Levine (1982) note that entry into the group is often marked by some ceremony or ritual. This is especially true of established or formal groups and organizations, although somewhat less typical of informal friendship and peer groups. These initiation ceremonies can take different forms ranging from a warm welcome, with the novice receiving rewarding and favourable treatment, to a distinctly unpleasant (not to say painful) experience in which the newcomer is mocked, embarrassed or even physically assaulted. Examples of the former type include the fringe benefits and privileges which some organizations bestow on their new employees and the celebrations which accompany the achievement of full membership of some religions (e.g. the Jewish Bahmitzva). Examples of negative entry experiences are numerous. Anthropologists have noted the prevalence of initiation ceremonies in a wide variety of culture (e.g. van Gennep, 1960). These are used to mark transitions in status or role within a society – what van Gennep (1960) termed 'rites de passage' – and may involve the inflicting of pain or some act of bodily mutilation (e.g. circumcision rituals). Such entry proceedings are not restricted to non-industrialized societies. Joining military organizations frequently involves a series of humiliating experiences as Lodge (1962) has chronicled in his novel *Ginger You're Barmy*. Stanley Kubrick's film, *Full Metal Jacket*, chillingly portrays a group of marine cadets undergoing the same process (see also Dornbusch, 1955). Some North American college fraternities still engage in practices of 'hazing' new or potential members. These require initiates to perform some degrading or humiliating activities for the amusement of existing members of the fraternity. Similar phenomena can be observed at the workplace. Vaught and Smith (1980) describe in some detail the process of 'making a miner' in a Kentucky coal mine, a process which they report involves physical assault and occasional sexual debasement.

Why should groups go to these lengths to mark the entry of new members into their ranks? There are several possible reasons. The first is that they may serve a symbolic function both for the newcomer and for the group itself. For the newcomer it helps in the process of identity transition that we discussed earlier. As van Maanen (1976) put it in talking about socialization to work: 'Transition rites provide a temporal reference point which allows the individual to say, "I am not what I used to be" (van Maanen, 1976, p. 101). The group, too, may need symbols to define its boundaries. In so far as the initiation involves the acquisition of characteristic markings or the donning of new clothing, it helps to underline the group's distinctiveness from other groups, an important feature of intergroup relationships (van Gennep, 1960, pp. 72–4; Tajfel, 1978a; see also chapter 8). Secondly, some entry procedures may serve as a kind of apprenticeship for the individual, introducing him or her to the normative standards of the group and relevant skills needed for effective functioning in the group. We shall return to this process of norm socialization later in the chapter. A third function served by initiation rituals may be to attempt to elicit some loyalty from the new member. This applies particularly to initiations which involve favourable treatment or special dispensations for the novice. The gratitude and perhaps even guilt which these favours may induce in the newcomer may enhance his or her commitment to the group's goals and activities (Lewicki, 1981).

The widespread occurrence of initiations which involve negative experiences is more puzzling, however. Although these may still serve the symbolic functions just noted, intuitively they would seem to act as a deterrent for the would-be member rather than as an inducement to join and identify with the group. Aronson and Mills (1959) proposed a rather ingenious explanation to account for these unpleasant experiences. They suggested that for most people the experience of group life is rarely completely positive. Attracted though they may be to the group, there will still be some aspects which do not appeal. This, then, may lead to a weakening of the cohesion of the group. However, Aronson and Mills suggested that groups can counter these effects by having group members undergo a painful or discomforting initiation. This will happen, they argued, because people's awareness that they have undergone the unpleasant experience to gain entry to the group is inconsistent with their subsequent discovery that there are things about the group which are not as they had anticipated. Drawing on Festinger's (1957) famous *Theory of Cognitive Dissonance*, Aronson and Mills reasoned that this perception of inconsistency (or dissonance) is psychologically uncomfortable and that people will look for ways to reduce it. Since the initiation may be too vivid or painful to repress easily, one avenue to reduce dissonance is to enhance one's evaluation of the group: 'if I went through all that to become a member of this group, it must be really attractive for me.' This led Aronson and Mills to the non-obvious hypothesis that the more severe the initiation, the more attractive the group would appear.

They tested this hypothesis in a now classic experiment (Aronson and Mills, 1959). Women college students were recruited to take part in group discussions on the 'psychology of sex' which, they were led to believe, would involve them joining an ongoing discussion group. Before doing so, however, they were asked to take part in a pretest which was described as a 'screening test' designed to assess whether or not they would be capable of taking part in the group discussion without being too embarrassed. The test (or initiation) involved the subjects reading out some sexually orientated material. The nature of this varied in the different experimental conditions. In the 'severe' initiation condition the women were asked to read out loud some lurid passages from sexually explicit novels. In the 'mild' condition, on the other hand, they simply had to read out five words which had some sexual connotation but which were not obviously obscene. There was also a 'control' group who did not have to read anything. Given the context in which the study was conducted (late 1950s), it is reasonable to assume that the 'severe' treatment was more embarrassing for the women students than the 'mild' or 'control' conditions.[1] On some pretext, the subjects were actually prevented from joining in the subsequent group discussions which they had expected, but they were permitted to listen in on a discussion which appeared to be already in progress. In fact, however, the discussion was pre-recorded and was identical for all subjects. And pretty dull it turned out to be. Far from the interesting discussion on the psychology of sex which had been promised, the excerpt which they heard was a tedious and stilted conversation about the secondary sexual behaviour of lower animals! Afterwards, the subjects were asked to rate both the discussion and the group on a number of scales. Exactly as predicted, these ratings were influenced by the severity of the initiation procedure. Despite the fact that they had all heard the same boring discussion and had been allocated to conditions randomly (thus ensuring initial equivalence between them), those who had experienced the 'severe' treatment rated both the discussion and its participants more favourably than those in the 'mild' or 'control' conditions.

In a subsequent experiment, Gerard and Mathewson (1966) confirmed this finding and showed that the results could not simply be attributed to, for example, the possibly greater sexual arousal in the 'severe' condition, or to feelings of 'relief' at discovering that the discussion group was not as embarrassing as the pretest. They accomplished this by modifying Aronson and Mills' design in a number of ways, the most crucial change being that real electric shocks ('mild' or 'severe') were used as the initiation procedure.[2] This was designed to circumvent the 'sexual arousal' alternative explanation. All subjects received these shocks, although in the control condition it was alleged that they were simply part of a 'psychological experiment', whilst in the experimental conditions they were clearly linked to a forthcoming group experience. This was to test whether it was the unpleasant experience itself (and subsequent 'relief' afterwards) which caused the effects, or the fact that it was an unpleasant *initiation*. The results were clear cut. Evaluations of the (boring) group discussion and its participants were in general more favourable when the electric shocks were seen as an initiation rather than as simply part of an experiment. The effects of altering the severity of the shock depended on this factor also. As can be seen from figure 2.1, those people who believed that the shocks were really an initiation test gave higher ratings of the group when the shocks were 'severe' than when they were 'mild'. In the control condition, this result was reversed.

Whether the underlying psychological process here is really one of dissonance reduction or some other mechanism is still a matter of controversy,[3] but there seems little doubt about the phenomenon itself: undergoing an unpleasant initiation experience does result in greater

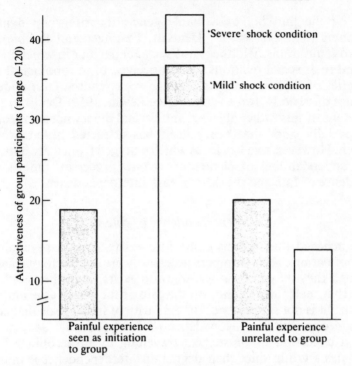

Figure 2.1 Effects of severity of initiation on the attractiveness of the group (from Gerard and Mathewson, 1966)

attraction to the group and hence may be used by groups as a device to bolster loyalty and cohesiveness.

Interdependence and group process

We have already encountered quite a range of different groups in an equally wide variety of social settings. Crowds, industrial work groups, military institutions, ethnic and gender categories, and the ubiquitous *ad hoc* laboratory group have all cropped up so far in the discussion. However, despite their diversity, there is one factor which is common to many, if not all, these groups. This is that their members are usually *interdependent*; one person's experiences, actions and outcomes are linked in some way to the experiences, actions and outcomes of the others in the group.

The importance of interdependence in the formation and functioning of groups was first noted by Lewin (1948), who had a profound effect on the thinking of a whole generation of group dynamics researchers (e.g. Cartwright, Deutsch, Festinger and Rabbie). The idea arose out of his field theory of social behaviour in which individuals and their social relations were conceived of in topological terms as a series of 'life spaces' (e.g. family work, church etc.) under the influence of various 'force vectors' (see Lewin, 1952; Deutsch, 1968). The details of this rather abstract and formal theory need not concern us, especially since the theory itself has attracted little systematic research. However, two key ideas which emerged from it are important to an understanding of elementary group processes. One is interdependence of fate and the other is task interdependence.

Interdependence of fate

Lewin believed that groups come into existence in a psychological sense not because their members necessarily are similar to one another (although they may be); rather, a group exists when the people in it realize that their fate depends on the fate of the group as a whole. As he put it: 'it is not similarity or dissimilarity of individuals that constitutes a group, but interdependence of fate' (Lewin, 1948, p. 165). Thus, a collection of passengers travelling in an aeroplane hardly constitutes a group since their degree of interdependence is minimal. However, the appearance of hijackers with grenades transforms them from 'passengers' into 'hostages' whose fate is now very much interconnected. Anecdotal evidence from survivors of such events confirms the power of this interdependence to weld the participants into a cohesive group (Jacobson, 1973). Indeed, sometimes that cohesion extends even to the hijackers themselves about whom hostages have been known to speak quite sympathetically, despite the fact that they were the ostensible cause of their ordeal. Mary McCarthy (1979) in her novel *Cannibals and Missionaries* has provided a compelling account of these phenomena.

The importance of interdependence of fate – or 'being in the same boat' as it is colloquially known – was demonstrated experimentally by Rabbie and Horwitz (1969). Stimulated by Lewin's ideas, they set out to establish what were the most minimal conditions for the formation of a group. Dutch school children who were strangers to each other were first divided into small groups (of four persons) on a random basis. The groups were labelled 'green' and 'blue' allegedly for 'administrative reasons'. They then worked individually on some irrelevant tasks for a few minutes. Then, depending on experimental condition, one of a number of things happened. Some of the children were told that one of the groups was to receive a reward (some new transistor radios) for helping with the research, whilst the other would not, apparently due to a shortage of resources. This common outcome of 'reward' or 'deprivation' was decided by the toss of a coin, by the experimenter in an arbitrary fashion or by one of the two groups themselves. In Lewin's terms all these groups experienced 'interdependence of fate', whether they obtained the radios or not. However, in the remaining control condition this experience was omitted; the group members thus had nothing more in common than their colour label. Finally, the participants were asked to rate each other privately on a number of sociometric scales. The question was: would these impressionistic ratings of what were more or less complete strangers be influenced by their respective group memberships and thus indicate that some primitive group had formed? The results showed that in the conditions in which some interdependence existed there did indeed seem to be clear signs of group influence on the ratings. Those who came from the children's own group were consistently rated more favourably than those from the other group. This was true regardless of whether they had been 'rewarded' or 'deprived' and irrespective of how that fate had been decided. On the other hand, the ratings from the control condition appeared to show no such favouritism; the ratings of ingroup and outgroup members did not differ. Rabbie and Horwitz (1969) concluded from these results that mere classification itself was not sufficient to form a group and influence people's judgements along group lines. What seemed to be necessary for group formation was some elementary sense of interdependence.

Actually, as we shall see in chapter 8, that conclusion turned out to be premature. Under the right conditions, simply being arbitrarily categorized into one group rather than another does reliably generate forms of group behaviour. Indeed, Rabbie and Horwitz themselves found indications of this when, in a follow-up study, they increased the size of their control group. With the larger sample (and hence greater statistical power) some significant ingroup–outgroup differences were then visible even in this most minimal of group situations (Horwitz and Rabbie, 1982). Nevertheless, these biases were still much weaker than those observed in the 'common fate' conditions, thus confirming Lewin's initial surmise about the importance of interdependence of fate.

Task interdependence

Interdependence of fate – simply experiencing similar outcomes at the same time as others – is the weakest form of interdependence. Much more important as far as group process is concerned, argued Lewin (1948), is some interdependence in the goals of group members: where the group's task is such that each member's achievements have implications for his/her fellow members' achievements. These implications may be positive or negative. In the former case one person's success either directly facilitates others' success or, in the strongest case, is actually necessary for those others to succeed also. Thus, in a sports team one player's brilliance (or ineptitude) has beneficial (or deleterious) consequences for the other players in the same team. In some kinds of teams there is a high degree of complementarity between the members, with each person playing a crucial role. A group of scientific researchers comprised of theoretical specialists, technical designers and computer analysts would be a case in point. In negative interdependence – known more usually as competition – one person's success is another's failure. The practice in some companies of providing financial incentives based on individual performance relative to other individuals is an example of negative interdependence.

This emphasis on the nature of the group's task and the relationship amongst the group members sprang from Lewin's concern to find an explanation for the uniformity of group behaviour. He believed that it was implausible to explain this uniformity in terms of individual motivational concepts such as those provided by psychoanalytic theory (Freud, 1932), or one of its offshoots at that time, frustration-aggression theory (Dollard et al., 1939; see chapter 6). Such theories require the many individuals in the group to be in the same state of psychodynamic tension simultaneously for uniform group behaviour to be explained (Tajfel, 1978b). On the other hand, Lewin's own account in terms of movement to or away from similar 'goal regions' made much less of an assumption of equivalence of psychological states. Whatever the individual dispositions of group members, so long as they shared a common objective they would be likely to act in concert to achieve it.

What evidence is there for the importance of task interdependence in determining group process and what exactly are its consequences? To begin with we should note that for a great many groups the very rationale for their existence is explicitly defined in terms of some common goal or objective. In the written constitution of my trade union, for example, the first paragraph of substance spells out the 'objects of the Association' which are the advancement of University Education and Research, the regulation of relations between University Teachers and their employers, the promotion of common action by University Teachers and the safeguarding of the interests of the members' (Association of University Teachers 1985). Defining a group in terms of its task objectives in this way seems to be a common phenomenon. In a survey of some 300 voluntary associations, Zander (1972) observed how the public descriptions of their activities nearly always referred to the purposes (or objectives) of the group.

What effect does defining the group's task in different ways have on the subsequent process in the group? The first serious attempt to answer this question was made by Deutsch (1949a), who developed Lewin's ideas into a number of testable hypotheses. Deutsch began by defining formally the terms 'cooperation' and 'competition' in terms of the goal interdependence between a person (X) and several others. In situations of positive (or what Deutsch called 'promotive') interdependence the actions of others towards their goals directly benefit X's goal attainment, as we have already noted. It follows, argued Deutsch, that under such conditions X will be motivated to cooperate with and help these others, will tend to like them also and the group as a whole will be propelled strongly towards its goal. On the other hand, in situations of negative (or 'contrient') interdependence X will be more motivated to compete with others, will like them less and the overall group force in the direction of the goal will be lessened. Associated with these effects should be a greater amount of communication about the task and higher group productivity in the promotively interdependent situations.

Deutsch (1949b) tested these hypotheses using a small number of student groups attending a psychology course. Half the group members were informed that they would be evaluated according to the performance of their group. In fact, all members of the group would receive the same grade, this being determined by comparing their group's performance with other groups in the class. These people were therefore positively interdependent on each other. The remaining students were informed that they would receive individual grades according to how well they performed in the group; the best students receiving the best grades. Thus, these were negatively interdependent on one another. Over a period of five weeks the groups worked on a series of human relations and logical problems and their discussions were monitored by observers. In addition, self-report measures of attitudes towards the task and fellow group members, and objective measures of performance were taken. As expected, the groups working under conditions of positive interdependence showed more cooperativeness towards one another, appeared to participate and communicate more in the discussion tasks, liked one another more, were less aggressive and on various indices were actually more productive than the groups working under negative task interdependence.

Although this experiment was important in establishing the importance of task interdependence as a major influence on what went on in the group, it was flawed in several respects. There were only ten groups and they were not randomly formed. The method of creating task interdependence confounded both intergroup and intragroup variables.[4] The observation measures were of uncertain reliability and did not derive from completely independent observers. However, such is the robustness of the effects obtained by Deutsch, despite these deficiencies, that later research has largely confirmed his findings. For example, Rosenbaum et al. (1980) examined both group performance and group process in a tower construction task where the degree of positive or negative interdependence was carefully controlled. In groups of three, the object of the exercise was to build as high a tower as possible. Depending on which condition the group was in, they were financially rewarded in the following ways: as a function of the total number of blocks comprising the tower (maximum positive interdependence), according to who had contributed the most blocks to the construction – the winner receiving all the money (maximum negative interdependence) – or according to some combination of these two allocation systems. As can be seen from table 2.1, as the degree of interdependence amongst the group members becomes more and more negative the productivity drops off, the degree of coordination (indicated by turn-taking) declines, and the amount of interpersonal attraction decreases. Just as Deutsch had found some thirty years earlier, where the group task links its members in a cooperative structure the result is greater cooperation, increased cohesion and enhanced performance.

This superiority of cooperative task structures on performance was confirmed by Johnson et al. (1981) in an extensive review of studies of group performance. Of the 109 studies which compared cooperative with competitive structures, they found that sixty-five showed a superiority of the cooperative structure, and only eight the reverse. This apparently unassailable superiority of cooperation should cause us to question seriously the overwhelming emphasis on *competitive* arrangements in our educational institutions and workplaces. The evidence is that such arrangements are quite literally counterproductive (see also Slavin, 1983).

Table 2.1 Group performance and group process under different forms of interdependence Type of interdependence

	Type of interdependence				
	100% positive	80/20	50/50	20/80	100% negative
Productivity (no. of blocks)	110.5	84.5	88.4	75.6	69.0
Coordination (turn-taking)	0.8	0.7	0.7	0.7	0.5
Interpersonal attraction for other group members	27.2	26.1	22.4	24.5	23.2

Source: Rosenbaum et al. (1980), table 4. Copyright (1980) by the American Psychological Association. Reprinted by permission of the author

Achieving the task and maintaining relationships

Although Deutsch and other researchers in the Lewinian tradition convincingly demonstrated the importance of task goals for determining the subsequent group process in general terms, little of this work shed much light on how the task was actually achieved. Even those Lewinians who specifically addressed questions of communication in the group tended to be more concerned with the quantity and direction of communications rather than with a detailed analysis of their content (e.g. Festinger, 1950; Schachter, 1951).[5] This gap was filled by another group of researchers working at the same time as, and indeed in close geographical proximity to, Deutsch and his colleagues. At the centre of this group was the figure of R.F. Bales who, like Lewin, came to exert a considerable influence on post-war group psychology.[6]

Interaction process analysis

Bales's starting point was to assume that the *raison d'être* of any small group is the achievement of some task. Thus, for Bales, any activity in the group is seen as being ultimately directed towards this end.[7] From this basic standpoint, Bales went on to make a number of important observations.

The first and most fundamental is his distinction between task-related or 'instrumental' behaviour and socio-emotional or 'expressive' behaviour. Eventually, as we have just noted, Bales believes that people's actions in a group are geared towards the group goal. Thus, whether they be social workers in a case conference, jurors in a trial or engineers grappling with a design problem, what the participants say and do to one another will mainly revolve around the group's goal (recommend a course of action for a client, reach a verdict or solve the technical difficulty). However, in all this 'instrumental' activity certain problems may arise which threaten the stability of the group. People may disagree with one another over the way the group should tackle the task at hand; the discussion may expose conflicting value systems; or perhaps there is some urgency implied by an externally imposed timetable. These kinds of factors are likely to generate tensions which, suggests Bales, may impede the group's progress towards its goal. Accordingly, counteracting processes will come into play to deal with those tensions. Bales (1953) uses a cathartic metaphor to describe this; he suggests that the tensions in the group need to be 'bled off' by means of 'expressive' activities. These processes focus on interpersonal relationships and reveal themselves in behaviours which are directly expressive of the person's own emotions or which are concerned in some way with the feelings of others. They may take the form of outbursts of laughter or anger, or expressions of sympathy or rejection for another in the group. However, since these socio-emotional behaviours are essentially subservient to the task-related activities, they are more likely to take a positive (or reinforcing) form than to be negative or inhibitory. Bales describes it thus:

> Even in cases of successful solution of the sub-problems we assume that there is 'wear and tear' involved in the solution of sub-problems which demands periodic activity oriented more or less directly to the problem of distributing rewards accruing from the productive activity back to individual members of the system and re-establishing their feeling of solidarity or integration with it. (Bales, 1950, p. 61)

A second key aspect to Bales's theorizing – one which follows directly from his functionalist perspective – is his assumption that groups have a natural tendency towards equilibrium (Bales, 1953). Any action is likely to produce a *re*action. Questions will tend to elicit answers or attempted answers. 'Instrumental' activities need to be balanced by 'expressive' activities, and so on. This homeostatic principle is closely tied to Bales's conception of how groups go about the business of tackling their task. He proposed that this has three components: orientation, evaluation and control. The group must first orientate itself to the problem it faces and acquaint itself with all the relevant information. Typically, this will involve a high level of communication and exchange of opinions. These different ideas then need to be evaluated to enable the group to move towards some decision. As the decision time approaches, the members of the group will start to exert control over each other in order that the decision is successfully articulated and implemented. Typically, at this stage, there is also a need for an increase in socio-emotional activity to reduce any tensions aroused by the preceding stages.

On the basis of these ideas Bales (1950) devised a coding scheme for the observation and analysis of group interaction. In this scheme – called interaction process analysis (IPA) – the interaction in the group is broken down into a series of microscopic 'acts'. Exactly what constitutes an 'act' is rather ambiguous in the coding system. For example, a sentence in a verbal utterance, some non-linguistic vocalization and non-verbal behaviours such as facial expressions, gestures or bodily attitude could all be regarded as 'acts' in IPA. Essentially an 'act' is the smallest meaningful and discriminable piece of behaviour which an observer can detect, and through training some consensus is reached between judges as to how fine the distinctions should be. Each 'act' is classified by the observer(s) into one of the twelve mutually exclusive categories shown in figure 2.2, together with a note of the committer of the act and its intended recipient. The following brief excerpt from a transcript of a group discussion will illustrate how the coding categories apply. (Numbers in parentheses refer to my suggested classification of each 'act'.) The group consisted of six students role-playing social workers preparing a court enquiry report on a young delinquent.[8]

Mary	So we need to discuss this, perhaps, with the employer and ask what facilities they do have for recreation for him. (4)
Pam	Um-hmm. (3)
Mary	. . . in what ways. (4) Because that is really important for him, isn't it? (5)
Caroline	. . . not very convincing, is it? (5) (*Laughs*) (2)
Pam	We've got to keep him out of trouble, that's the main thing, (4) or . . .
Mary	Mm, (3) or try to. (5)
Pam	We've got to come to some agreement. (4)
All	(*Laughs*) (2)
Caroline	. . . We've been more or less agreed all the way along haven't we? (6) (*Laughs*) (2)
Mary	So are we going to visit the mother straightaway, (9) or visit the employers first? (9) And see? (9)
Karen	. . . the family first. (5)
Brian	Yeah (3) . . . I think . . . (5)

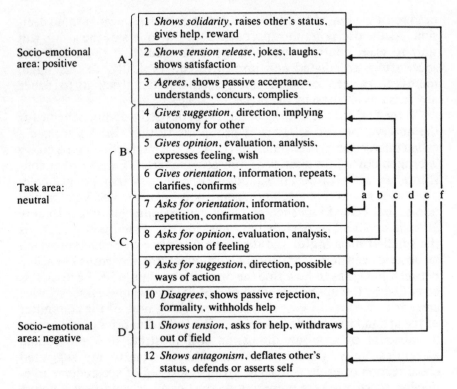

Figure 2.2 The coding categories in interaction process analysis and their major relations: (a) problems of communication; (b) problems of evaluation; (c) problems of control; (d) problems of decision; (e) problems of tension reduction; (f) problems of reintegration; (A) positive reactions; (B) attempted answers; (C) questions; (D) negative reactions (From Bales, 1950. Copyright © University of Chicago Press)

At the end of the period of observation it is possible to collate the observations in each category and provide an interaction profile of the group as a whole (in terms of the percentages of time spent engaged on the different categories of behaviour) or of individuals in the group, or (the most complete picture of all) the proportion of time each person spent interacting with each other and in what manner. These profiles have many uses. They can be used as data for the testing of particular research hypotheses about the consequences of certain independent variables on group process. Or they may be used in clinical and educational settings for analysing the recurrent interaction patterns in, for example, a family or a seminar group. Examples of studies which have used IPA are reviewed in Hare (1976).

Just how reliable and valid is IPA? After three or four months' intensive training, observers are reported to be able to achieve reasonable reliability both in the sense of agreeing amongst themselves and being reasonably consistent over time when re-scoring the same material (Borgatta and Bales, 1953; Heinicke and Bales, 1953). Mann (1961) found that varying the group's activity between a relatively task-orientated problem with a clear-cut solution and a more socioemotional issue involving value judgements and consensus did produce small but reliable differences in the amount of behaviour scored in several of the IPA categories, thus indicating that the system is responsive to presumed changes in the group's behaviour. Ultimately, however, the value of any methodological innovation lies less in these formal assessments of reliability and validity than in its ability to shed new light on the phenomena of interest. In this, IPA has been strikingly successful. One of its most important contributions has been to identify the regularities behind the apparently complex and chaotic web of communication which constitutes a typical episode of group interaction. Hare (1976) and McGrath (1984) have summarized some of the more important conclusions which have emerged from research with IPA: some group members consistently talk more than others; people who talk the most tend to receive the most attention from the group; the discrepancy between the leading initiator in the group and his/her peers increases with the size of the group – large groups are more likely to be dominated by a single individual; different people in the group often tend to predominate in particular coding categories suggesting a degree of role specialization (see chapter 3); the interaction profile for a typical laboratory discussion group is quite stable and consists of nearly two-thirds task 'acts', particularly attempted answers (categories 4–6), one-quarter positive socio-emotional behaviours (categories 1–3), and the remainder negative socio-emotional behaviours; however, other kinds of group reveal very different patterns. Children's groups seem to engage in more negative socioemotional behaviours, as do union–management groups, while therapy groups may spend more time in task-related activities (up to 75 per cent in some cases); in problem-solving groups there are consistent changes over time in the preponderance of different kinds of activities; for example, the proportion of informational 'acts' declines as the discussion proceeds, while positive socio-emotional 'acts' typically increase, especially during the final decision phase.

All these generalizations are based on the detailed objective observations of group behaviour which is the hallmark of IPA. Almost completely missing from all this work is the more subjective data from within the group itself. In his early work Bales deliberately eschewed this source of information but subsequently he has rectified this omission by turning his attention to the nature of relationships within the group as perceived by the group members themselves (e.g. Bales, 1970; Bales and Cohen, 1979). It is the most recent of these attempts that we now consider.

SYMLOG

SYMLOG is an acronym standing for a system for the multiple level observation of groups. This system, devised by Bales and Cohen (1979), builds on and considerably extends the earlier IPA scheme. Just as in IPA, at the heart of SYMLOG is the distinction between cognitively controlled task-related behaviours and those which are more reflective of emotional concerns or relate to the concerns of others (socio-emotional behaviours). In SYMLOG these are renamed as forward (F) movement (i.e. towards the group's goal) versus backward (B) movement (i.e. the absence or counteraction of goal direction). However, to this fundamental dimension two others are added. One is a dimension of value – positive (P) versus negative (N) – which simply denotes whether behaviours are friendly or unfriendly. The other is a dimension of power – upward (U) versus downward (D) – which gives an indication of dominance or submission. A second link to IPA is the emphasis on observed behaviour. Like IPA, SYMLOG is a system for coding and analysing behaviour in a group. Where it differs from IPA is that it also provides for the simultaneous analysis of social relations within the group by its members. Built into SYMLOG is an adjective rating scale whereby each member can rate every other member. These mutual ratings can be analysed according to the same three dimensional structure, thereby providing a subjective picture of the group to complement the behavioural data. This reveals one of the meanings of 'multiple level' in the name of the system: within the same conceptual framework the group can be analysed at an objective or a subjective level, or both. A further difference from IPA is that the coding categories in SYMLOG require more interpretation on the part of the observer. The aim of IPA is to provide a rather microscopic *description* of an interaction sequence; in SYMLOG the emphasis is rather on trying to give an *interpretative account* which will then be checked back against the perceptions of other observers and the participants. This seems to reflect a desire to provide a system which will be useful as a training or therapeutic tool in self-analytic or clinical groups, rather than merely as a methodological device for research purposes (Bales and Cohen, 1979, p. 189).

The three SYMLOG dimensions are assumed to be orthogonal to one another. If one divides each dimension into thirds – towards one pole or the other, with a neutral area in the centre – one can imagine a cube representing the twenty-seven different combinations of the three dimensions.[9] Thus, in a particular exchange one person might be simultaneously submissive, friendly and task-orientated whilst someone else might be dominant, unfriendly and expressive, and so on. These various combinations represent the system of coding categories, whether for observing behaviour or for the retrospective rating of fellow participants. As can be seen, this is more than double the number of categories in IPA, thus allowing a potentially more sensitive analysis. By aggregating the observations (or ratings) of the members of the group over the course of an episode one can locate each group member in this three dimensional space. Analysis of each person's position both in relation to the three dimensions and to his/her fellow group members then provides the basic data on the structure and dynamics of the group which may be used to test particular research hypotheses or as feedback in some therapeutic or educational intervention.

The main technique for such analyses involves the use of a field diagram which is a two-dimensional graphic representation of the three-dimensional SYMLOG space. Each person's location on the P–N and F–B dimensions is plotted from their 'scores' on these attributes derived from observational or rating data. Their score on the U–D dimension is represented by the size of circles drawn around these plots (larger circles = higher scores in the U direction). Examination of how and where these plots are clustered is said to reveal aspects of the group's functioning. Thus, if the group members tend to fall into two subgroups lying in different quadrants of the field diagrams then the group is said to be 'polarized' and to have a high potential for internal conflict. On the other hand, the members may all be clustered relatively close together in which case the group is said to be 'unified' and presumably more cohesive (Bales and Cohen, 1979, ch. 5). With the aid of a computer such field diagrams are not difficult to produce, and provide a convenient and readily accessible picture of the group which is easily comprehended even by those not well versed in SYMLOG technicalities.

The 'multiple level' nature of SYMLOG derives not only from the different methods of gathering data (interaction scoring or participants' ratings) but also from the different levels of coding involved in the interaction scoring itself. Each behavioural act is scored not only in terms of its type, who committed it and towards whom (as in IPA) but also in terms of its content or 'image'. If it was a verbal utterance the content is coded for whether the actor seemed to be in favour or against it, and which of six broad classes of referents it belonged to ('self', 'others', 'the group', 'the situation', 'society' or 'fantasy'). In this way it is claimed that SYMLOG provides a means for recording the development of group norms (Bales and Cohen, 1979, p. 168).

It should by now be clear that SYMLOG is considerably more sophisticated than its predecessor IPA. How well does it stand up to empirical and theoretical scrutiny? Although the system has not yet been widely adopted, the initial findings from studies assessing its validity and reliability seem mainly favourable. Take the three-dimensional model, for instance. There is converging evidence from a number of studies that social interactions in groups do, indeed, seem to be reducible to three basic factors and that these bear a close resemblance to the F–B, P–N, and U–D dimensions on SYMLOG (Stiles, 1980, Isenberg and Ennis, 1981; Bales, 1985). Further support for the validity of the SYMLOG rating procedure was obtained by Fassheber and Terjung (1985), who found that students' positions on the three dimensions correlated moderately well with teachers' judgements on related attributes, although hardly at all with subsequent academic performance. Bales and Cohen (1979) report reliability data on both the rating scales and scoring system which seem satisfactorily high, although there is some doubt about whether the three dimensions are really orthogonal to one another. There are indications that people who score highly on the U–D dimension tend also to come out positively on the F–B and P–N dimensions. That is, higher status members of the group tend to be seen as task-orientated and friendly. On the other hand, this is counteracted slightly for a tendency for task orientation and friendliness to be *negatively* correlated (Bales and Cohen, 1979, pp. 265–6).

Nevertheless, despite this supportive evidence, SYMLOG does have some limitations. First of all, it is only really applicable to small face-to-face groups and perhaps only to some of these. Like IPA, the empirical foundations of the system derive from study groups in educational settings, groups which are either concerned with particular tasks or which are explicitly self-analytic. As Sherif (1971) has pointed out, such activities are not typical of a great many groups in society (e.g. families, peer groups). Furthermore, by restricting itself to interacting groups, the system excludes from consideration larger social categories which often exert a strong influence on our behaviour. There are thus doubts about the generalizability of SYMLOG.

A second limitation, which is also inherited from IPA, is its over-emphasis on *intra*group processes and its almost total neglect of *inter*group relations. As we have seen, its prime objective is to provide a method and framework for analysing behaviour within the group; but in so doing it provides little opportunity for incorporating intergroup factors into its analysis. However, as Sherif (1966) showed so convincingly, changes in the external intergroup situation (for example, from group coexistence to outright conflict) will have dramatic repercussions on the process and structure within the group. Similarly, the successes or failures of a group in its dealings with others will have consequences for its morale and internal structure, as one can often observe in political parties after victories or defeats (see chapter 7). If SYMLOG is to fulfil its claim to be 'The new field theory in social psychology' (Bales, 1985), then some way of extending its scope to include the context in which groups exist needs to be found.

A third and closely related issue concerns its applicability to situations involving interaction between members of different groups, for example, negotiations between unions and management. Because the aim of SYMLOG is essentially to conceptualize members of the same group within a three-dimensional space, it may not be so well suited for the study of two or more groups, perhaps with fundamentally different goals and value systems. Although some SYMLOG studies of intergroup negotiations have been carried out (e.g. Hare, 1985; Hare and Naveh, 1985), it would be instructive to compare such analyses with those obtained from observation systems specifically designed for intergroup encounters. One such system is conference process analysis devised by Morley and Stephenson (1977).

A final limitation of SYMLOG is its relative neglect of the substantive content of the group's deliberations. SYMLOG seeks to extract the underlying structure and relationships from the complex interchanges which make up a sequence of interaction. Although it does incorporate some content analysis in terms of the type of 'image' conveyed in an utterance and the attitude expressed towards it, the reduction of image contents to one of six categories and attitudes to 'pro' or 'con' seems hardly to do justice to the huge variety of norms, attitudes and ideologies which groups may evolve. The development and acquisition of such normative systems – the fourth of our elementary group processes – is discussed below.

The acquisition and development of group norms

In the previous section much of the emphasis was on the regularities in the patterning of behaviour which seemed fairly consistent across a wide variety of groups. In this section, by contrast, the key word is *idiosyncrasy* rather than communality. For, as even the most superficial observation confirms, groups have various ways of viewing the world; they hold different values and attitudes; and, in the last analysis, they behave quite uniquely. Underlying all this diversity are systems of norms, systems which are to be found in every imaginable human group – from the loosest knit collection of friends to the most structured of institutions. Because of the universality of such systems and because of their importance in governing people's behaviour, the factors involved in the acquisition and development of norms represent the last of our 'elementary group processes'.

Just what is a norm? Paraphrasing Sherif and Sherif (1969), we can say that a norm is a scale of values which defines a range of acceptable (and unacceptable) attitudes and behaviours for members of a social unit. Norms specify, more or less precisely, certain rules for how group members should behave and thus are the basis for mutual expectations amongst the group members.[10] Examples of group norms in action would include the different styles of dress and appearance adopted by various subgroups in Britain, ranging from the colourful unorthodoxy of 'punks' to the bizarre traditionalism of the royal enclosure at Ascot. The varied life styles and mores of different sections of society (those favourite topics for Sunday newspaper exposés) also reflect the operation of different normative standards as do, in a much wider context, the rich variety of cultural practices around the world which have been documented by social anthropologists (e.g. Mead, 1935; van Gennep, 1960).

Earlier in this chapter we saw what happens when people join a group for the first time. I want now to return to this theme to illustrate how group norms come to be incorporated by the new members. One of the earliest attempts to document this process was Newcomb's study of an American college in the 1930s, the Bennington Study (Newcomb, 1965). Bennington College was a small private college with strong liberal political ethos. However, despite its progressive outlook it recruited mainly from very conservative upper middle-class families. What Newcomb showed, by a careful longitudinal study of cohorts of students through the college, was that their initially conservative attitudes underwent a radical reversal during their college career. Just one example will suffice to illustrate this. During the study the 1936 US presidential election occurred and within the college a mock election was also held. Newcomb was able to analyse the votes cast in this mock election. From the first-year students, who had only been at the college a month or two, there was a solid majority for the conservative Republican candidate over the more liberal Roosevelt (62 per cent versus 29 per cent). This was entirely consistent with their conservative family backgrounds. However, the third- and fourth-year students, whose families were no less reactionary, voted 54 to 19 per cent in favour of Roosevelt and fully 30 per cent of them even voted for the Communist/Socialist candidates! (versus only 9 per cent of the first years). The impact of Bennington's liberal norms on its students seems clear.

Of course, it could be objected to Newcomb's findings that the different year groups within the college may not have been strictly comparable. For instance, the senior students were also older. Perhaps what he had discovered was simply a maturational effect rather than any effect of group norms. That this is an unlikely explanation was shown by Siegel and Siegel (1957) in a rather similar study. Like Newcomb, they were interested in the political attitudes of entrants to a private American college. In this college there were two kinds of housing available to students. There were the traditional and rather conservative sorority-type residences and there were more liberal dormitories and halls of residence. Allocation to these different types of housing was essentially random, names being drawn out of a hat. Siegel and Siegel exploited this almost perfect natural experiment by measuring students' attitudes in these different residences at the beginning and end of their first year at the college, using the authoritarianism scale which is basically a measure of political conservatism (see chapter 6). Because the groups had been formed randomly (as in a good laboratory experiment) they should have been very nearly equivalent at the start of the year. Their authoritarianism scores confirmed this: the mean score in the sorority group was 103 as against 102 in the other group. However, by the end of the year the effect of the different group norms prevailing in the two residences was plain: the mean authoritarianism score in the liberal group had dropped by nearly fifteen points, while in the more conservative sorority it had declined by a trivial four points.

In these two studies the impact of the group's norms on individuals' behaviour could only be indirectly inferred from changes in their attitudes, and the actual process of acquistion was studied in a rather gross fashion. However, detailed observational research on new entrants to children's groups has revealed how individuals come to incorporate pre-existing group standards into their own behaviour. For instance, McGrew (1972) studied the behaviour of young Scottish children (3–4 years) over the first few days in their nursery. He noticed how the new children tended not to join in the communal activities at first but spent most of their time in careful observation of the others at play. Similar findings were obtained in the USA by Feldbaum et al. (1980), who observed that some of the differences between the newcomers and their 'hosts' persisted for as long as four weeks after entry. It seems as if new members of children's groups spend some time trying to discover what the appropriate 'ground rules' are before joining in fully. Experience of my own children going to nursery and then to primary school confirms for me the reality of this 'probationary period'. Putallaz and Gottman (1981) analysed the behaviour of 'popular' and 'unpopular' children upon entry to the group and concluded that the 'popular' entrants were those who tended to join in the ongoing activities rather than try to impose new games on the others, supporting observations of Phillips et al. (1951) some years previously.

Individual and social functions of norms

There seems little doubt, then, that the group's norms, whether these be long-established traditions or merely informally evolved patterns of activity, have considerable significance for group members. What functions do these norms serve and why are they so fundamental to an understanding of group behaviour? We can answer this question in two ways: first by considering what functions they serve for the *individual*; and then by assessing their *social* significance from the perspective of the group itself.

For the individual, norms act as frames of reference through which the world is interpreted. They can be seen as construct systems with associated values which bring order and predictability to a person's environment. Thus, the norms which my students and I evolve over the first few meetings of a seminar group about the extent of preparatory work which will be needed and about how the seminar discussions should proceed help me – and I hope them also – to function more effectively in the seminar. Norms are especially useful in novel or ambiguous situations where they can act as pointers as to how to behave. Hence the wariness of those nursery children in the studies discussed above; without a clear idea of what was socially appropriate, they hung back and watched.

The idea of norms as 'signposts' guiding the individual through unfamiliar territory was beautifully illustrated by Sherif (1936) in what is justly regarded as one of the single most significant experiments in the history of social psychology. In this experiment Sherif made use of an optical illusion known as the autokinetic effect. The illusion can be experienced by staring at a minute pin-prick of light in a completely dark room. Very soon the light appears to move erratically even though the source itself remains stationary.[11] Sherif confronted individual subjects with this illusion and asked them to estimate orally how far the light moved on each occasion. Over a hundred trials, Sherif found that each subject's estimates tended to stabilize around some idiosyncratic mean value. Sherif then ran exactly the same experiment in groups of two and three subjects and made a remarkable discovery: the subjects' estimates of movement rapidly converged until they were giving almost indistinguishable answers from one another. They had, in other words, developed a primitive group norm which served to constrain their judgements within quite narrow limits. Intriguingly, this norm continued to be influential even when they were retested on their own, their subsequent estimates deviating very little from the previously established value.

An obvious interpretation of these findings is that the judgements of the others took the place of the usual physical cues which aid visual perception (Gibson, 1966). The group norm served as a useful frame of reference in what was otherwise a completely unstructured and perhaps somewhat anxiety-provoking situation.[12] And there is no question that this norm must be a genuinely social product. Objectively the light is fixed and so there can be no right or wrong judgements. Consequently, left to their own devices people report widely different amounts of movement. It is only when they are exposed to the influence of each other that they converge to a common point of view.

Norms created in the autokinetic paradigm have a powerful and persistent effect. One can manufacture a deliberately extreme norm by asking confederates to give exaggeratedly large estimates (e.g. 30 cm). The other naive subjects will tend to converge to those high values. If one gradually substitutes more naive subjects for the confederates and the original subjects until none of the original participants remains, the extreme norm will persist through several such 'generations', only gradually decaying to the median value for the population, usually around 10 cm (Jacobs and Campbell, 1961; MacNeil and Sherif, 1976). The survival of these essentially arbitrary norms is quite surprising when one considers that it occurred in the absence of any social sanctions and social control which normally accompany normative systems in the world outside the laboratory (see below and chapter 4).

If norms are useful to individuals in helping them to construe and predict their world, they serve equally useful social functions also. First, they help to regulate social existence and hence help to coordinate group members' activities. To return to my seminar example. If we did not have those norms concerning the conduct of the seminar (e.g. that people should not all talk simultaneously), it is doubtful whether the group could really function as a learning unit at all. This social regulatory function is, of course, closely related to the predictability which norms contribute on an individual level. Secondly, norms will be closely tied to the goals of the group, which we have already seen as being of critical importance. Once a group develops a clearly defined goal inevitably norms encouraging goal-facilitative actions and discouraging inhibitory behaviours will emerge. An example of this was observed by Coch and French (1948) in their study of group productivity in a factory. A worker was transferred to a new department which had a well-established production norm of around fifty units per hour. After a few days the newcomer's productivity started to creep up to nearly sixty units per hour. This was regarded by the others in the group as contrary to the group's interests since it might be seen as giving management the chance to worsen their working conditions, and so they put strong pressure on the new member to come into line with the group norm. Of course, it goes without saying that group norms do not always inhibit productivity (see Schachter et al., 1951). Finally, norms may serve to enhance or maintain the identity of the group. This is particularly true of norms concerning particular styles of dress or forms of linguistic or cultural expression. Unorthodox clothing, hairstyles or distinctive dialects, while not directly functional in themselves, help to demarcate members of the group from non-members and thus define that group's identity more clearly (see chapter 8).

Variations in norms

It should not be thought that norms always prescribe exactly how group members should behave. Depending on the domain to which they refer and the person's position in the group, the range of acceptable behaviours – what Sherif and Sherif (1969) call the 'latitude of acceptance' – may be quite broad or very narrowly defined indeed. General norms and norms which refer to peripheral aspects of group life will have wide tolerance, while on issues which are central to the group's existence, or which concern one's loyalty to the group, the bounds of acceptable behaviour will be quite restrictive. Thus, while in many communities there may be some latitude regarding such matters as clothing, appearance and personal eccentricities, on such antisocial behaviours as theft or physical assault which threaten the viability of the group, the limits of acceptability are finely drawn. A person's standing in the group will have a great influence on how closely he/she must adhere to established norms. Typically, high-status members will be able to deviate much further from norms than their subordinates. However, once again, on key group activities and particularly activities relating to dealings with outgroups, leaders will be expected to be a model group member and stick strictly to the 'party line'. Witness the watchfulness displayed by many rank-and-file trade unionists when their leaders conduct negotiations with employers on their behalf.

Much of the evidence to support these conclusions was uncovered by Sherif and Sherif (1964) in their pioneering study of adolescent gangs in the USA. Groups of teenage boys in several different American cities were infiltrated by participant observers, who made a detailed study of each group over several months. These observers were able to identify clear norms in all the groups over a number of issues. Most groups had given themselves names and had adopted various insignia (e.g. tattoos). Often these were associated with rivalry with neighbouring groups. The type of clothing permitted in each group was often very rigidly defined which may seem surprising over such an apparently inconsequential matter. However, it is clear that for these particular subcultural groups, style of dress was a crucial marker distinguishing one gang from another; hence the importance attached to clothing norms (see also Sherif et al., 1973 for a similar finding amongst teenage girls). Each group had its own well-defined sexual mores and rigid codes of conduct for dealings with 'outsiders' (e.g. parents, police). As already noted, leaders in the groups could get away with much more (for example, being able to commit fouls in games which would not be permitted from lower-status members) except in certain critical areas. The Sherifs report how one of the gang leaders was criticized by his fellow gang members for being picked up by the police in possession of an offensive weapon, an incident which threatened the existence of the group.

It is not just between members of the group that one can observe variations in norms. Norms may also change over time in response to the changing circumstances faced by the group. For instance, in the Coch and French (1948) study mentioned above the researchers witnessed a dramatic change in production norms in three work groups following the implementation of a new management policy. Two of the groups were consulted by management before the change and were able to participate to some degree in the formulation of the policy. The third group was simply informed of the change that was to occur. In the days following the change the work rate of the two 'participative' groups rose steadily, whilst for the 'non-participative' group it fell. By the end of the evaluation period, the norms of the participative groups had diverged by nearly 50 per cent from the non-participative group. This is another example of how a change at the intergroup level (in management–worker relations) has effects at the intragroup level (in norms within the work group), underlining one of the central themes of this book: the interrelatedness of between and within group processes.

Of course, not all norms are subject to change. Many group practices and traditions are remarkably stable. Sherif and Sherif (1967) report a follow-up study of one of their adolescent groups through three generations. They were able to locate former members of the gang, then in their twenties and thirties, as well as the current group. They found that very little had changed. Although the individuals comprising the group had come and gone, the customs were very similar to those observed in the original study. The same rivalry with a nearby gang persisted. Interestingly, the erstwhile members of the gang still saw each other socially and still referred to each other by the special names they had had as teenagers. This lasting impact of adolescent group norms was confirmed by Newcomb et al. (1967) in their continuation study of Bennington College and its former graduates. They managed to trace a substantial proportion of the students they had studied so intensively twenty years previously. It was clear that many of the progressive values imparted by the college in the 1930s had stayed with the students. On a number of comparisons they were politically more liberal than a variety of groups of similar age and socioeconomic status. And it was not just the individuals who showed stability; a careful analysis of the college itself revealed that it, too, had retained much of the radical ethos with which it had been founded all those years previously.

No discussion of the acquisition and development of group norms would be complete without considering the social processes whereby they are enforced. However, that discussion properly belongs under the heading of 'social influence' and so is deferred until chapter 4 where the impact of majorities and minorities in shaping and changing group members' normative judgements is investigated in detail.

Summary

1 Becoming a member of a group has implications for the way we see ourselves. We are more likely to define ourselves in terms of that group
membership which may then have positive or negative consequences for
our self-esteem, depending on the fortunes of the group.

2 Initiation into the group is often marked by some ritual, frequently
involving embarrassment or pain. The function of the ritual may be
symbolic – to delineate more clearly who belongs to the group and who
does not. The associated discomfort may serve to increase the subsequent
commitment to the group through processes of dissonance reduction.
Having endured some costly experience may lead group members to
rationalize their judgement of the group retrospectively and evaluate it
more positively.

3 One of the most elementary aspects of group formation may be the
experience of common fate, the understanding that one's outcomes are,
through change or design, bound up with those of others.

4 An even stronger form of interdependence is that shaped by the task goals
of the group. Where these bring people into a *positive* relationship with
one another – where their outcomes are positively correlated – then
cooperation, cohesion and enhanced group performance are likely.
Negative interdependence, on the other hand, leads to competition, reduced
liking for others in the group and, usually, lower performance.

5 A fundamental distinction in group life is that between behaviours focused
on achieving the group's goal and behaviours concerned with feelings for
and towards others in the group. This task/socio-emotional dimension can
be discerned by careful observation of interacting groups. One useful
observation system is Bales's interaction process analysis (IPA). Using
IPA, it is possible to identify several regularities in the ways problem-
solving groups behave.

6 Recent theoretical developments suggest that two further dimensions are
important. These are status and friendliness. Whether one uses subjective
ratings by group members themselves or objective behavioural analysis, it
is possible to characterize people and relationships in the group pictorially
in terms of these dimensions. The system which has been developed for this
purpose is Bales's and Cohen's SYMLOG. Useful though SYMLOG is, it
is limited by its overconcentration on particular kinds of groups and its
neglect of intergroup relations.

7 All groups evolve systems of norms which define the limits of acceptable and unacceptable behaviours. Norms help the individual to structure and predict her/his environment and they provide a means by which behaviour in the group can be regulated. They also facilitate the achievement of group goals and express aspects of the group's identity.

8 Normative limits vary depending on the centrality of the issue for the group and the status of the group member. Norms may change with changing circumstances, but can also be highly stable over many years.

Further reading

Bales, R.F. and Cohen, S.P. (1979) *SYMLOG: a system for the Multiple Level Observation of Groups*, chs 1-5. New York: Free Press.

Cartwright, D. and Zander, A. (eds) (1969) *Group Dynamics*, 3rd edn, chs 31, 34, 35. New·York: Harper and Row.

Moreland, R.L. and Levine, J.M. (1982) Socialization in small groups: temporal changes in individual–group relations, in Berkowitz, L. (ed.) *Advances in Experimental Social Psychology*, vol. 15. New York: Academic Press.

Sherif, M. and Sherif, C.W. (1969) *Social Psychology*, chs 9-10. New York: Harper and Row.

CHAPTER 3

Structural Aspects of Groups

This book is concerned with various processes within and between groups which govern our social behaviour. 'Processes' signify movement and change over time and, to be sure, group relations are often in a state of flux. However, this should not blind us to the fact that there are facts of group life which show some stability. Most prominent of these are those which reflect the *structure* of the group – the framework within which the elementary processes discussed in chapter 2 take place. This chapter is concerned with those structural aspects.

Sherif and Sherif (1969), defined group structure as 'an interdependent network of roles and hierarchical statuses' (p. 150) and, following their lead, the first two sections of the chapter deal with *role* and *status* differentiation. Both 'role' and 'status' refer to predictable patterns of behaviour associated with not so much *particular* individuals in the group but with the *positions* occupied by those individuals. They are, if you like, the parts and script of a play rather than the actors who perform in it. The main difference between role and status is one of value. The various roles in a group can be of equal worth whereas different status positions are, by definition, differentially valued.

The existence of status differences is closely related to a social process which constitutes the second of this book's three major themes – that of social comparison. As I shall show, social comparisons take place within – and, indeed, often give rise to – status hierarchies, and it is suggested that this strongly implicates self-evaluation as the motive underlying them. By locating ourselves in the group's status structure we gain insight into our abilities relative to our peers. One type of group member who possesses more status (and power) than most is the leader. It is natural, therefore, that the next major portion of this chapter is given over to a discussion of leadership. Leadership is examined as a personal attribute, as an outcome of situational determinants, as an interaction of personality *and* situation, and finally – recalling some ideas from chapter 2 – as a *process* of negotiation between leaders and followers. The final section deals with communication structures and how these influence group performance and morale.

Role differentiation

In chapter 2 we saw how important norms were in generating expectations about how group members should or should not behave. Mostly, the norms we considered were general rules applying more or less strictly to everyone in the group. Often, however, we find that different expectations are associated with particular people or positions within the group. This is what is meant by role differentiation and it is an exceedingly common feature of group life.

Sometimes roles are formally prescribed. Thus, in a factory a worker may be paid to carry out certain specific functions within the production team (e.g. lathe operator, welder). Similarly, in institutions like schools there will usually be well-defined roles of head teacher, departmental head, class teacher, student, and probably various designated positions within each class. In smaller units, such as a sports team or group of mountaineers, the various participants are also designated different jobs (e.g. mid-field player; medical support). Sherif et al. (1961) observed exactly such a differentiation of roles in groups of boys in a summer camp. After just two or three days of interaction the groups of strangers had developed a clear structure with boys being allocated different tasks. However, in a great many groups such clear demarcation of roles is not immediately visible. Amongst friends or in informal discussion groups, for instance, it is rare for different role positions to be explicitly referred to. Nevertheless, it is possible to identify role differentiation as having occurred even in these apparently amorphous groupings.

One of the earliest studies to do so was by Slater (1955). Using Bales's IPA system, he observed twenty problem-solving groups over four consecutive sessions. In addition, he obtained subjective ratings from the participants themselves on who they regarded as having the best ideas in the group, who exerted the most guidance and whom they liked the best. A number of interesting findings emerged. First, the person who was regarded by his peers as being the most influential was not usually the person who was liked the most; there was some positive correlation between the two attributes but not a very strong one, and it became progressively weaker over time. This suggested to Slater that Bales's primary distinction between instrumental and expressive behaviours (see chapter 2) might be reflected in two basic roles in a problem-solving group: the task specialist (the 'ideas' person) and the socio-emotional specialist (the person whom everyone liked). Sure enough, when he divided his sample into those ranked high on 'ideas' and those ranked high on 'liking', some clear behavioural differences were visible. 'Ideas' men were observed to spend more time than 'best-liked' men on task-related activities (IPA categories 4–9), but correspondingly less on positive socio-emotional behaviours (IPA categories 1–3). Interestingly, although they spent their time in the group doing different things, Slater found that these two kinds of specialist interacted with each other more than one would have expected by chance, suggesting that the two roles might be complementary.[1]

Some of the clearest examples of role differentiation are to be found in that most important of all small groups, the family. Whether we consider the nuclear family typical of the industrialized West or the variety of other family arrangements around the world, it is nearly always possible to identify a number of formally ascribed positions (e.g. parent, child, caretaker), as well as some more socially functional roles (e.g. those associated with emotional support or with discipline). Scott and Scott (1981), in an analysis of nearly 300 primary groups of different types in Australia, found the family to be easily the most role (and status) differentiated. Zelditch (1956), in a cross-cultural analysis of ethnographic reports of fifty different societies, found that more than three-quarters of them showed some differentiation between task and socio-emotional roles within the family.

Parsons and Bales (1956) argued that Zelditch's findings implied that the family should be regarded merely as one particular kind of small group and, as such, it faced the usual problems of reconciling instrumental and expressive behaviours. Since they also believed that it was difficult for one person to carry out these functions simultaneously (recall that task and socio-emotional orientations are assumed to be inversely related within the IPA and SYMLOG systems, see chapter 2), this suggested to them that the most effective and cohesive families would be those where there was a clear division of roles between different family members. They went on to argue that this role specialization would be universally effected by allocating the roles along sex lines with fathers adopting the instrumental role and mothers fulfilling expressive functions. This suggestion was based on psychoanalytic theorizing about the assumed need for children to be able to achieve identification with the same sex parent. Zelditch's data appeared to support this idea since in both matrilineal and patrilineal societies the allocation of roles was predominantly by sex. Furthermore, there is a wealth of evidence – mainly, it is true, from Western sources – indicating a bias in personality style towards socio-emotional orientation in women and towards task orientation in men (Carlson, 1971; Spence and Helmreich, 1978).

Although some differentiation of role in families undoubtedly does occur, and occur quite frequently, the idea that this necessarily has to coincide in an invariant way with two principal parents, or indeed has to be allocated between different family members at all, is rather questionable. There are several reasons for saying this. First, as Slater (1961) pointed out, the Parsons–Bales theory of the family rested on the assumption that task and socio-emotional activities were always incompatible. Actually this is not the case, as Slater's own earlier study had shown (Slater, 1955). Although he had found some differentiation into task and socio-emotional specialists, the correlation between subjective ratings along these two dimensions was *positive*, although not strongly so. This suggests that the same individual can sometimes fulfil both roles, and Slater (1961) unearthed additional anthropological evidence to suggest that in several societies this is indeed what happens. Alternatively, role differentiation in the family may not fall *along* the task–socio-emotional dimension but orthogonal to it. For instance, both parents could be equally 'instrumental' in family affairs but perhaps in different domains (e.g. garden and kitchen). Nor is it clear that a high degree of differentiation is always associated with internal family solidarity. Although Scott and Scott (1981) did observe a general trend across all the types of groups they studied for role differentiation and solidarity to be positively correlated, within the subset of families the relationship was actually significantly *negative*. Perhaps too rigid a family role structure creates more problems than it solves (see Minuchin, 1974).

There is also evidence from experimental studies of family problem-solving activity which contradicts the presumed universal correlation between sex and the adoption of instrumental or expressive roles. Leik (1963) found that the conventional differentiation only occurred in artificially constructed 'family' groups (e.g. a man, a woman and a teenage girl – all strangers); in natural families representation of mothers and fathers in the task and socio-emotional behavioural categories was much more even. A similar conclusion was reached by O'Rourke (1963), who compared the same families' interaction patterns in their home settings with those in the novel environment of the laboratory. It was only in the latter setting that the fathers seemed more task-orientated than the mothers. At home, they appeared to display more positive socio-emotional behaviour than their wives (see also Waxler and Mishler, 1970).[2] Finally, Bartol and Martin (1986) conclude in a recent review that the nature of men's and women's behaviour in task groups may depend on the sex composition of the group. Where women are in the majority the 'usual' differentiation by sex may be less evident. There is thus good reason to be cautious in accepting too readily the notion of a universal sexual division of labour in group dynamics.

At the beginning of this section it was noted that role differentiation is a pervasive feature of group life. Why should this be? One obvious reason is that roles imply a division of labour amongst the group members which can often facilitate the achievement of the group's goal, an important motivating factor as we saw in the last chapter. As we shall see later in our discussion of leadership and communication, one of the problems faced by a group is to find ways to share the work and responsibility amongst the group members to prevent the leader(s) from becoming physically or cognitively overloaded. This is why so many committees, political groups and clubs find it useful to designate people to the roles of chairperson, secretary, treasurer etc., each with its own range of duties and functions. This also means that the adoption of roles may be situation-specific as the group goals change. A child at school might play a minor role in the academic setting of the classroom but emerge as a key figure in a school sports team.

A second function of roles is similar to that provided by normative systems: they help to bring order to the group's existence. Like norms, roles imply expectations about one's own and others' behaviour, and this means that group life becomes more predictable and hence more orderly. The emergence of task and socio-emotional roles, in so far as this occurs, is important in this respect since group members will quickly learn who to look and respond to at certain points in the group's existence or in particular situations.

Finally, roles also form part of our self-definition within the group, our sense of who we are. Having a clearly defined role – as secretary, parent etc. – undoubtedly contributes in important ways to our identity. This is revealed when a person's role becomes ambiguous, overloaded or in conflict with other roles. If any of these conditions becomes too acute, whether this happens in a large organization or in the micro-context of the family, problems may result both for the individual and for the group itself. These reveal themselves in various ways; for example, in job dissatisfaction and reduced organizational effectiveness (Katz and Kahn, 1978; van Sell et al., 1981) or in mental illness and family dysfunction (e.g. Minuchin, 1974).

Status differentiation

Not all roles taken on by different group members are equally valued, nor do they carry the same power to exert influence or control over others. Each member is respected or liked to a different degree. In a classroom, the teacher has more prestige than the pupils and usually has the power to dispense sanctions and rewards to them. Once in the playground some children may be faster, stronger or more popular than others and, as a result, may be deferred to in making decisions about choices of activities and so on. When they return home, these same children will again occupy a subordinate position, this time in relation to their parents or an older brother or sister. In other words, closely tied to the pattern of roles in a group is the existence of a status hierarchy (Scott and Scott, 1981).

How should status be defined? This question has long preoccupied social scientists, and from the wealth of different answers which have been put forward I want to pick out two recurring themes (see Cartwright and Zander, 1969 for a full discussion). One is that high status implies a *tendency to initiate ideas and activities* which are taken up by the rest of the group. This is the view taken by Bales, as we have seen, and by Sherif and Sherif (1964) whose work we touched on in chapter 2 and to which we will return shortly. The other important aspect of status is that it implies some *consensual prestige*, a positive evaluation or ranking by others in the group. This is the position of Homans (1950) among others. These two indicators of status are nearly always highly correlated with each other and are worth distinguishing only because sometimes one may not have access to both. In an observational study, for instance, one tends to rely on the first aspect, whilst in a questionnaire or interview schedule the second may be easier to elicit.

However, two classic studies which documented the existence and importance of status differentiation in the group were able to tap both aspects in their methodology. The earliest of the two was Whyte's (1943) study of an Italian immigrant community in the USA. By living in this community for three years Whyte was able to build up a detailed picture of the various gangs and cliques that made it up. One of these was the Norton gang whose leader Whyte became friendly with. From conversation with the various gang members and from careful observation of their relationships and activities, Whyte concluded that the thirteen members formed a hierarchy. At the head was 'Doc'. Beneath him were three 'lieutenants' whom Doc deferred to more readily than to the other members of the group, who in turn could be ranked in terms of how much influence they exerted and how well they were regarded. 'Doc' described to Whyte how he had achieved his position:

> Nutsy was the head of our gang once. I was his lieutenant. He was bigger than me, and he walloped me different times before I finally walloped him . . . After I walloped him, I told the boys what to do. They listened to me. If they didn't, I walloped them. I walloped every kid in my gang at some time . . . [but] it wasn't just the punch. I was the one who always thought of the things to do. (Whyte, 1943, p. 4)

This combination of 'Doc's' physical dominance and his ability to take the initiative was reflected in many of the gang's activities, including ten-pin bowling where some quantitative assessment of each member's standing was possible. Invariably, he came out near the top even though, as we shall see in a moment, others in the gang were probably athletically superior to him.

The prevalence of status hierarchies in informal groups was confirmed by Sherif and Sherif (1964) in their study of adolescent gangs. In addition to analysing the normative systems in these gangs (see chapter 2), the Sherifs' participant observers were able to obtain quantitative data on the various group structures both from within the gang itself (from the participant observers and the group members) and from outside the group from independent observers. One of the measures involved ranking the members in terms of being able to take effective initiative in various group activities. In all the groups this proved possible, indicating that hierarchical structures were indeed a common phenomenon – and a genuine one, as comparisons of the different rankings revealed. The rank orderings of the independent and participant observers correlated very highly with each other (around + 0.9), thus providing good evidence for the reliability of the method. These 'objective' rankings also corresponded very closely (again around + 0.9) with the rank orders the group members themselves produced, suggesting that the measures were tapping something psychologically significant. Interestingly, the correlations between these status rankings and rankings of popularity ('Who would you like to hang around with?'), although always positive, were somewhat lower, echoing Slater's (1955) findings in the laboratory which indicated a distinction between task effectiveness and liking.

The ease and regularity with which status differences may be observed in groups should not mislead us into thinking that the hierarchy will necessarily remain fixed. Both Whyte and the Sherifs noted changes in the positions in the group structure as members entered and left the group. Another source of instability is the changing intergroup context in which the group finds itself. For instance, one of the groups in the Sherifs' study developed an interest in basketball. In the ensuing contests with other groups it soon became apparent that the existing leader was not the best player and his high-status position was soon taken by a more athletic gang member. A similar change in group structure as a result of changed intergroup relations was found in one of the summer camp studies also undertaken by the Sherifs (Sherif et al., 1961). There they found that as a conflict between two groups of boys intensified, a new and tougher leader emerged in one of the groups (see chapter 7).

What are the origins of this widespread occurrence of status differentials in groups? One explanation is to be found in the by-now familiar theme of the need for predictability and order. We saw in the last section that role positions carry with them expectations of the *kind* of behaviour that the person occupying them will engage in. So it is with status positions, only here the expectations concern people's *competence* in various domains. We believe that different people in our group are better or worse than us at this activity or that, which then enables us to allocate people (and be allocated ourselves) to certain tasks in an appropriate manner. Ordering the group in this way may help to stabilize the group and allow it to concentrate more effectively on achieving its goals.

Sometimes this can generate self-fulfilling prophecies so that people conform to the level expected of them, even though actual abilities may be higher or lower than this. Some years ago I taught in a secondary school which grouped its pupils by presumed ability in certain subjects after their first year. I well remember the experience of teaching fourth- and fifth-year students who had been designated as 'low ability'. Their actual level of competence was well below that of some of the 'low ability' first-year children who had not yet been so labelled. Even making allowances for their monumental lack of motivation, it was quite clear that, after three or four years' occupation of the 'bottom set' status position, they had actually internalized the official view that they were academically not very able, and performed accordingly. That this anecdote is not a completely idiosyncratic experience is confirmed by better documented accounts in the literature of group dynamics. Whyte (1943), in the study referred to earlier, recorded how in the gang's various sporting activities the lower-status members always seemed to play badly, even though in other contexts they were actually better athletes. Here is his description of 'Frank', ranked seventh in the gang, at a baseball match:

> In the basis of his record, Frank was considered the best player on either team, yet he made a miserable showing. He said to me: 'I can't seem to play ball when I'm playing with fellows I know . . .'. Accustomed to filling an inferior position, Frank was unable to star even in his favourite sport when he was competing against members of his own group. (Whyte, 1943, p. 19)

For another example of status generating expectations we can turn to Harvey's (1953) experiment carried out among established groups of adolescents. Harvey arranged for a darts contest to take place but with a blank sheet of paper covering the divisions of the dartboard so that people's scores were not easy to ascertain. Before each contest, he obtained predictions from the group members regarding each person's likely performance (which only he had access to). Sure enough, the high-status members of the groups were predicted to do better than subordinate members. However, these predictions showed a consistent bias. The estimated scores of the high- and intermediate-status members by their peers were consistently *above* what they actually obtained, whilst the predictions of the lower-status people were slightly below (high-status members: + 2.7; intermediate-status members: + 1.3; low-status members: – 0.2; a positive difference means that a person's performance was overestimated; Harvey, 1953, table 3). In this novel situation, the status rankings in the club were used as anchors to structure the group's activity.

Self-evaluation through social comparison

In the last chapter I described how social norms could serve both social and individual needs. So, too, can status differentials. Not only do they provide useful functions for the group as a whole but, by acting as a kind of social yardstick, they also assist the individual in the crucial business of self-evaluation. If roles help us to know *who* we are, our status position helps us to know *how good* we are.

One of the first people to recognize the psychological importance of self-evaluation was Leon Festinger. Some thirty years ago he proposed a theory to explain how self-evaluation may be achieved and what happens when it is. That theory, 'A theory of social comparison processes' (Festinger, 1954), can with some justice be regarded as one of the landmarks in the history of social psychology since its influence has spread far beyond its original concerns, extending to such diverse phenomena as the experience of emotion, interpersonal attraction, resource allocation and social unrest. The centrality of the notion of social comparison within social psychology generally is reflected in the study of group dynamics. Time and again in the chapters which follow we will find that social comparison processes provide a vital clue in understanding different facets of group behaviour.

Festinger (1954) begins by proposing that there is a universal human drive to evaluate our opinions and abilities.[3] The basis for this bold assumption is Festinger's belief that life would be difficult, if not impossible, unless we had a way of correctly appraising our abilities. As an example illustrating the survival value of accurate self-evaluation, consider what would happen if we did not know how well we could drive a car. Not only our own life but that of others too would be in jeopardy·if we took to the road without some inkling as to our competence in this sphere. Indeed, one of the tragedies of the influence of alcohol on one's driving ability is precisely that it can lead drivers to overestimate their competence to control their vehicle, all too often with fatal consequences. At a less life-threatening level, consider the decision of teenagers regarding a choice of career. Surely a critical component of that decision is their assessment of their particular abilities. Someone who regards him/herself as innumerate is unlikely to choose a career in accountancy, just as a person whose athletic prowess is in doubt will not seek trials for Manchester United Football Club.

How do we come by this self-knowledge? The most obvious and reliable method is to find some objective means of assessment. If I want to know how fast I can run, I can time myself over a known distance. However, often such objective measurements are not so readily available. I happen to be learning the guitar. For such an activity I do not have access to the musical equivalent of a tape-measure and stop-watch to be able to know how well I can play. In situations like this Festinger suggests that we turn to others to obtain information about our abilities: by comparing myself to other guitarists I can get some sense of my own musicality. Such social comparisons are important even if an objective evaluation is possible. Suppose – to return to my athletics example – I discover that I can run the 1500 metres in six minutes. Does this mean I am a fast or a slow runner? Without some knowledge of how fast others can run such a question has little meaning. Similarly, intelligence tests, believed by some psychologists to be objective measures of cognitive ability, are in reality measures of an individual's performance *relative* to some population of other individuals. In other words, to quote Menander (343–292 BC), commenting 2000 years ago on the famous Delphic oracle: In many ways the saying "know thyself" is not well said. It were more practical to say "know other people" (quoted in Bartlett, 1962, p. 27).

Of course, not just any 'other people' will do. In order to make a realistic appraisal of our abilities, we need to choose people who will provide the most – and the most reliable – information for us. To know how fast I can run does it make sense for me to compete against Sebastian Coe or Daley Thompson? To know how well I can play the guitar should I compare my rendering of Albeniz's *Leyenda* with that of John Williams? Festinger suggested that comparisons such as these between people so wildly different in competence are not very informative and that typically we will choose for comparative purposes others who are like ourselves. The achievements of others who are similar to us in ability act as a guide to our own likely achievements. This is why status differentiation in the group is so important. Since it provides group members with a rough rank ordering of ability on various attributes, it permits them to choose *comparable* others for purposes of self-evaluation.

This was nicely revealed by Radloff (1966), who examined the accuracy of self-evaluations amongst groups of sailors performing a pursuit rotor task. This task was said to be a good measure of eye–hand coordination which would be useful to them in the operation of naval equipment. The sailors were thus highly motivated to know how good at this task they were. The experimenter artificially manipulated their apparent performance in practice trials so that there were always two 'average' members, one 'above-average' and one 'below-average' performers. Following Festinger (1954), Radloff reasoned that those designated as 'average' would be capable of the most accurate self-evaluations since they had someone similar to compare themselves with. So it turned out. As a measure of accuracy, Radloff correlated everyone's estimated performance (their self-evaluation) with their *actual* performance and found that the allegedly 'average' members' correlations were markedly higher than the 'superior' or 'inferior' members' correlations taken together. Of the former, 43 per cent achieved correlations significantly greater than zero whilst only 21 per cent of the latter did.

If Festinger's similarity hypothesis is examined carefully, it seems rather circular. The whole point of social comparison activity is to discover the ability of another person so that we may infer our own ability. But if we already know they are similar to us in ability, why do we need to make the comparison in the first place? Goethals and Darley (1977), noting this tautology, suggested that what we really do in seeking out 'similar others' for comparative purposes is to look for others who are similar to us on *attributes which are related to* the ability in question. As any parent or school teacher will confirm, a common preoccupation of young children is to know how good they are – how fast, how clever, how strong – compared to others *of their age*. They assume, quite reasonably, that many of these abilities are correlated with the attribute of age and hence disregard the superior performances of their older siblings or peers and concentrate on their immediate contemporaries.

This was shown very convincingly by Zanna et al. (1975), who asked college students which other group's average score on a cognitive ability test they would like to know, given a rough idea of their own score. They were given the option of choosing between students of the same or opposite sex, or students taking the same or different degree subjects as their own, or with non-students. Almost unanimously (97 per cent of those participating), they chose to learn the score of some-one of their own sex. There was also a clear but less strong tendency to choose people taking the same degree, and virtually none opted to see the score of non-students. The students had clearly made the assumption that sex was related to cognitive ability and hence knowing the scores of same sex students would give them some indication of their own ability. Very similar results were obtained by Wheeler et al. (1982), who used the related attribute 'amount of practice' at the experimental task. Those who had been told that practice was related to eventual performance were more likely to compare themselves with someone who had practised the same amount as them than those who were told that practice was irrelevant to performance. Following Goethals and Darley's (1977) argument, then, we can see that our status position in the group acts as a kind of general 'related attribute'. By observing the performance of others of similar status at some particular activity, we are able to infer our own competence in that same domain.

So far we have considered the social comparisons which people engage in as if they were affectively neutral behaviours from which people disinterestedly made inferences about their abilities. Naturally, things are not quite so simple. To begin with, any inference about our own abilities has consequences for our self-esteem – we feel better about ourselves if we have done well at something. Since high self-esteem is preferable to its absence, this might suggest that we would be motivated to avoid comparisons with those who are better than us since the outcome of those comparisons is likely to be invidious. Moreover, from a strictly logical point of view, comparisons with our betters may not be all that informative for us, as Harvey and Smith (1977) have pointed out. As I have learned to my cost, knowing that my guitar teacher can play a particular piece is not a very good guide as to the likelihood of my being able to master it also! More reliably, I see what another beginner like myself is playing and know that there is some chance that I may be able to manage it too.

However, comparing with those of lower standing in the group is not without its problems either. To be sure, if we do better at some task it confirms our superiority, but only if we can assume that they were trying just as hard as us. If we cannot then the inference becomes unclear. Furthermore, there is always the risk that the outcome of such a comparison might be unfavourable for us which leads to a much more unambiguous inference of inferiority than from the same negative outcome *vis à vis* a high-status person.

Finally, as Festinger (1954) pointed out in the original theory, in many Western cultures at least there is a value on better performance which will motivate people to try to excel each others' achievements. Festinger called this a 'unidirectional drive upwards' and suggested that it would have two general effects on status relations in the group. First, it would introduce some instability as the group members jockeyed with one another for position. Secondly, people would tend to compare upwards rather than downwards in an attempt to improve their standing. Taking all these considerations together, the broad conclusion is that people will tend to choose others who are just slightly better than themselves for comparison purposes. As Goethals and Darley (1977, p .275) sum it up: 'it would seem that the individual has little to gain and much to lose by comparing downward and much to gain and little to lose by comparing upward'.

There is certainly evidence that this is what people do. Wheeler (1966) gave groups of students a fake personality test leading them to believe that it would be used for selecting people for a new seminar course. Each person in the group was given their own exact score and rank position although, unknown to them, they all received the same score and were led to believe that this was the median value (fourth in a group of seven). They were also given the approximate scores of the best and worst person and then asked which other person's score in the group they would like to know, given only their rank positions. As expected, there was a strong tendency to compare upwards rather than downwards: 87 per cent chose one of the three people above them, and this was most pronounced for the person *just* above them. Nearly 50 per cent of the sample chose to learn the score of rank position three, the person immediately above them in the hierarchy. This preference for those 'slightly better' was confirmed by Nosanchuk and Erickson (1985) in their study of a contract bridge club. They asked club members who they would like to discuss various hypothetical game situations with (e.g. a contract which just failed to make; a contract which was won against the odds, etc.). In nearly every case they found that the players opted to seek advice (or consolation) from someone who was a better player than themselves, as determined by a consensually accepted league table of bridge-playing success.

Important though similarity is in determining comparison choice, there are occasions when it may be as useful to know the *range* of abilities in the group. This was shown by Wheeler et al. (1969), who investigated the effect of depriving people of this information. They gave groups of students a bogus personality scale which was said to measure intellectual traits. Each person in the group was (privately) told what he had scored and that this had been the median value for the group. Half the subjects were then given information as to the approximate scores of the highest and lowest performers in the group, whilst the others were not. As usual, the critical question concerned which other people's scores in the group they would like to know. The results were clear. Of those who did not know the range of scores in the group, 70 per cent asked for the score of the top-ranking member as compared to only 24 per cent of those who already knew the range. For the latter, those immediately above or below them were the main focus of their choices. Moreover, the second choice of comparison amongst those who did not know the range was predominantly for the *bottom*-ranked person, a device which hardly featured at all amongst those who did (61 versus 12 per cent). Gruder (1971) found similar results in his replication. Thus, there are circumstances when Festinger's similarity hypothesis gives way to a preference to know about *dissimilar* others (Mettee and Smith, 1977).

One aspect of social comparison processes which we have not yet examined is their consequence for people's actual performance rather than their estimated performance. Festinger (1954) derived two implications from his theory. One, which followed directly from his hypothesized drive upward, was that people would tend to try to improve their performance, especially in relation to those similar to or immediately above them. The other, rather less obviously, was that high-status members would be motivated either to attempt to improve the performance of those below them (by coaching or practice) or, failing that, they might actually perform below their capability so as not to become too different from others in the group. In both cases the higher-status individuals are attempting to maintain comparability (i.e. similarity).

Compared to the plethora of studies investigating self-evaluations and comparison choices, these hypotheses have received very little attention. One of the few relevant experiments was that by Rijsman (1974), who examined what happened to people's reaction time when presented with feedback on the reaction time performance of another similar person. In a pretest session, the other person was said to have done very much worse, very much better or exactly the same as the experimental subject. Rijsman then measured the change in the subject's reaction time over the following ten trials. As expected from social comparison theory, he found that the biggest improvement came from those who believed that they had done as well as the comparison person (see figure 3.1). Those who received the negative or positive feedback or who believed that they were participating alone changed their performance significantly less. Rijsman (1974) also reports one other intriguing finding. When this same experiment was repeated but with the modification of telling the subject that he came

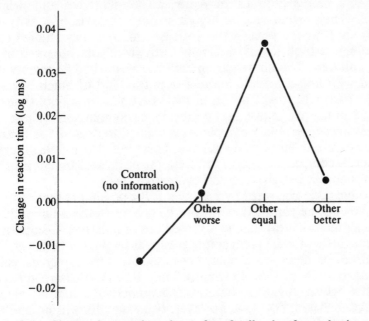

Figure 3.1 Change in reaction time after feedback of another's performance (from Rijsman, 1974, figure 3)

from a different category from the comparison person – they were said to be of different physiological types – the large change in the 'similar performance' condition disappeared. If anything, there was most improvement when subjects believed that they were being compared to a superior category. We obtained a rather similar result in some conditions of another experiment involving intergroup comparisons (Brown and Abrams, 1986). Taken together, these findings suggest that comparisons within the group may not serve the same functions – or have the same effects – as comparisons between groups.

As we have seen, Festinger's (1954) theory provides a useful framework for understanding the causes and effects of status differentiation in groups. Nevertheless, despite its undoubted historical significance, one or two cautionary notes are necessary before we leave it. First, we may question his assumption that the self-evaluation needs thought to underlie social comparison behaviours are indeed universal. Although there is precious little cross-cultural evidence on this issue, there are suggestions from developmental research within one culture which indicate that self-evaluation needs to take some time to appear. Frey and Ruble (1985) conducted an observational study of children's peer groups in an American kindergarten and primary school. They found that although social comparison activity was clearly in evidence even in the younger children they studied (five-year-olds), it took a very different form from that observed in the older children. The kindergarten children seemed to be mainly concerned with non-academic matters (e.g. the kind of lunch-box their friends had) and it was not until their first year in school that they showed an interest in task and performance comparisons. These classic Festinger-type ability comparisons seemed to drop off as the children progressed through the school. Frey and Ruble (1985) suggest that social comparisons serve different purposes at different ages and may not always be driven by self-evaluative needs.

Another issue neglected by Festinger is the possibility that comparisons may not be confined to within the group. In the original theory Festinger made it clear that he regarded this as unlikely: 'Comparisons with members of a different status group, either higher or lower, may sometimes be made on a phantasy level, but very rarely in reality' (Festinger, 1954, p. 136). In chapter 8 I shall be discussing a variety of evidence which suggests that this phenomenon is not as rare as Festinger believes. For now, however, two examples will suffice. One comes from Runciman's (1966) classic analysis of class relations in Britain in the early 1960s. One question in his survey asked respondents 'what sorts of people are doing noticeably better than you and your family?' a prototypical exercise in social comparison. Most answers to this question supported Festinger's contention regarding the within-group nature of comparisons: over 60 per cent of the responses from the manual and non-manual groups studied mentioned either some-one earning more than themselves (a personal reference) or other workers of a similar type. However, fully *one-fifth* of the responses in both groups mentioned a *different* status group (non-manual and manual workers respectively). An even more dramatic example of intergroup comparisons across status levels is provided by Abeles (1976) in his study of black militancy in the USA. One of his surveys, conducted in 1968 at the height of civil rights activity, revealed that in answer to the same question which Runciman had used 31 per cent of his black respondents mentioned whites, 14 per cent Cubans and only 25 per cent mentioned (the same status) blacks. In both these cases, then, we have clear evidence that people can and do make comparisons with groups in reality, and not just 'in phantasy' as Festinger sug-gested. Some of the origins and consequences of those intergroup comparisons will be outlined in later chapters (see chapters 6 and 8).

Leadership

In this section I want to focus particularly on one aspect of the status structure, those occupying high-status positions – otherwise known as leaders – and their interactions with the rest of the group: the leader-ship process. We have seen that one of the key characteristics of high-status group members is that they have a tendency to initiate ideas and activities in the group. In other words, they have some means of influencing group members to change their behaviour. However, since social influence is always a reciprocal process (as we shall see in chapter 4), perhaps it would be more precise to say that what really characterizes leaders is that they can influence others in the group more than they themselves are influenced. In everyday language the word 'leader' has dozens of synonyms: shop steward, team captain, line manager and director are just some of the many terms in frequent use. Equally various are the methods by which leaders come to attain their position. Election, appointment, usurpation or 'spontaneous' emergence are some of the most common of these. As we shall see, each can have quite different consequences for the morale and effec-tiveness of the group.

Leaders: personality types or products of the situation?

'Leaders are born not made', so the saying goes. This commonly held view about leaders is that they possess certain personality characteristics which distinguish them from 'ordinary' people. Thus, political leaders around the world – past and present – are all thought to have traits in common which have enabled them to attain their positions of power and allowed them to exert a controlling influence over their peoples. Just what are the characteristics which link a Ronald Reagan with a Golda Meir, a Fidel Castro with an Augusto Pinochet, a Margaret Thatcher with a Nelson Mandela or a Mahatma Gandhi with a Genghis Khan? Perhaps not surprisingly, in the face of this diversity, proponents of the 'great man' (or, more properly, 'great person') theory (as it is known) have found it hard to be precise, usually resorting to such vague terms as 'charisma' or 'genius' to explain the success of these 'heroes' (Carlyle, 1841). However, when examined more carefully, this personality explanation of leadership proves to be of little worth. Stogdill (1974), reviewing a large number of empirical investigations of leadership traits, could find few reliable correlates. In general, it seems, leaders tend to be slightly more intelligent, self-confident, dominant, sociable and achievement-orientated than their followers. They may also be older, more experienced and taller. But all these associations tend to be rather inconsistent across different studies, averaging out in most cases to correlations of less than 0.30, thus explaining less than 10 per cent of the variation in leadership behaviour.

In complete contrast to the personality theory is an explanation in terms of the functional demands of the situation. According to this view, expressed by Bales (1950) amongst others, the most effective leader in a given context is the person who is best equipped to assist the group to fulfil its objectives in that context. In another time or another place someone else may emerge as leader. This was well illustrated by Sherif et al.'s (1961) summer camp studies alluded to briefly above. When competition with another group was heightened, one of the groups underwent a change in leadership, with a boy of greater physical prowess replacing the previous leader. The new situation confronting the group had presented it with different problems, requiring a new leader for their resolution. An experimental demonstration of the same point was made by Carter and Nixon (1949). They gave pairs of high school students three different tasks to perform: an intellectual task, a clerical task and a mechanical assembly task. Contrary to the 'great leader' hypothesis, they found little evidence of the same person emerging as leader in all three tasks. Those who took the lead in the first two situations seldom were the same people who dominated in the mechanical task. The conclusion from these findings is then, as the novelist J.G. Farrell put it, that 'nobody is *superior* to anyone else, he may only be better at doing a specific thing' (Farrell, 1975, p. 154).

A more extreme form of the situationalist hypothesis is to deny any influence at all to the leader. An early adherent of this view was the Russian writer Tolstoy, much of whose epic novel *War and Peace* was devoted to a critique of the 'great leader' versions of historical analysis current in the nineteenth century (and still to be found today in some history classrooms). In Tolstoy's opinion, 'To elicit the laws of history we must leave aside kings, ministers and generals, and select for study the homogeneous, infinitesimal elements which influence the masses' (Tolstoy, 1869, p. 977). Although Tolstoy did much to discredit the naive leader-centred approaches to history, to disregard the leader completely would be unwise. In a test of Tolstoy's hypothesis, Simonton (1980) analysed the outcome of more than 300 military battles about which he could find reliable archival evidence on the generals and their armies. Although he did indeed find that situational factors – for example, the size of the army and the extent to which the command structure was diversified – *were* highly correlated with the number of casualties inflicted on the opponents (in line with Tolstoy's prediction), he also found that some personal attributes of the commanding general were reliably associated with victory in battle. The most important of these were the experience and previous battle record of the generals and their willingness to take the offensive. This indicates that the general does have some influence over the outcome of military encounters (contrary to Tolstoy). The kinds of personal characteristics identified by Simonton seem more in line with the 'right person at the right time' version of the situationalist hypothesis than the strict personality trait approach which we rejected earlier.[4]

The idea of leadership as a product of the situation is, as we have seen, more useful than simply regarding it as a characteristic possessed by some but not others. However, the situationalist approach is not entirely satisfactory either. It still does not tell us very much about what leaders actually do; nor, crucially, does it tell us much about the process by which they emerge in a given situation. It is these omissions which are the focus of the following sections.

The behaviour of leaders

If it is not who you are that is important to leadership success then perhaps it is how you behave, or so at least argued Lippitt and White (1943) in one of the earliest and most influential studies of leadership. They believed that an important function of the leader was to create a 'social climate' in the group, and that the group's morale and effectiveness would be dependent on the nature of the climate engendered. Accordingly, they set up an experimental situation using young school boys engaged in after school clubs. The leaders of these clubs were confederates of the researchers and each was trained in the adoption of three quite different leadership styles. In the first, the leader acted *autocratically*, organizing the group's activities, telling the children what should be done at all times, and generally remaining rather aloof from the group, concentrating on the task at hand. In the second, labelled the *democratic* style, the leader made a point of discussing all decisions and activities with the group and allowing the children to choose their own work partners. In general, the leader adopting this style attempted to become a 'regular group member'. Finally, there was a *laissez-faire* style in which the group was left to its own devices with minimal intervention by the leader. Each leader stayed with his group for seven weeks and for that period maintained a consistent style of leadership.

Then the leaders changed groups (twice) and at each change they also changed their behavioural style. This meant that any effects observed in the groups could be attributed to the leaders' behaviour rather than to their underlying personalities. And effects there were. The 'democratic' leaders were liked more than either of the other two types. The atmosphere in these groups tended to be friendly, group-centred and reasonably task-orientated while with the 'autocratic' leaders there was more aggression, a greater dependence on the leader and a more self-centred orientation. The 'laissez-faire' leaders tended to elicit considerable demands for information and were reasonably well liked, but more of the children's time was spent in play rather than work. As far as measurable productivity was concerned, the autocratically led groups worked the hardest but only so long as their leader was actually present. When, on a pretext, the 'autocratic' leader left the room they more or less stopped work altogether. The democratically led groups, although a little less productive, were affected hardly at all by the leader's absence. In the 'laissez-faire' groups the productivity actually seemed to increase when the leader left the room. These results led Lippitt and White (1943) to a strong endorsement of

the democratic leadership approach, both on grounds of group autonomy and morale, and for overall effectiveness.

At about same time as this work was going on, Bales (1950) was
developing his IPA system (see chapter 2) and, along with it, a theory
of leadership. Earlier in this chapter I described how Bales identified
the role of task and socio-emotional specialist in the group (Slater,
1955). These, in Bales's theory, correspond to the leaders of the
group. He placed most emphasis on the former role, arguing that the
person most likely to emerge as the 'task specialist' was the one perceived to be best equipped to assist the group in the performance of its
current task. Behaviourally, these kinds of people can usually be easily
distinguished: they tend to be the biggest participators in the group's
activities and their behaviour is particularly concentrated in the task
interaction categories, particularly those concerned with offering
opinion and direction. On the other hand, the socio-emotional specialist spends more time paying attention to and responding to the
feelings of other group members. Bales implies that these two roles are
difficult for the same person to occupy simultaneously and suggests
that most often they devolve onto separate people. Casual observation
of some real-life groups tends to support this dual-leader notion. In
the world of football management, for example, one often finds an
abrasive task-orientated manager in tandem with a more sympathetic
trainer or physiotherapist: the highly successful partnerships of Brian
Clough and Peter Taylor at Nottingham Forest and Bill Shankley and
Bob Paisley at Liverpool in the 1970s are good examples.

It is probably no coincidence that Bales's task versus socio-
emotional dichotomy bears such a close resemblance to Lippitt's and
White's autocratic versus democratic experimental distinction. Shorn
of their ideological overtones, one of the key differences between
these two leadership styles was a concern with directing the task as
opposed to paying attention to the concerns of the group members.
This same polarization recurs even more clearly in yet another
research programme, the Ohio state leadership studies (e.g.
Fleishman, 1973; Stogdill, 1974). These consisted of a large number of
investigations among mainly military and industrial groups in which,
through questionnaires to subordinates and other measures, the
behaviour and effectiveness of group leaders were assessed. The first
major finding from this work came from people's descriptions and
ratings of their leader's behaviour. Underlying all these ratings two
main themes could be discerned: one was a concern for *initiating
structure* and the other was a *consideration* for others. These, of
course, are very close indeed to Bales's two orientations just discussed.

However, in one respect the two formulations are crucially different: in Bales's theory, it is assumed that the task and socio-emotional orientations are bipolar opposites whereas the Ohio state researchers concluded that they could be better regarded as independent dimensions. The main evidence for this is derived from factor analyses of questionnaire data in which the two factors emerged not as inversely related (as Bales would have expected) but as largely *orthogonal* to each other. This means that, in theory, one could have a leader who is high in both structure and consideration, or high in one and not the other, or high in neither.

This brings us to the second conclusion from these studies. This concerned leader effectiveness. The best leader, it seemed, was the person who was rated above-average on both attributes: someone who could organize the group's activities while remaining responsive to their views and feelings (Stogdill, 1974). This has recently been confirmed in a longitudinal experiment involving detailed observations of twelve problem-solving groups (Sorrentino and Field, 1986). Those who were elected by their peers to be group leaders at the end of the five-week testing programme were those who had been consistently observed to score highly in both the task and the socio-emotional category classes in Bales's system. However, the situation may not be quite as simple as this, as Fleishman (1973) has pointed out. For instance, it appears that consideration and structure do not have a straightforward association with group morale. At very high or very low levels on either dimension, the relationship seems to disappear, thus producing overall curvilinear relationships. Furthermore, the two attributes may not be symmetrically complementary. A high level of consideration by the leader may help to offset too little concern with structure, but the reverse may not be true. However concerned with structure one is, one cannot compensate for a complete absence of consideration.

Despite these subsequent complexities, the Ohio state studies were valuable in providing strong empirical confirmation of the importance of the task – socio-emotional distinction in the leadership process. Added to the work of Lippitt, White, Bales and others, there is now a large body of data testifying to the importance of these two quite different orientations. However, in concentrating so much on the leader's style of behaviour we must not overlook the powerful situational determinants of leader effectiveness and, perhaps more importantly, we should also be aware that the leader's behaviour and these situational factors may interact.

Interaction of leader style and situation

With the demise of the trait view of leadership, the Lippitt/White and Ohio state approaches seemed to command the field: what was needed for effective leadership, it seemed, was the right combination of task-centredness and consideration for others. Fiedler (1965) was one of the first to notice the shortcomings of this simple dictum. Drawing on data from quite a variety of different kinds of groups (e.g. basketball teams, aircraft crews), he observed that there was no straightforward relationship between the leader's predominant style and the effectiveness of the group. Sometimes very task-orientated leaders seemed to be effective; in other situations, the socio-emotional leaders did best. Fiedler's resolution of these puzzling findings was to propose an interactionist model of leadership in which effectiveness was seen as *contingent* upon the match of the leader's style with the kind of situation which he/she faced. In a nutshell, the type of leader attitude required for effective group performance depends on the degree to which the situation is favourable or unfavourable to the leader (Fiedler, 1965; p. 182 of 1978 reprint).

Fiedler accepts the basic distinction between task-orientated and socio-emotionally orientated leadership styles which Bales and others have identified but has developed a measuring instrument in an attempt to quantify the difference. This scale – called the least pre-ferred co-worker (LPC) scale – simply asks would-be leaders to think of all the people they have ever known and then describe the one person with whom it has been most difficult to work. They do this by rating this individual on eighteen bipolar scales (e.g. pleasant–unpleasant, boring–interesting, friendly–unfriendly etc.). High scorers (high LPC) on this scale (that is, those who evaluate their least preferred co-workers relatively favourably) are thought to be those who habitually adopt a relationship-orientated or considerate leader-ship style, while low scorers (low LPC) are assumed to be more task-orientated kinds of people.[5] There are two important points to note here about Fiedler's distinction between high and low LPC leaders. The first is that he regards a person's LPC score as reflecting a rela-tively fixed personality characteristic which is consistent across situa-tions and over time. In a way, therefore, Fiedler is resurrecting part of the old trait theory of leadership. The second is that he does not view the high and low LPC categories as completely exclusive. Rather, the high and low scorers differ in the relative importance which they attach to person and task aspects of the group. In his terms, they have dif-ferent 'motivational hierarchies': high LPC means that people are primary and the task is secondary, and *vice versa* for low LPC (Fiedler, 1978).

Having distinguished between two basic leader types, Fiedler then goes on to identify three elements which he believes determine the 'favourableness' of the situation for the leader. The first, and most important, is the atmosphere of the group, which Fiedler calls *leader-member relations*. A leader who enjoys the confidence, loyalty and affection of the group will find his/her work easier than one who does not. Second in importance is *task structure*: a group with clear instructions for achieving a well-defined goal is thought to be easier to manage than one whose job is less well formulated and which has a number of possible outcomes. The obvious contrast here is between a production work group on a factory assembly line and a design team attempting to discover a new process or product. In the former case the components of the job are usually specified in the most minute detail and the end product is known in advance. In the latter, by definition, the outcome is uncertain and often the means of achieving it are equally ambiguous. Finally, the leader may have attained – or may be invested with – more or less *power*. Leaders may have many rewards and sanctions at their disposal and be able to exercise considerable authority or, alternatively, their position may be weak and they may have little competence or few means to influence the group members.

Suppose, now, every leadership situation can be defined as 'high' or 'low' in each of these three factors. This produces eight possible combinations or degrees of 'favourableness', ranging from good leader-member relations, high task structure, and high position power to the opposite of these three. Because Fiedler assumes leader–member relations to be most important followed by task structure and power, this suggests the order for the intermediate degrees of favourableness shown at the foot of figure 3.2. Fiedler's basic hypothesis is that low LPC leaders will be most effective in situations which lie towards either end of this eight level continuum, whilst high LPC leaders will excel in the situations falling in the middle. The rationale behind this prediction is complex: when the situation is very favourable for leaders (they are well liked by the group, the task is straightforward and their authority is unquestioned) they need waste no time in worrying about the morale of the group members and they have the means and the power to be wholly task directive. A similar style is called for at the opposite extreme, although for different reasons. Here, things are so unfavourable for the leaders (disliked by the group, an ambiguous task and little power) that they have little to lose by being fairly autocratic. Attempts to win over the group by a more considerate approach will probably fail anyway, resulting in lost time and hence lowered effectiveness. At the intermediate levels, on the other hand, the leader may, by adopting a suitably relationship-orientated style, be able to improve the leader–member relations sufficiently to compensate for an ill-defined task or a lack of authority. Taken together, these three lines of reasoning suggest that if one correlates the effectiveness of the group (according to some performance criteria) with the leader's LPC score, the sign and size of the correlation should vary across the eight situational combinations, being clearly negative at either end but positive in the middle. This predicted pattern of correlations is shown as the dashed curve in figure 3.2.

How well does this fit with observed correlations from leadership studies? In an early paper, Fiedler (1965) summarized the findings from a dozen published studies which generated more than fifty separate correlations between LPC and effectiveness. These correlations were allocated to their appropriate situational classification and the median correlation for each of the eight situations was determined. These are shown as the solid line in figure 3.2 and the fit is apparently quite close. In a later review, Fiedler (1978) presented evidence from further experiments which seemed largely to confirm the original picture except for octants II and VII where in both instances he found a more positive median value than had been predicted.

However, Hosking (1981) has pointed out that presenting the median correlations from a number of studies in this way is potentially misleading. First, because it obscures the considerable variation in the correlations around the median value and, secondly, because several of the original correlations were small in absolute size, many of them being not different from zero statistically. In her review of methodologically adequate tests of the theory she concludes that not only is the inverted 'U' shape of the solid curve in figure 3.2 rather exaggerated, but that in most of the octants the full range of positive *and* negative correlations has been observed. The only situational combinations showing clear support for Fiedler's theory, according to Hosking, are I (clear negative correlation between LPC and effectiveness) and V (clear positive correlation).

But this conclusion has itself been disputed. Strube and Garcia (1981), in a meta-analysis[6] of 178 empirical tests of the theory, concluded that there was substantial support for it, although their review did resurrect the doubts about the second and seventh octants which Fiedler had already identified (Fiedler, 1978; see also Vecchio, 1983; Peters et al., 1985). Given the very extensive range of studies on which

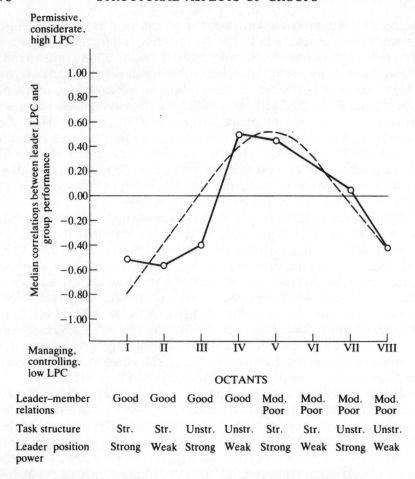

Figure 3.2 Optimal leader attitudes and behaviour required by various group task situations. Dashed line, pattern predicted by contingency theory; solid line, observed pattern of median correlations (from Fiedler, 1965)

Strube and Garcia's review was based, it does seem that the contingency theory provides a reasonably good model to explain leadership effectiveness, even if there remain some doubts as to its completeness. We will return to these problems shortly, once we have considered some of the implications of the model for leadership training.

Training leaders to be effective is now big business. Industry and the armed forces spend large sums of money every year sending their managers and officers on training courses. What happens on many of these courses is that attempts are made to alter the trainees' behaviour (or leadership style) so that they may return to their organizations and elicit enhanced performance from those in their charge. The preferred style will depend on the orientation of the training consultants, the occupations of those being trained and the likely leadership situations they will face, but the underlying objective is usually the same: to change the leader in some way. Fiedler, however, argues that this traditional aim is misconceived because, in his view, leaders' behavioural styles are deep-rooted reflections of their personalities and hence are rather difficult to modify. Thus, while he would applaud those training and selection schemes which attempt to match the leadership style to the work situation, he believes that this 'match' is best achieved not by trying to change the leaders but by the leaders either altering the situation, or moving to another situation more suited to their personality. This is the essence of his leader match training programme (Fiedler et al., 1976).

The programme takes the form of a self-administered set of readings, exercises and problems which are designed to teach trainees how to assess situations in terms of leader–member relations, task structure and position power, and how to identify which of these elements is most amenable to change so as to bring the situation more into line with their personality (assessed with the LPC scale). Fiedler (1978) reviews several studies in both civilian and military contexts in which leader match has been used and concludes that it is successful in enhancing performance. Indirect evidence for the idea that leaders have to be matched to situations was also provided by Chemers et al. (1985) in a study of university administrators. From these respondents the researchers obtained LPC scores, subjective assessments of 'situation favourability' and measures of general health and job stress. Just as the model predicts, those administrators in an inappropriate job (e.g. low LPC in a 'moderately' favourable situation) showed higher levels of stress and more physical symptoms of ill health than those who were better matched (e.g. high LPC in a 'moderately' favourable situation or low LPC in a 'very' favourable situation).

If Fiedler's training model is correct, the ironic consequence of some training schemes can be that they may actually lead to lowered rather than enhanced group performance. This can happen if they bring about changes in the situation which mean that a leader with a certain style is no longer operating in the most appropriate environment. This is what appeared to happen in an experiment conducted by Chemers et al. (1975). Army cadets were put in charge of student groups to solve coded messages. The leader–member relations of these groups were poor, the task was relatively unstructured and the cadet leaders had little power. The initial situation was therefore towards the most unfavourable end of Fiedler's continuum (octant VIII). Half the leaders were given a training course designed to reduce the complexity and difficulty of the task and by so doing move the subsequent leadership closer to octant VI. All leaders were then classified as high or low on the LPC scale, and their effectiveness assessed by measuring the group's productivity. As figure 3.3 shows, the low LPC leaders who had been trained actually did *worse* than the low LPC leaders who had not. For the high LPC leaders the reverse happened. The authors' explanation for this was that training had had the effect of improving the person–situation 'match' for the high LPC leaders (since the model predicts them to perform better on octants IV to VI), but of worsening it for the low LPC leaders who were already well matched to their poor situation before the training began!

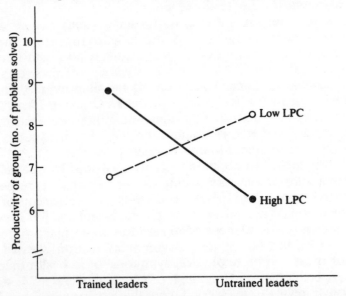

Figure 3.3 Differential effects of leadership training on high and low LPC leaders (from Chemers et al., 1975. Copyright (1975) by the American Psychological Association. Reprinted by permission of the author)

In spite of supportive evidence like this, Fiedler's theory has excited considerable controversy over the past twenty years. A central issue in this debate has been the extent to which a leader's style should be considered a 'given', unaffected by circumstances. There are at least three grounds for doubting whether the leader's orientation is as immutable as Fiedler claims. First, the claim is based on a trait view of personality which suggests that people will be consistent over time and across situations. But this conception of personality has attracted much criticism. For example, Mischel (1968) and Argyle and Little (1972) have convincingly shown that there is, in fact, very little temporal and cross-situational consistency in people's behaviour. This implies that personality traits may not be quite the fixed entities that Fiedler believes them to be. Indeed, if people's leadership style was so difficult to alter, how could Lippitt and White (1943) have so successfully trained their confederates to adopt different styles in the study described earlier? Further evidence of the instability of people's leadership orientation comes from attempts to establish the test–retest reliability of the LPC scale. Rice (1978) notes that these have produced correlations varying from 0.01 to 0.93 with a median of around 0.67. While the latter figure is comparable with reliability coefficients from other personality scales, it still implies that more than half the variance at the second time of testing is unaccounted for by the first set of scores. Rice points out that the lowest reliability figures were obtained in environments designed to bring about change (e.g., training courses), further suggesting that any traits underlying the LPC score are not completely unaffected by the situation. One might imagine, for instance, that changes in the leader–member relations in a group (one of Fiedler's key situational variables) could well affect the way the leader behaved towards even the 'least preferred' members of the group. All in all, then, there are grounds for questioning Fiedler's assumption that a leader's personality is fixed.

A second question about the contingency theory concerns Fiedler's assumption that the eight different situation types form an ordered continuum of favourableness, with each octant being equally distant from the next. There are two problems here. The first is that the order of importance attributed to the three situational factors was essentially arbitrary in the original formulation of the model (Fiedler, 1965). With a different ordering – for example, by assuming that task structure was more important than leader–member relations, the predicted pattern of LPC–effectiveness correlations would look very different. Although Fiedler (1978) was later able to offer some empirical support for his *a priori* ordering, he still assumed that the octants formed an approximately interval scale. However, Singh et al. (1979) have suggested that this assumption may also be problematic. They asked respondents to rate a number of situations, which varied systematically along each of Fiedler's three factors, for their favourableness to the leader. As expected, each factor did indeed prove to be an important determinant of perceived favourableness. Somewhat less expected, however, was the relative importance of the three factors. When judged in terms of how much variance each accounted for in the subjects' ratings, leader–member relations proved to be the most important factor in only two out of the four studies. In all four, position power was a powerful influence, the strongest in two of the studies. This is especially difficult for the contingency theory since this is conventionally assumed to be the *least* important factor of the three! Singh et al. (1979) further showed that if the octants were positioned according to how favourably they are actually perceived (rather than being equidistant from each other on *a priori* grounds), a rather more regular pattern of LPC–effectiveness correlations results. Perhaps this might help to explain the equivocal findings in some of the octants (Hosking, 1981). If the octants were re-ordered and re-positioned along the favourableness dimension, some of the ambiguities might disappear.

A third limitation of Fiedler's theory is its neglect of the dynamic aspects of leadership. Its main objective is to identify the factors which will maximize a leader's effectiveness in terms of some measurable performance outcome, and it pays almost no attention to the *process* by which leaders emerge in the group or are deposed. It is questions like these to which E. P. Hollander has principally addressed himself.

Leadership as a process

In chapter 2 we saw the importance of norms in regulating behaviour in the group, and noted that everyone within the group was influenced by these norms with – in some domains most central to the group – the leaders being more so than the followers. And yet, the whole discussion in the last three sections has emphasized the leader as an agent of *change* in the group, a person who is able to alter the prevailing norms and hence 'influence others more than he/she is influenced by them' (as we defined a leader earlier). This, then, raises a fundamental paradox: how can a leader be both a loyal group member (in adhering faithfully to the group's norms) *and* an effective and powerful deviate (in persuading the group to adopt new norms)?

The solution to this paradox was suggested by an early experimental study by Merei (1949). This was carried out in a Hungarian nursery school, where Merei observed the behaviour of groups of young children when an older child was introduced to the group. This child was someone who had earlier shown characteristic leadership behaviours in the sense of having been an 'initiator' rather than a 'follower' in his/her own peer group. Naturally, Merei expected the newcomers to assume a dominant position in these new groups, if for no other reason than that children at this age are very sensitive to age differences. However, what was of interest was the manner in which they achieved this leadership role. Would they assert their authority from the very beginning or would the process be more gradual than this? Merei concluded that those children who attempted the former strategy turned out to be unsuccessful leaders who were largely ignored by the other children. The successful leaders – as judged by the extent to which they were eventually followed by the younger children – adopted a more cautious approach. To begin with they tended to follow the existing games and 'traditions' of the group, suggesting only minor variations. It was only after a few days of this accommodative behaviour that they began to suggest completely new activities or radical departures from the old routines. Merei's observation of one of these 'successful' leaders sums up the emergent nature of the process of acquiring influence:

> It was at this point that a new leader was added. He tried to suggest new games but was not accepted. Then he joined their traditional game and slowly took over the leadership. The first day there were only two instances in which he led, the second day there were already nine. However, he was the one being modeled, taking over the group's habits. He accepted those habits but introduced minor changes. For example, he joined in the block game traditional with the group, but demanded that always the red side of a block be on top. (Merei, 1949, p. 30)

This sequence of first conforming to the group norms and then introducing new ideas is central to Hollander's theory of leadership (Hollander, 1958; Hollander and Julian, 1970). Hollander suggests that what leaders must do in the early stages of their 'reign' is to build up 'credit' with the rest of the group. This 'credit' is what gives them the subsequent legitimacy to exert influence over those same group members and to deviate from the existing norms. Hollander terms this 'idiosyncrasy credit' because it may eventually be expended in novel or innovative behaviour by the leader. Essentially, the more credit one builds up the more idiosyncratic behaviour will be subsequently tolerated by the group.

How does the leader establish a good credit rating with the group? One way, as Merei's (1949) findings suggest, is to adhere initially to the group norms. Hollander (1982) suggests at least three other sources of legitimacy for the leader. One stems from the methods by which the leaders achieve their position: were they elected by the group or simply appointed by an external authority? Hollander believes that the former method usually gives the leader greater legitimacy than the latter. The leader's competence to fulfil the group's objectives is also a critical factor. Someone seen to be exceptionally able in task-relevant behaviours will accrue more credits than the less able person. Finally, the leader's identification with the group may also be important. Those perceived to share the group's ideals and aspirations will have more legitimacy than those who are seen to identify more with some other grouping. Let us look at some of the research which has investigated these four factors.

Hollander (1960) examined the role of initial conformity in permitting the leader subsequently to influence the group. Experimental confederates were introduced into laboratory problem-solving groups. The groups had a series of problems to solve, and over the course of these false feedback from the experimenter established that the confederate was consistently suggesting correct solutions. This, it was thought, would give the confederate some initial legitimacy. Before each problem the group was required to discuss the best procedure for tackling the task. It was in this discussion phase that the critical variation in the confederate's behaviour was introduced. Every so often he would depart radically from the group consensus view as to the most appropriate procedures. Depending on the experimental condition, this 'idiosyncratic' behaviour occurred *early* in the sequence of problems or *late*. The measure of his influence was the frequency with which the group followed his suggestions as to the correct solution to the problem. As predicted, when the idiosyncratic behaviour occurred early in the group's mini-history there was much less conformity to the confederate's suggestions than when it occurred later.

Hollander and Julian (1970) showed that the method by which the leaders achieved their position can also be important. In this experiment, leaders of groups who thought they had been elected to their position by their group were more likely to suggest solutions to the task problem which appeared to differ from the group's own solution than were leaders who thought they had been appointed by an outside expert. The 'elected' leaders believed they were more competent at the task and enjoyed more support from the group and thus, in Hollander's terms, had more credit to expend in suggesting controversial solutions.

The method of attaining power may not affect just the leader's behaviour and the group members' perceptions of them, however. It may also have demonstrable effects on group performance. This was shown by Pandey (1976), who combined Hollander's concept of leader legitimacy with Fiedler's analysis of leadership effectiveness in a study of group creativity. The group's task was to generate the maximum number of original solutions to some topical social problems. Each group was led either by a task-orientated or by a relationship-orientated leader, as determined by their scores on Fiedler's LPC scale. The leader was variously elected, appointed or was apparently part of a rotational leader arrangement. From Pandey's description of the experimental situation, it seems safe to assume that the leadership context fell into either octants III or IV in Fiedler's model (see figure 3.2): the leader–member relations were probably fairly good, the task was unstructured and, depending on the method of leader selection, the positional power of the leader was either weak (in the 'appointed' or 'rotation' conditions) or strong (when elected by the rest of the group). Consistent with this assumption, the high LPC leaders were generally more effective than the low LPC leaders, which, it will be recalled, is what Fiedler expects in these octants (see figure 3.2). However, rather problematically for Fiedler's model, increasing the position power of the leader by having him elected did not favour the task-orientated leader as it should have. In fact, it was in this situation that this style of leadership was *least* effective, significantly less so than the relationship-orientated leader.

The strength of the leader's identification with the group – the fourth of Hollander's proposed sources of legitimacy – has been little studied. One of the few attempts to investigate this was Kirkhart (1963), who examined choice of leader in predominantly black college fraternity houses. Those selected most frequently as leaders tended also to be those who identified most strongly with blacks as a social group. One of the interesting aspects of this result was that several of the hypothetical situations in which the students were asked to nominate leaders involved dealings with outside groups over issues concerning black-white relations. The fact that the social identification of the leaders was implicated in these kinds of *intergroup* contexts reminds us yet again of the close interdependence between intragroup and intergroup processes.

Overall, then, it can be seen that Hollander is principally concerned with the changing relationship between leaders and their followers. In this, his approach contrasts quite sharply with Fiedler's. For Fiedler, the leader's style is seen as an enduring personality attribute, with his/her relationship with the group and position power as relatively static and independent components of particular situations. Hollander, on the other hand, views leadership as a much more dynamic process in which the leader's power to influence the group changes over time *and* critically depends on the developing leader–member relations. In this respect, his theory avoids two of the criticisms levelled at Fiedler's model at the end of the previous section.

However, although Hollander provides a good account of temporal changes in leadership behaviour stemming from forces *inside* the group, one omission which his theory shares with Fiedler's (and, indeed, with almost all current theories of leadership) is a neglect of intergroup relations, their impact on leadership structures and *vice versa*. The significance of changing intergroup relations for the internal group hierarchy has already been noted more than once in this chapter: recall the Sherifs' summer camp experiments and their studies of adolescent gangs described above. What has been less often studied is the effect of a changing leadership position on the group's subsequent intergroup orientation.

This was the focus of Rabbie and Bekkers' (1978) experiment which varied the stability of a leader's position and examined the effects of this on the leader's intergroup behaviour. They found that leaders who were rather uncertain of their position – they could be easily deposed by their group – were much more likely to choose a competitive bargaining strategy in a union–management simulation than those whose position was more secure. This was particularly likely when the ingroup's position *vis à vis* the other side was apparently strong. As Rabbie and Bekkers (1978) point out, their experimental findings have many parallels in international politics. Political leaders experiencing unpopularity on the home front will often need little excuse to engage in an aggressive foreign policy. Witness the British government's decision to send the Falklands invasion force in 1982, an event which coincided with the lowest poll rating for several months for the British prime minister, Mrs Thatcher. Whatever the process at work here, it is becoming abundantly clear that our theories of leadership must recognize the important role which the intergroup situation plays in the internal workings of the group.

Communication networks

Like many other large organizations, the university where I work has a very hierarchical and centralized decision-making structure. All major decisions about the university's present and future policy are taken by a small group consisting of the Vice-Chancellor and two or three of his colleagues, and these are disseminated downwards to the various faculties, thence to the staff belonging to these, and eventually to the students. In theory, decisions can also be made at these lower levels and communicated upwards through the hierarchy although, to those of us inhabiting these lowly quarters, this seems to be an ever-more infrequent event! Furthermore, there are very few formal channels of communication which follow a *horizontal* course; they are nearly all up or down. Departmental chairs report to faculties, faculty deans report to Senate, the Senate to the Vice-Chancellor, and so on. What are the effects of organizing group communication networks in this way?

This was one of the questions which concerned Bavelas (1969). He suggested that a useful way of understanding the effects of different communication structures is to think of the group members as being related in terms of information 'linkages'. He pointed out that how those linkages are arranged topologically is much more important than knowing how close in units of physical distance various members of the organization or group may be. A direct telephone link between the White House and the Kremlin means that in communication terms the national leaders of the USA and USSR can be much closer to one another – if they choose to be! – than they may be to most members of their own country living many thousands of miles nearer by. Borrowing from topological mathematics, Bavelas devised various quantitative indices by which it is possible to describe different kinds of networks. One of the most important of these is the notion of 'distance' which is simply the minimum number of communication links which must be crossed for one person in the group to communicate with another person. Thus, in figure 3.4d a person occupying the position at the join of the Y is linked to three of the other positions at a distance of 1, and to the person at the foot of the Y at a distance of 2.

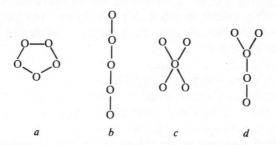

a   b   c   d

Figure 3.4 Some simple communication networks: (a) circle; (b) chain; (c) wheel; (d) Y-shaped

On the other hand, the distance from the last position to the other extreme is 3 since at least three linkages must be crossed. Using this system, one important measure for the system as a whole is the 'centrality index' which, in non-mathematical terms, is the extent to which the information flow in the group is centralized on one person or is dispersed more evenly amongst the members (see Leavitt, 1951).

Armed with this analysis, Bavelas and his colleagues devised on experimental paradigm in which the effects of different communication networks on group processes and productivity could be studied. A typical experiment is that by Leavitt (1951). The members of a five-person group were seated around a table separated by wooden partitions. The partitions had slots in them so that written messages could be passed between the group members. The slots were also fitted with 'doors' which could be closed by the experimenter to constrain the communication in various ways. This allowed different networks to be created and the four studied by Leavitt are shown in figure 3.4. In the 'wheel', for instance, the central group member could communicate to each of the others in the group directly but they could only communicate with each other through that central person. Each person was given a card with six symbols on it and the group's task was to discover which of these six was common to everyone's card, communicating only by written messages through the 'open' slots. The results were fairly clear. The groups arranged in a centralized fashion (networks b–d) made fewer errors on the task than the decentralized 'circle' arrangement. However, the morale and job satisfaction was higher in the latter, apparently because its members did not feel as 'left out' of things as did most of the members of the more centralized networks. This was apparent from analyses of the different positions in the network. Those in the central positions liked the task much more than the peripheral members and, interestingly, were almost invariably nominated as the group leader. This is a powerful illustration of a 'situational' leadership factor at work. Since subjects had been randomly assigned to their positions, no personality trait could possibly be influencing these choices.

The conclusion that centralized groups performed more effectively was soon challenged, however. Shaw (1964), in a close study of eighteen communication experiments, discovered that the nature of the task was a critical variable. In the early experiments the task was a very simple one involving a process of elimination and took a matter of a few minutes to solve. In these kinds of tasks, as we have just seen, the centralized groups performed better. However, on more complex tasks involving arithmetical problems, sentence constructions or discussion-type problems, the *decentralized* networks were clearly superior. Shaw showed that this was because the more difficult tasks required a much greater amount of information to be integrated for their success- ful solution. Since this integrative function typically fell on one person in a centralized network, this often resulted in 'cognitive overload' in that person and a consequent impairment of group performance. In the less-centralized networks, on the other hand, although the group members needed to send more messages to one another, the load was shared more evenly amongst them, resulting in a greater probability of a faster and more correct solution. Shaw also argued that centralized groups may result in lowered performance because of lowered morale and motivation among their members. Most people, he suggested, work better when they have some autonomy and this is denied to members of centralized networks since they are always dependent on someone else 'down the line' for information.

Of course, the networks used in these experiments are a far cry from the large and complex arrangements one finds in human organizations like the one I began this section by describing. Nevertheless, since the tasks faced by these real-life groups are many times more involved than even the most difficult of laboratory tasks, it seems safe to sug- gest that there are real dangers in centralizing the decision-making of organizations too far. Most of these problems stem from the cognitive limitations of those placed in those key central positions. Without delegation of many of their functions, such leaders may simply be unable to assimilate and process the huge volume of information necessary for the group's effective performance. In addition, whilst coping with such problems may prove gratifying to leaders' beliefs in their indispensability, the resulting lowered group member morale because of *their* sense of dispensability may be counter-productive. If we add to these difficulties other potential problems associated with collective decision-making in the presence of powerful leaders – the so-called 'groupthink' phenomenon (Janis, 1972; see chapter 5) – we are forced to conclude that a highly centralized communication net- work is not the optimal arrangement for most human groups. Perhaps democracy has, after all, a pragmatic social psychological justifica- tion, quite apart from any political and ethical considerations!

Summary

1 Two fundamental aspects of group structure are role and status. Roles are behavioural regularities or expectations associated with particular group members. Two key roles in many groups are the task and socio-emotional specialists. Role differentiation can facilitate division of labour in the group as well as contribute to people's identities.

2 Not all roles are equally valued; group members enjoy different amounts of power and prestige which gives rise to status hierarchies in most groups. Closely related to this status differentiation are processes of social comparison through which individuals can make appraisals of their abilities. These social comparisons not only influence our perceptions of ourselves and others but may also affect our actual behaviour and task performance.

3 Those in high-status positions are often referred to as leaders and it is often believed that certain individuals possess traits which equip them for this role. Most evidence suggests otherwise. Leaders are those who have attributes which can help the group achieve particular task goals, or are those whose personalities are well matched to particular situations. Where the match is poor the group is often less effective. Improving the fit between a leader and the situation is the objective of leadership training programmes, although controversy exists over whether to change the leader, the situation or both. The process by which a leader acquires influence over the group is also important.

4 The network of communication in a group is another crucial aspect of group structure. It is helpful to view communication channels in topological terms – as linkages – rather than in units of physical distance. Networks which are highly centralized may be more efficient at solving simple problems where the amount and complexity of information is not great. However, for more complex problems decentralized systems are superior. Morale is also higher in these, regardless of the type of problem.

Further reading

Cartwright, D. and Zander, A. (eds) (1969) *Group Dynamics*, 3rd edn, ch. 36. New York: Harper and Row.

Fiedler, F. E. (1978). The contingency model and the dynamics of the leadership process, in Berkowitz, L. (ed.) *Advances in Experimental Social Psychology*, vol. 11. New York: Academic Press.

Hollander, E. P. (1978) *Leadership Dynamics: a Practical Guide to Effective Relationships*. New York: Free Press.

Shaw, M.E. (1964) Communication networks, in Berkowitz, L. (ed.) *Advances in Experimental Social Psychology*, vol. 1. New York: Academic Press.

Suls, J.M. and Miller, R.L. (eds) (1977) *Social Comparison Processes.* Washington: Hemisphere.

CHAPTER 4

Social Influence in Groups

In chapter 2 we saw the crucial role that social norms play in group life both as cognitive constructs or 'signposts' for the individual and as social regulators for the group. An obvious indication that norms are at work is the existence of some uniformity of attitude or behaviour amongst the group members. Whether it be experimental subjects observing a pin-prick of light in a darkened room, the behaviour of adolescent gangs in American cities or factory workers controlling the production rate in their 'shop', such uniformity is not difficult to observe. Once people get into collective settings, it seems, they appear only too ready to conform to the majority in the group and to abandon their own personal beliefs and opinions. This conformity can be demonstrated even more dramatically in situations in which individuals are so influenced by the majority that they apparently deny the evidence of their own eyes. As we shall see, in the first part of this chapter, this turns out to be a remarkably robust and culturally near-universal phenomenon.

One of the most persuasive attempts to explain this widespread prevalence of conformity is Festinger's social comparison theory, which we encountered in chapter 3 in the context of discussing people's needs for self-evaluation. In addition to making comparisons about abilities, argues Festinger, we also need to assess the correctness of our beliefs and this too is accomplished primarily by reference to others. The information gleaned from these comparisons is particularly potent if it reveals the existence of a social consensus since that strongly implies a 'correct' way of looking at things. Accordingly, Festinger suggests that groups are motivated to establish and maintain uniformity in the group. From this he predicts a number of consequences for group cohesiveness and communication patterns amongst group members as the majority seeks to influence any dissenters to come around to its way of thinking.

So pervasive are conformity phenomena, both inside and outside the social psychology laboratory, that for many years 'social influence in groups' was simply equated with 'conformity to the majority'. Little attention was given to the possibility that a dissenting minority might itself have some impact on the majority. However, the past twenty years have seen a number of empirical demonstrations of precisely that. Minorities, it turns out, are not completely passive recipients of influence from the majority but can elicit some change of opinion in that majority by behaving in a certain manner. One of the main architects of this growth of interest in minority influence has been Moscovici, and his work and that of his colleagues dominate the second part of the chapter.

One of Moscovici's central arguments is that the processes of majority and minority influence are different in kind and effect. This claim will be examined and contrasted with a recent model of social influence which suggests that, on the contrary, majority and minority influence are essentially similar processes, and differ only in the strength of their social impact on group members.

The power of the majority

The pervasiveness of conformity

A British television documentary, which examined the causes of civil aviation accidents ('The Wrong Stuff', BBC2, February 1986), attributed one of the major causes of such accidents to human error, particularly arising out of the group dynamics of the flight crew. In the programme, a serious airline accident, was recreated using the actual sound recording of the final few minutes interaction in the cockpit of the plane. The accident had been caused by the captain of the plane totally misjudging his landing approach. Only eight miles from his destination he was approaching the airport 40 knots too fast and 200 ft lower than he should have been. Here is what took place between the captain (John), his co-pilot and the flight engineer as the co-pilot realized from his instruments that something was wrong and called the attention of the captain to the incorrect glide slope.

Captain	(*in a relaxed voice*) Well, we know where we are; we're all right.
Engineer	The boss has got it wired.
Co-pilot	I hope so.
Captain	No problem.

Co-pilot	(*cautiously*) Isn't this a little faster than you normally fly this John?
Captain	(*confidently*) Oh yeah, but it's nice and smooth. We're going to get in right on time. Maybe a little ahead of time. We've got it made.
Co-pilot	(*uncertainly*) I sure hope so.
Engineer	You know, John, do you know the difference between a duck and a co-pilot?
Captain	What's the difference?
Engineer	Well a duck can fly!
Captain	Well said!
	(*Pause of several seconds.*)
Co-pilot	(*anxiously*) Seems like there's a bit of a tailwind up here, John.
Captain	Yeah, we're saving gas – helps us to get in a couple of minutes early too.
	(*Another pause.*)
Co-pilot	John, you're just a little below the MDA here.
Captain	Yeah, well we'll take care of it here.

The captain then attempted to leapfrog the plane up over the glide slope in an attempt to compensate for the incorrect altitude. This caused the plane to be much higher than it should be for a safe landing and the accident was unavoidable.

If one had to choose a group that would be resistant to internal conformity pressures one might well have thought that a small group like this, consisting as it did of three highly skilled professionals, would be a safe bet. Each could clearly see the instruments revealing the danger signals and were well trained to respond to them. Yet only one of the three saw any cause for alarm and, significantly, the majority not only chose to ignore his increasingly anxious comments but actually ganged up together at one point to ridicule him. The dissenting voice, it seems, was as unwelcome here as it is in other groups the world over.

Real-life examples of conformity like this are inevitably complicated by such factors as the status relationships in the group, the personalities of those involved and the complex nature of the group task which they have to undertake. Is it possible to demonstrate the existence of conformity to group pressure in conditions where such variables are either absent or experimentally controlled? This was the question posed, and answered, by Asch (1956) in a series of experiments which, like those of Sherif (1936) some years earlier, have rightly come to assume classic status in the history of social psychology.

The basic procedure used in Asch's experiments is as follows: subjects are recruited for what they are told will be an experiment in visual judgement. On arrival at the laboratory the subject is shown to a room where a number of other subjects are already seated, having apparently arrived a few minutes earlier. The experimenter explains that their task is to compare the lengths of some vertical lines which will be presented to them. On each presentation there is a standard line and their task is to identify which of three comparison lines is the same length as the standard. They call out their answers in turn. This seems a simple enough task and, sure enough, in the first two trials everyone calls out the obviously correct answer. Then, on the third trial – and on eleven others occurring at intervals – the others in the room give what appears to be a completely wrong answer. What is more they are unanimous in their error, giving their answers confidently and calmly. In fact, of course, those already in the room before the start of the experiment are confederates of the experimenter who have been carefully briefed to give incorrect answers on two-thirds of the trials. Asch's interest was in the behaviour of the one genuine subject: how would he/she react to the testimony from these apparently quite unexceptional people which contradicted so dramatically the evidence of his/her own eyes? Asch's findings were surprising: fully three-quarters of those 'naive' subjects gave at least one incorrect response on the critical trials when the confederates went astray. Looking at the results another way: out of all the genuine subjects' responses on the critical trials, over 36 per cent of these were either the same as or in the direction of the incorrect majority.

What gave these results such impact was the unambiguous nature of the task. There could be no doubt as to the correct answer as Asch confirmed in a control condition where people gave their answers as their own. Here the number of errors was virtually zero. What Asch had demonstrated, therefore, was an apparent willingness on the part of people to deny this obvious veridical judgement in order to 'go along with' the majority. And that, according to Asch, was precisely the motivation behind most of the conforming responses. From detailed debriefings of the subjects, Asch established that it was rare for the compliant subjects actually to have 'seen' the lines as the same when they were different. Rather, they lacked confidence in their own judgement, assuming that the others in the experiment were privy to some additional information that was guiding their responses. Others, on the other hand, while not actually doubting what they saw, simply conformed so as not to be different. These reactions suggest that we should distinguish between conformity which involves a private perceptual or cognitive change – seeing the world differently – and conformity which is merely a behavioural or public compliance – 'going along with the others' (Festinger, 1953). The latter seems best to characterize the subjects in Asch's experiments, while Sherif's (1936) experiments with the autokinetic effect seemed to elicit the former reaction (see chapter 2). It will be recalled that one of Sherif's interesting findings was that the previously established group norm persisted even when the subjects were subsequently tested on their own. Later in this chapter we shall encounter other examples of such internal changes.

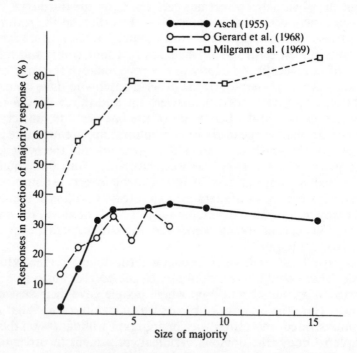

Figure 4.1 Group size and conformity (from Asch, 1955; Gerard et al., 1968; Milgram et al., 1969)

In other experiments, Asch (1955) explored the effects of altering various aspects of his conformity-inducing situation. The most obvious factor to vary was the size of the confederate majority. Asch's results are shown in the solid curve of figure 4.1. From this, it seems that with just one confederate there is negligible conformity on the critical trials. However, with the addition of one or two further confederates the conformity level rises sharply, only to level off with the addition of further confederates. Indeed, Asch reported that fifteen confederates seemed to elicit slightly less conformity than four. This rapid increase in conformity with majorities of two or three has been confirmed in subsequent research, although the reduced conformity which Asch observed with large majorities has not generally been replicated. For example, Gerard et al. (1968), using a modification of Asch's paradigm but with a similar judgemental task, found a general linear effect of group size (dashed line in figure 4.1). Milgram et al. (1969), in a naturalistic study of the influence on passers by of different-sized crowds staring upwards apparently at nothing, found that the number of people who also looked up was linearly related to the size of the crowd, although there was a tendency for the relationship to flatten off with larger crowds (dotted line in figure 4.1). All in all, then, it seems safe to conclude that large majorities do elicit more conformity than small ones, although continually increasing group size seems to have only marginal effects on the level of conformity.

Another variation which Asch (1955) introduced was to break up the consensus produced by the confederate majority, and this proved to be crucial. In one experiment, there were two naive subjects facing the incorrect majority. Immediately, the level of conformity dropped to around 10 per cent. In another experiment, one of the confederates was instructed always to give the correct answer and this resulted in even less conformity, a negligible 5 per cent. However, it was clear that it was the breaking of the unanimity that was the critical factor rather than simply the presence of an 'ally'. This was revealed in a third experiment in which one of the confederates was instructed to deviate from the majority but still give incorrect answers. In some conditions this incorrect answer fell between the majority's and the true answer; in others, it was even more incorrect than the majority's. Both conditions reduced the level of conformity but, interestingly, the latter condition had even more powerful effects than the former. Subsequent research has confirmed Asch's findings on the importance of dissent for reducing conformity, although for some sorts of behaviours – particularly those involving subjective opinions rather than objective judgements – it is apparently necessary for that dissent also to support the subject's own position (Allen, 1965, 1975).

Exact replications and various modifications of Asch's experiments have been conducted in a large number of different countries and the basic conformity phenomena which he discovered seem to be remarkably persistent. Although there are often substantial variations in the level of conformity observed, very few of these cross-cultural studies have failed to find any conformity at all (Mann, 1980).[1] Perhaps more interesting than this near-universal prevalence of conformity are the reasons for the cultural differences in its manifestation. One intriguing theory has been advanced by Berry (1967) which relates the degree of conformity to the nature of the economy in different societies. Berry suggests that in societies whose economies require a high degree of interdependence – for example, high food accumulating cultures – there will typically be greater pressures to conformity (and socialization practices consistent with this) than in societies where food accumulation is less important and where people are more independent of one another. Adapting Asch's judgement task, Berry found evidence in support of this idea. The Temne of Sierra Leone, who depended on a single crop each year and are thus high food accumulators, showed substantially more conformity than groups of Eskimos who rely on regular hunting and fishing trips for survival. As one Temne tested by Berry explained it: 'When Temne people choose a thing, we must all agree with the decision – this is what we call cooperation' (Berry, 1967, p. 417).

Not only do the absolute levels of susceptibility to the influence of others differ from culture to culture, but so too do the sources of that influence vary. This was established by Bronfenbrenner and his colleagues in a number of cross-national studies examining children's conformity to conventional moral values (e.g. Bronfenbrenner, 1970). Their technique involved asking children to resolve a number of simple moral dilemmas in which they were required to choose between some conventional (adult) standard of behaviour and some mildly antisocial action endorsed by a peer group. In the control conditions the children believed their answers would be confidential whilst in the two experimental variations of the task it was intimated to the children that *either* their parents *or* their peers would subsequently be able to see their responses. By examining discrepancies between the control and experimental conditions, it was possible to discern whether children in particular cultures were more responsive to adult or peer norms. As usual, gross levels of conformity varied considerably between countries with children in the USSR showing most adherence to conventional mores and those in Switzerland least. However, the potency of the different group influences also varied. In Israel, for example, the peer group seemed to be a particularly powerful influence, whereas West German children seemed more orientated towards adults (Shouval et al., 1975).

Why do people conform?

Conformity to the opinion of others is not restricted to the judgements of line lengths in experimentally contrived settings. A moment's reflection will confirm that we have a rather general propensity to change our attitudes and behaviour so as to bring them into line with others around us. This seems to be as true of the relatively minor issues of clothing fashion and musical taste as it is of more fundamental moral values and sociopolitical action. The question is, then, what underlies this widespread tendency towards uniformity in groups?

One of the most influential explanations of these conformity pressures has been put forward by Festinger (1950). He proposed that there are two powerful processes which result in individuals being influenced by the majority in the group. The first concerns the social construction of reality. Festinger started from an assumption that all of us hold a number of beliefs about the world. These act for us, he suggests, like mini-theories, guiding our actions and helping us to interpret social events. Because of this, it is important for us to have some way of verifying or testing our theories. But, unlike more formal scientific theories, we usually do not have any objective means of agreed procedures for doing so. Anticipating his later social comparison theory (Festinger, 1954; see chapter 3), Festinger hypothesized that what we do instead is to turn to other people for information about the correctness (or otherwise) of our beliefs. Where everyone else appears to agree with us then that offers some reassurance that our beliefs are not completely at variance with reality. Festinger concluded that this validational function provided by social comparisons would mean that people will generally value uniformity in groups and will often behave so as to maintain it.

Pressures towards that uniformity are likely to increase in novel or ambiguous situations since here are fewer 'objective' ones to guide our judgements. Recall Sherif's (1936) autokinetic effect experiment. Here, it will be remembered, subjects in a completely dark room were asked to make a highly subjective judgement of how far a spot of light appeared to move. Faced with this uncertainty, the subjects' judgements very quickly converged. Social consensus becomes still more valuable not only when the truth cannot be readily ascertained but where our decisions also have important consequences. Perhaps that is why many judicial systems have required juries to reach unanimous, or near unanimous, verdicts in their deliberations.

The second determinant of conformity identified by Festinger is the presence of some important group goal. When a group has a clearly defined objective this may, by itself, induce some uniformity of action amongst the group members, especially where achievement of the goal is dependent on the simple aggregation of their efforts. The effectiveness of a tug-of-war team, for example, critically depends on their success in maximizing and coordinating their pull on the rope. However, with more complex group tasks it is also vital that the group members can agree not just on the goal itself but on the means to the achievement of that goal. Without that uniformity of opinion the group members' efforts are likely to be fragmented and the attainment of the goal rendered less likely. This may be one reason why political parties devote so much time to appeals for unity in their ranks, particularly when confrontation with rivals is imminent. The following excerpt from a speech by Neil Kinnock, leader of the British Labour Party in the run up to the 1987 general election, captures this sentiment exactly:

> I have no time, and this party has no time, for those who would rather win an argument with friends than win an election against enemies . . . we make it categorically clear that the people at the fringe of our movement have no influence and will get no influence over the leadership, the policies or the direction of our party. They are numbered in tens. They do not represent the policies or the character of a party of over 300,000. (As reported in the *Guardian*, 5 March, 1987)

The power of a new goal to bring about attitude change in group members was convincingly demonstrated by Lewin (1965). As part of a health education programme after the war to persuade American families to eat more of various unfashionable, but nutritionally rich, cuts of meat (e.g. heart, kidney), Lewin compared the effectiveness of a lecture by a nutrition expert to a participative group discussion. In both cases the participants were housewives and the key measure was whether or not they would subsequently attempt a recipe at home with one of these novel ingredients. Nearly a third of those who had taken part in the group discussion were persuaded enough so to experiment, whilst a negligible 3 per cent of those who had only heard the lecture did so. One of the key differences between the two methods of persuasion was that in the discussion groups each session ended with the group deciding *as a whole* to give the new recipes a try; in the lecture, on the other hand, there was no such clearly defined group goal, merely an exhortation by the lecturer. Moreover, the active participation of the members of the discussion groups ensured that the group goal was internalized and not imposed from outside. A similar outcome was observed by Coch and French (1948) in their study of organizational change in a pyjama factory. One work group, allowed to participate in the managerial decision-making leading up to the change, showed pro-management changes in their attitudes and productivity. Another group, however, was simply *ordered* to change their working practices and, as a result, showed a strong shift in opinion *against* management and a decline in output (see chapter 2).

Both of these motives for conformity presuppose that the group has some initial attractiveness for its members. The other people in the group – and their opinions – matter to the person subjected to the influence. Presumably, the more they matter (i.e. the more cohesive a group is) the more conformity we should expect. This seems to be the case. Festinger et al. (1950), investigating relationships in a student housing project, found a strong positive correlation between the degree of cohesiveness of student groups and how effectively group standards were maintained. This was confirmed by Lott and Lott (1961) who found a similar association between the cohesiveness of friendship cliques and the amount of conformity they showed in an experimental task. There was also a positive relationship between cohesiveness and the amount of communication in the group, suggesting how the conformity came about.

Important though these motives for conformity are, neither seems adequate to explain the compliance observed in Asch's experiments. In the first place, there was no ambiguity in the situation. People's opinions on the lengths of lines are easily and objectively verifiable; why then should the confederates' (incorrect) opinions have been so influential? Furthermore, there was no real or cohesive group. The subjects were taking part in what they thought was an experiment in *individual* perceptual judgement; there were none of the usual criteria to mark a group's existence (face-to-face interaction, interdependence, categorization etc.; see chapter 1). Thus, pressures arising from attempts to achieve a group goal (the second of Festinger's proposed motives) should not have been present.

Noting these anomalies, Deutsch and Gerard (1955) suggested a third reason for conformity which is really the obverse of the social reality function which Festinger had proposed. People may have conformed, they suggested, not because they were relying on the confederates' judgements to define reality for them but rather to avoid the possibility of social ridicule, of being the 'odd one out'. There is a great deal of evidence that we are attracted to others with similar attitudes to us (Byrne, 1971) – or, perhaps more accurately, *repelled* by those with dissimilar attitudes (Rosenbaum, 1986) – presumably because of the social validation (or disconfirmation) such people provide. Thus, if we dislike others who disagree with us we may reasonably anticipate that others will dislike *us* if we express very different opinions from them. Assuming that most people prefer to be liked than disliked, then this might give them a motive to conform to the majority's opinion in situations such as those devised by Asch. If this really is a reason for conformity then conformity should be reduced if people make their responses privately.

Deutsch and Gerard (1955) designed an experiment which would simultaneously test this idea and the earlier hypotheses put forward by Festinger. The experiment involved several modifications to Asch's procedure. In one condition (the closest replication of Asch) subjects gave their responses in a face-to-face situation where there was an incorrect majority of three. In half the trials responses were made whilst the stimuli were still visible (as in Asch's experiment); in the remainder the stimuli were removed before the judgements were made. It was thought that this would enhance the uncertainty and ambiguity of the situation and hence, according to Festinger, increase the reliance on others for information. The next condition was identical to the first except that the subjects could not see each other and the responses were given anonymously. It was thought that this would reduce any conformity which is due to the need to be liked. In a third condition Deutsch and Gerard stepped up the conformity pressures by informing the subjects that they constituted one of twenty groups in the experiment and that the five groups which made the fewest errors in the experiment would receive an attractive prize (some Broadway theatre tickets). In this way a clear group goal was introduced which was expected to increase cohesion and conformity. Finally, Deutsch and Gerard devised three conditions in which subjects had to commit themselves by writing down their answers before hearing the responses of others and before giving their own responses: some had to write their answers on paper which they subsequently threw away ('private

Table 4.1 Mean number of socially influenced errors in Deutsch and Gerard's (1955) experiment (range 0–12)

Condition	Stimuli present	Stimuli absent
Group goal	5.7	6.9
Face to face	3.0	4.1
Anonymous	2.8	3.2
Private commitment A	0.6	0.7
Private commitment B	1.6	2.3
Public commitment	0.9	0.5

commitment' A); some used a 'magic pad' which could erase their response on each trial ('private commitment B'); and some wrote their answers on notes which they signed and which they knew would subsequently be handed to the experimenter ('public commitment').

Deutsch and Gerard's results confirmed that all three motives were significant influences on conformity (see table 4.1). Notice, first of all, that as the group was made psychologically more significant by providing a collective goal, the number of errors (or level of conformity) increased. This was despite the fact that the group goal was to make the fewest errors! This clearly supports Festinger's second hypothesis. It is also clear that Festinger's first hypothesis – the need for information in ambiguous situations – is supported by the greater conformity consistently found in the more uncertain trials where the stimuli were removed before responding. The need to be liked must also have been influential. When subjects responded anonymously there was less conformity than in the face-to-face situation. This conformity dropped still further when subjects first committed themselves by writing down their judgement. Perhaps this acted as an additional source of information when making their response proper. However, it is interesting that even in these prior commitment conditions conformity did not disappear completely, as it had in Asch's control conditions when no confederates were present. This strongly suggests that there was some residual influence due to the confederates, even though the stimulus situation was clear-out *and* the individuals could be assured of complete anonymity from their peers.

Such persistence of social influence when both 'informational' and 'normative' pressures for it (to use Deutsch and Gerard's terms) are virtually absent, poses something of a difficulty for the explanations for conformity we have considered so far. Recently, Turner (1987) has proposed a rather different explanation for conformity which may help to resolve this problem. Turner's starting point is to assume that a fundamental feature of group membership is that it provides people with a social identity – it helps them to define who they are. (This is already a familiar idea which we discussed in chapter 2; it is one to which we will return in later chapters, especially chapter 8.) When people identify with a group, argues Turner, they categorize themselves as members of it and, as a consequence, mentally associate themselves with the attributes and norms which they perceive as being part of that group. This process may be analogous to those actors who claim that their best performances occur when they quite literally become the person whose part they are playing. The outwardly visible aspect of the role – the spoken lines and the costume – is reflected in an internal personality change as they attempt to assimilate the attributes of the character in the play. In Turner's theory, the script and the costume are the objective features of a social category which became salient or 'visible' in certain situations. The corresponding internal change is the cognitive matching of oneself with the group's perceived characteristics, what Turner calls 'self-stereotyping'. It is this self-assignment of ingroup characteristics and behaviours which Turner believes is the key to understanding conformity. Thus, his explanation of the presence of conformity in Deutsch and Gerard's (1955) experiment, even when all attempts had been made to eliminate it, is to assume that the subjects believed that others in the experiment belonged to the same ingroup (they could reasonably infer that they were college students like themselves) and hence perceived their rather unusual actions as being normative for that group in that situation. The subjects' self-categorization as 'college students' then led them to assimilate those same actions for themselves.

If this theory is correct then people should be much more affected by sources of influence which appear to come from their ingroup than from some outgroup. There is some evidence that this is the case. For example, Boyanowsky and Allen (1973) found that the ethnic composition of the confederates in an Asch-type conformity experiment affected levels of conformity. Borrowing Asch's idea of introducing social support for the subject by having one of the confederates consistently offer the 'correct' opinion, Boyanowsky and Allen arranged for that supporter to be either black or white. Then, using only highly prejudiced white subjects (for whom ethnic identity was probably quite important), they confronted them with three kinds of conformity task. Two were neutral – visual perception and matters of general opinion – whilst a third was highly relevant to their identity since it concerned attitudes and beliefs held by them personally. On this latter task, but not on the other two, it was found that the ethnicity of the 'social supporter' had a dramatic effect. When the supporter was white (same ingroup as the subject) the degree of conformity dropped markedly, just as Asch had found. However, the presence of a black supporter had *no* effect on conformity; subjects preferred to continue to agree with the white majority than accept the support for their views offered by a black confederate. A similar effect was reported by Hogg and Turner (1987) using artificially created categories rather than real-life groups. In their experiment, subjects were always exposed to three people who agreed with them – and three people who disagreed – on the social desirability of various personality traits. However, in the experimental conditions the three supporters came from an alleged 'ingroup' and the three others from an apparent 'outgroup'. In the control conditions these labels were omitted. Conformity towards the supporters' view was significantly higher when they were seen as ingroup members, despite the fact that, in Festinger's terms, the amount of information (or 'consensual validation') they provided was the same as the supporters in the control conditions. There is more to conformity, it seems, than simply 'defining social reality'; it all depends who is doing the defining.

On being a deviate

The main result of conformity is, of course, greater uniformity amongst the group members. How does this uniformity come about? In most experimental demonstrations we have discussed so far it seemed to happen as a result of individuals cognitively restructuring the situation, either to justify giving an 'incorrect' response or perhaps to reinterpret the meaning of the stimuli themselves (Allen and Wilder, 1980). But conformity is not always as private a phenomenon as this. Very often the majority will act directly to bring pressure on those with deviant opinions. Indeed, this was another central hypothesis to emerge from Festinger's (1950) theory. He argued that those in the majority in a group would direct most of their communications towards those in the minority subgroup in an attempt to persuade them to change their position. The greater the discrepancy between minority and majority, the more communications one would expect. Since the object of these communications is to exert influence on the deviants, if these influence attempts are unsuccessful (that is, if the deviants maintain their non-conformist stand) Festinger believed that the other members of the group will eventually reject the deviants and show that rejection by expressions of dislike or even, in extreme cases, expelling them from the group altogether.

Schachter (1951) put these ideas to the test. He observed the behaviour of student discussion groups who had been set the task of solving some 'human relations' problem involving a delinquent boy and his family. Unknown to the half-dozen or so real participants in each group, Schachter introduced three experimental confederates into the group. One was instructed to take up a deviate position in the group. Once the group's views on the case began to crystallize, his job was to argue for a point of view directly contrary to this using a standard set of arguments. The second confederate was also instructed to be a deviate initially but about a third of the way through the discussion he had gradually to change his position and come into line with the rest of the group. He was dubbed the 'slider'. The third confederate (the 'mode') had an easier role since he simply had to go along with the prevailing opinion in the group throughout. Schachter carefully monitored the number of remarks each person addressed to these three bogus group members and the results are shown in figure 4.2.

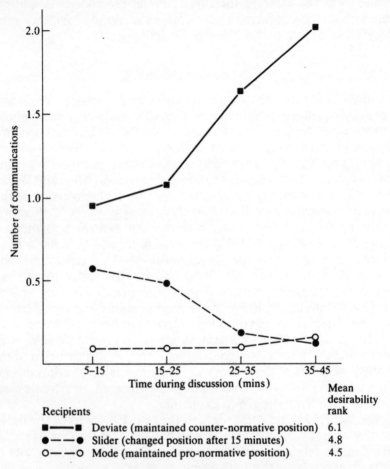

Recipients

	Mean desirability rank
■——■ Deviate (maintained counter-normative position)	6.1
●– – –● Slider (changed position after 15 minutes)	4.8
○— —○ Mode (maintained pro-normative position)	4.5

Figure 4.2 Number of communications (per person) addressed to 'deviate', 'slider' and 'mode' in Schachter's (1951) experiment

As can be seen, most attention was paid to the deviate. In the first ten minutes of the discussion each group member addressed about one communication on average to this confederate which rose to over twice that by the end of the session. In contrast, the slider, who initially received nearly as many communications as the deviate, was increasingly ignored, especially after he had apparently changed his mind. The mode was virtually ignored throughout; since he already agreed with the group, there was no need for them to pay him any heed. These findings were neatly paralleled by some sociometric data which Schachter also collected. At the end of each session, everyone was asked to rank order their fellow discussants in terms of their desirability as group members. The mean ranks given to each confederate are shown at the bottom of figure 4.2 and it is clear that the deviate was given a consistently lower ranking than the other two, and well below the median rank of 5. Just as Festinger had predicted, the deviate who resisted the group's social pressure was not well regarded by his peers.

The discovery that deviates are not particularly liked has stood the test of time. Some years later Schachter and seven colleagues conducted an enormous cross-cultural study which used a very similar procedure to the experiment just described, but which omitted the 'slider' and 'mode' roles (Schachter et al. 1954). Nearly 300 groups of schoolboys from seven European countries were observed discussing a project to build a model aeroplane. A number of prototypes were available. Most were highly attractive motor-driven models and were generally preferred by the boys. One of the models, however, was a glider and this was the model which the deviate always 'preferred' in the ensuing discussion to choose which model they would build. In the rank ordering measure at the end (this time to elect a group leader), although there were some slight national variations, the deviate's mean rank was below the median *in every single country tested*, confirming once again that deviates are seldom very popular members of the group. Furthermore, as Mann (1980) has noted, there was a strong correlation between the tendency of groups to reach uniformity and rejection of the deviate. More recently still, Miller et al. (1987) found that members of the majority in a group consistently rated each other as more likeable than they rated the deviate, even when experimental instructions made it quite clear that a majority decision by the group would be quite acceptable and that unanimity was not necessary.

There was one further intriguing result from the study of Schachter et al. (1954). In the first table of their paper the authors present the number of groups sampled from the different countries. At the right-hand margin of that table there is a column marked 'Additional groups' which, as the text beneath the table explains, shows the number of groups in each country in which the stooge was not a deviate. In such groups, *either the subjects had not reached agreement among themselves or they were so enamoured of the glider that they eventually unanimously agreed with the stooge in his choice* (Schachter et al., 1954, p. 408, my emphasis). What is significant about this column is the number of groups it contains. There were in fact some 95 groups (or 32 per cent of the total sample) which, in the researchers' view, could not be used because the deviate was not truly on his own against a consensual majority. Even more fascinating are some further findings presented a few pages later which make it clear that of these 95 groups, fully 26 of them (or 9 per cent of the total) came around completely to the deviate's point of view and chose the glider, despite their initial preference for the motor-powered models! In other words, in a small but nevertheless not negligible proportion of the experimental groups it was a minority person who managed to persuade those in the majority to change their minds, and not the other way around! Quite how and when minorities are able to exert influence like this is the subject of the next section.

The influence of the minority

There is a particular irony that this little-known finding was reported in a paper which is so frequently cited as demonstrating the coercive power of the majority. Indeed, the study was specifically designed to test some hypotheses from Festinger's (1950) theory which, as we have seen, stresses the dependence of the individual on the rest of the group for information (reality testing) and the need for groups to achieve uniformity for the achievement of goals. For Festinger, social influence is a unidirectional process: the deviant individuals are seen as the passive *recipients* of pressure from the rest of the group (see figure 4.3). But what those 26 influential deviates from Schachter et al.'s (1954) study show is that such a view of social influence may not be either accurate or complete.

This, at least, is the contention of Moscovici (1976), who has inspired some radical changes in the way social influence should be understood. Moscovici begins by asking how change comes about in social systems. If groups are dedicated to achieving uniformity of opinion, as Festinger implies, how do their norms and values ever change? One immediate answer to this question is that groups change as a response to new *external* circumstances. If the situation confronting a group presents a new goal to achieve or task to perform (perhaps because of an altered intergroup relationship) then one would expect the group to adapt accordingly, which might result in changes within the group.

Thus political parties alter their manifestos to take account of their rivals' policies, popular opinion and changing economic conditions. Another source of change within the group might be people with superior status and power. As we saw in chapter 3, a characteristic of leaders is that they are able to influence the group more than the group is able to influence them.

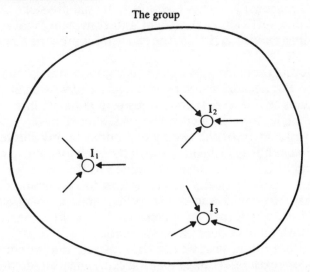

The group

Figure 4.3 Festinger's view of social influence. Deviate individuals (I) are subject to social influence pressures from the rest of the group

Although these reasons for change are undoubtedly important, Moscovici points out that several historical examples of change cannot easily be explained by them. Take the change in popular thinking brought about by Freud's psychoanalytic theory, for instance. While the influence of Freud's ideas may not have been unrelated to social and economic changes occurring in Europe in the first half of this century, it is not immediately obvious how these changes should have facilitated the acceptance of this particular psychological perspective. Moreover, Freud himself hardly enjoyed any great position of power. Indeed, as we know, his writings have often been subject to ridicule and abuse by establishment figures (Jones, 1964). Moscovici argues that the success of psychoanalysis in infiltrating Western culture was due not so much to any external influences, and hardly at all to Freud's status in society, but to the strategy which Freud and his colleagues adopted in propagating it. One feature of this strategy in particular, Moscovici believes, was crucial and that was that Freud was unusually persistent in maintaining the validity of his theory, even in the face of the most virulent criticism from others. According to Moscovici, this behavioural consistency created intellectual conflicts with existing scientific ideas and value conflicts with prevailing social mores, and it was from these conflicts that the changes sprung. Minority influence is possible, argues Moscovici, because no group is perfectly homogeneous; it always contains potential divisions. Deviants, if they act in a sufficiently consistent and convincing manner, make those divisions explicit and from the resulting conflict new norms may emerge.

In promoting these ideas Moscovici is a good advertisement for his own theory. For decades social psychologists had written about influence in groups as if it were synonomous with *majority* influence; that minorities might have influence too was almost never recognized. Even as I write, eight of the twenty text books on my shelves do not even mention minority influence, and in the twelve which do most give the topic only cursory treatment compared to the extensive coverage of conformity to the majority. It was against this dominant climate of opinion that Moscovici and a few others started to publish their 'deviant' ideas, which they have continued to do in a consistent and persuasive fashion over the past dozen years.

An important initial task was to demonstrate that minority influence did indeed exist, and one of the first experiments to do this was by Moscovici, Lage and Naffrechoux in 1969. They used a similar procedure to that which Asch had used. A group of subjects was asked to make some perceptual judgements – this time about the colour of some bluish-tinted slides. However, they turned Asch's set-up on its head by employing a *majority* of naive subjects (four in all) and a *minority* of two confederates who had been instructed by the experimenter to call out the colour 'green' in response to the slides in a predetermined manner. In one condition, both confederates were consistent with one another, responding 'green' on every trial. In another condition, the confederates were not so consistent, sometimes calling out 'blue' along with the real subjects. The primary measure of influence was how often the real subjects responded 'green' also to the obviously blue slides. The results were clear. Fully 32 per cent of the subjects in the first experimental condition made at least one 'green' response, and over 8 per cent of their responses overall were 'green'. This compares to the virtually zero 'green' response in the control condition (where there were no confederates), and a negligible 1 per cent of the other experimental condition where the confederates behaved inconsistently. The figure of 8 per cent as a measure of influence may not be very startling, especially when we compare it to the 36 per cent conformity rate reported by Asch (1956), but it must be remembered that this was achieved by a deviant *minority* against a majority twice its size. From this perspective, and in contrast to the dominant view that majorities are more powerful than minorities, that there was any influence at all is quite significant.

In an extension of this experiment, Moscovici et al. (1969) followed up their standard procedure with an individual assessment of the real subjects' colour thresholds. A second experimenter, supposedly conducting some independent research, entered the laboratory after the group perception task and administered a standardized test of colour discrimination. Each subject was tested individually with no knowledge of other people's responses. The results showed that the experimental subjects had a significantly lower threshold for the perception of green than the control subjects: that is, blue–green slides were more likely to be seen by them as 'green'. These ancillary findings indicate that minority influence is effective not just in changing people's overt behaviour (their public responses in the first part of the experiment), but may have internalized cognitive consequences as well. This conclusion is strengthened by one last result from this experiment. Those groups of subjects who were resistant to the minority in the first phase showed a greater shift in their colour threshold measured in the second (private) phase than did those who had initially changed their public response.

These findings were confirmed in a subsequent experiment which compared directly the influence exerted by minorities and majorities. Using the same colour perception task, Moscovici and Lage (1976) employed three conditions of minority influence: one was identical to their earlier experiment (i.e. two confederates always calling out 'green'); one was a single confederate who was also consistent; in the third, the two confederates were inconsistent with one another. There were also two conditions of majority influence, similar to those employed by Asch, i.e. a unanimous or a non-unanimous majority. Of the minority influence conditions only the consistent pair of deviates were able to exert any noticeable influence as compared to the control condition where there were no confederates at all. Just over 10 per cent of the responses in this consistent minority condition showed evidence of conformity (versus 1 per cent in the control). While this was clearly less than the 40 per cent conformity rate in the unanimous majority condition, it was comparable to the 12 per cent found with the non-unanimous majority. However, in the subsequent colour discrimination test, those in the consistent minority condition were the *only* subjects to change their blue–green thresholds significantly compared to the control baseline. So, despite the greater overt compliance found with majority influence, it was the *minority* which was apparently able to shift people's internal colour codes.

Minority influence is not restricted to these rather unusual perceptual tasks, however. Wolf (1979) found clear evidence of it in a simulated jury study. She asked her subjects (in groups of four) to consider an injury compensation case. The case materials presented strongly suggested that an award of compensation in the region of $20–30,000 should be made, and this was indeed the figure most subjects initially endorsed. However, during the discussion one of the group appeared to argue consistently for a much lower figure of only $3000. As a result, by the end of the discussion period, the rest of the group were favouring an award which was over $3500 *lower* than their original judgement. Interestingly, the influence of the deviate was even more marked in highly cohesive groups than in the less cohesive ones. Thus, the very pressures towards uniformity which Festinger (1950) had identified can, paradoxically, create the conditions for a persistent minority to increase its influence.

There seems little doubt, then, that minority influence is a genuine phenomenon (see Maass and Clark, 1984 for a review of other studies not mentioned here). If so, then we are forced to accept Moscovici's argument that the traditional view of social influence as the exclusive property of the majority in a group (see figure 4.3) is incomplete. Minorities, it seems, are not simply passive recipients of pressure from the group but may be active agents, sometimes acting as catalysts for change by provoking conflict in the cognitions and perceptions of the majority. This leads to the view of social influence as the reciprocal and bi-directional process depicted in figure 4.4.

For Moscovici, as we have seen, consistency is a key factor determining a minority's ability to be able to influence the rest of the group. Part of its importance may be due to the changes it brings about in the casual attributions of the majority. In fact, Moscovici draws explicitly on Kelley's (1967) attribution theory to suggest that by maintaining a steadfast position over time ('consistency information' in Kelley's model) and by appearing to be in agreement amongst themselves ('consensus information'), members of a minority can create an impression in the minds of the majority that what they stand for is not a passing whim or a personal idiosyncrasy but may really have some substance.

But consistency is just one of several 'behavioural styles' which Moscovici (1976) has suggested affect minority influence. Another

The group

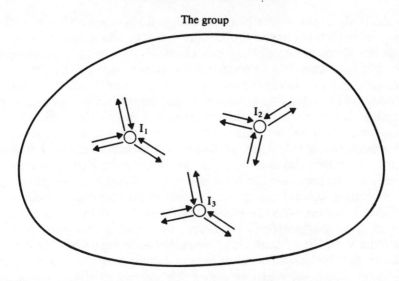

Figure 4.4   Moscovici's alternative view of social influence. Deviate individuals (I) are both recipients and emitters of social influence

may be the extent of *investment* which the minority is perceived to have made in promulgating its views. Those who are seen to have made personal or material sacrifices for their cause are likely to be taken more seriously than those for whom the endorsement of minority views has been fairly painless.

A third factor may be *autonomy*, the extent to which the minority is seen to be acting out of principle and not from ulterior motives. A famous personality's endorsement of an unpopular campaign will be much more credible if we are sure that she or he is not being paid large sums of money for it.

A fourth factor is *rigidity* (versus *flexibility*) with which the minority argues its case and this, in the view of Mugny (1982), is the major variable qualifying the effects of consistency. Mugny points out that minority members, by remaining consistent, run the risk of being seen as dogmatic and unyielding. Such unfavourable perceptions are likely to lessen their ability to influence the majority since they may be dismissed as 'cranks' or 'extremists'. However, Mugny and Papastamou (1975-6) have shown that such perceptions can be counteracted if the minority adopts a style of negotiation which is both consistent *and* flexible. They must give the appearance of reasonableness and open-mindedness whilst still maintaining their position.

Mugny and Papastamou (1975-6) elicited from their subjects their opinions about the causes of environmental pollution. After a week's delay, they then presented those same subjects with a communication from an 'Environmental Research Group' which purported to agree (*or* disagree, according to experimental condition) with the opinions each subject had initially expressed. The manner in which this communication was worded was varied. For half the subjects it was presented in rather strident tones with uncompromising proposals, whilst for the remainder it was written in more temperate language with apparently more moderate conclusions. This rigidity/flexibility variable had little effect on those who received the 'agreeing' communication; both groups moved somewhat in response to the message, although, in the absence of a control group who received no communication, it is difficult to assess whether this change was due to influence or was merely a temporal effect. However, the more interesting changes occurred with the 'disagreeing' message. Although both the 'rigid' and the 'flexible' messages were seen as equally consistent, it was only the latter which evinced any noticeable change in the subjects. As Mugny concludes: 'Consistency is certainly necessary, but it is not sufficient to account for social influence' (Mugny, 1982, p. 34).

The perceptive reader will by now have realized that there is a clear conflict between these strategies for successful influence advocated by Moscovici, and those proposed by Hollander (1958) in his theory of leadership. In the last chapter we saw that Hollander suggests that in order to influence group members the (minority) leader should first conform to group norms to gain 'credit' in their eyes before proposing the novel opinions. Moscovici, on the other hand, believes that the minority needs to make its deviant position clear from the start and maintain it throughout. This contradiction was noted by Bray et al. (1982), and they designed two experiments to allow a direct comparison of the efficacy of the two approaches. In both studies a single minority person (or two persons in the second experiment) argued against the prevailing opinion in a group discussion. In half the groups the deviate(s) adopted the 'Hollander strategy' of agreeing with the group initially and then arguing for the minority viewpoint. In the other groups the deviate(s) took up a contrary position from the start, the 'Moscovici strategy'.[2] The result were clear. First of all, as Moscovici and Lage (1976) had found, a pair of deviates in a group were much more influential than a lone dissenting voice. Secondly, generally the 'Hollander strategy' was more effective in getting the others to change their view, although there were indications that this was particularly true for groups of men. However, comparison with a control group, who were not exposed to any minority influence, revealed that, though less powerful, the 'Moscovici strategy' did have some effect, at least in groups where the deviate was not an isolated individual.

In the studies discussed so far the minority has been defined by its disagreement with the normative opinion in the group. However, outside these laboratory contexts, as we know, those with minority views in society are not simply 'people who disagree with us', they are often categorized as belonging to various outgroups as well. Thus, those with homosexual preferences are labelled 'gays', those with radical political views 'the loony left', and so on. What happens to processes of minority influence when they are overlaid with an intergroup division in this way? This was the question posed by Maass et al. (1982). They arranged for groups of men to discuss two issues: the abolition of the death penalty which, at the time in which the experiment was conducted in the USA, was still a fairly controversial issue; and the liberalization of abortion legislation, for which there was more public support. The men taking part in the study generally had rather conservative views on both these topics, being opposed to both proposals. Maass et al. infiltrated the groups with two confederates who were *either* both male (like the rest of the group) *or* both female and hence something of an outgroup. These confederates had been instructed to argue consistently but flexibly for a liberal/progressive point of view on both issues. The results are shown in figure 4.5, where it can be seen that the confederates only exerted appreciable influence on the abortion issue. On the question of the death penalty, where public opinion was more deeply entrenched, there was little or no change compared to the control groups, who had not been confronted with the minority point of view. What is interesting (although not statistically significant) was that there seemed to be a tendency for the male (ingroup) confederates to exert more influence than the female (outgroup) confederates.

That outgroup minorities may be less influential than ingroup minorities was confirmed in two experiments by Martin (1987). Using sixth-form school children as subjects and the level of state financial support for sixth-form students as the issue, he found that a minority viewpoint attributed to an ingroup source (either someone from the same school or someone of the same gender) was consistently more influential in changing opinions than a message from an outgroup source (different school or gender). Interestingly, however, this was only true for opinions which were to be expressed *publicly* to other members of the ingroup. In other experimental conditions, where they expressed their views privately (i.e. known presumably only to the

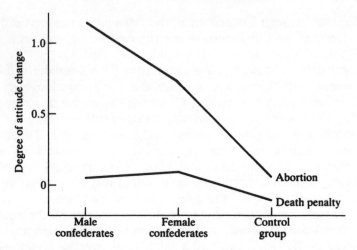

Figure 4.5 The effect of topic and categorization of minority on social influence (from Maass et al., 1982. Copyright (1982) by John Wiley and Sons, Ltd. Reprinted by permission)

experimenter), the difference in influence between the ingroup and outgroup message disappeared. There may be circumstances, therefore, where a minority, even when categorized as an outgroup, can still have some effect on prevailing norms.

Two influence processes or one?

In the last section I was concerned to demonstrate that minority influence does exist and to examine some of the factors which affect its strength. An important question still remains, however: are the social psychological processes which govern minority influence the same or different from those which underlie majority influence? As often happens in social psychology, answers to this question fall neatly into two conflicting camps. On the other hand, we find Moscovici (1976) and several of his associates arguing forcibly that there are qualitative differences between the two forms of influence, both in the factors that give rise to them and in the effects that they have. On the other side, Latane and Wolf (1981) and Tanford and Penrod (1984) and others have tried to show that the differences between the two forms of influences are primarily differences of *degree* not of kind, and that the same fundamental processes are at work in both. Let us examine the terms in which this debate has been conducted and the evidence which bears on it, beginning with the 'two processes' school of thought.

Moscovici, as already noted, believes that the means by which majorities and minorities come to have their effects are different. Following Festinger and others, he suggests that majorities primarily elicit *public* conformity from individual group members for reasons of social or informational dependence. By contrast, minorities, he believes, are successful mainly in bringing about *private* changes in opinion due to the cognitive conflicts and restructuring which their deviant ideas provoke.

That such different processes may be at work in the two kinds of influence is strongly suggested by two studies which examined creativity in response to majority and minority pressure. In the first, Nemeth and Wachtler (1983) elaborated the usual Asch paradigm in which subjects are asked to make comparisons between a standard stimuli and a number of others. In this experiment the stimuli were, in fact, taken from a standard psychological test in which a pattern is embedded in a complex background. The subjects' task was to pick which of the six comparison embedded figures matched the standard (there might be more than one). One of the correct comparison figures was always easy to detect, two were much harder since they contained more distracting designs, and the other three, though just as complex as these two, were 'incorrect' since they did not contain the standard pattern. As usual, there were some confederates who had been primed to give certain answers: *either* to respond correctly with both the easy and one of the difficult comparison figures *or* to respond correctly with the easy figure but to make an incorrect choice from the difficult set. In half the groups, there were two confederates and four naive subjects (minority influence); in the other half, there were four confederates and two naive subjects (majority influence). What happened? Those exposed to the majority influence were much more likely to copy the confederates' responses exactly, whether these were right or wrong. This is the usual conformity effect. However, when the subjects' *novel* responses were examined, i.e. those which had *not* been made by the confederates, then it was those in the *minority* influence condition who not only made a higher percentage of new responses overall, but also produced a greater proportion of these which were actually correct, regardless of whether or not the confederates had given a correct answer too! Nemeth and Wachtler (1983) argue that the minority's deviant responses had stimulated the subjects to think more creatively about the difficult figures, and hence recognize more of the correct answers. The majority, on the other hand, seemed more likely to elicit unthinking compliance. This conclusion was strengthened in a second experiment which observed people's (private) associations to the colours blue and green after being exposed to minority or majority influence in the perceptual task devised by Moscovici et al. (1969). Nemeth and Kwan (1985) found not only that those exposed to minority influence made more colour associations in total than those under majority influence, but also that these associations tended to be more original.[3] Once again, it appears that a minority stimulates a different kind of internal cognitive activity from that produced by a majority.

Further differences between majority and minority influence were identified by Maass and Clark (1983, 1986). In three experiments they examined people's attitude change (towards gay rights) after reading a summary of a group discussion in which a majority and minority viewpoint could be easily discerned. Whether these positions were for or against gay rights was systematically varied. The participants then had to indicate their own attitudes towards the issue and for half of them this was done anonymously and hence privately; the others believed that their responses would be seen by others taking part in the session with them. Attitudes in this public condition showed clear evidence of being influenced by the majority views they had read. When these were anti-gay their attitude hardened also; when the majority was pro-gay, so were they. However, those responding *privately* were influenced mainly by the minority view (see figure 4.6).

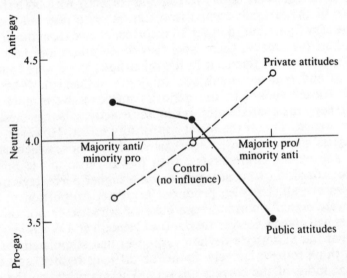

Figure 4.6 Public and private attitude change in response to majority and minority influence (from Maass and Clark, 1983, experiment 1)

The distinction between the overt public compliance produced by majority influence and covert private conversion is central to the 'two processes' hypothesis. Remember that in the early demonstrations of minority influence by Moscovici et al. (1969) and Moscovici and Lage (1976) the effects of the deviant confederates were not restricted to the perception task where responses were all made in public but extended into the subsequent, and individually administered, colour discrimination test. An even more dramatic illustration that minority influence can bring about internal, and perhaps even unconscious, changes which majority influence may be unable to do has been provided by a series of experiments by Moscovici and Personnaz (Moscovici and Personnaz, 1980, 1986; Personnaz, 1981). These experiments began with the blue–green colour task used in the earlier experiments. As before, there was a confederate who always called out 'green' to the obviously blue slides. Subjects were led to believe that this confederate was either representative of the general population (it was alleged that 82 per cent also tended to respond in the same way) or was unrepresentative (only 18 per cent responded in this way). In this manner the confederate seemed to be one of a majority or a minority. The ingenious twist which Moscovici and Personnaz now introduced into the procedure was to ask the subjects, after each slide had been turned off, to report privately the colour of the after-image they saw on the blank screen.[4] Now what most people do not know – and Moscovici and Personnaz state that their subjects did not know – is that the colour of an after-image is always complementary to the colour of the original stimulus. So, for blue slides the after-image should be yellow–orange; for green slides it would be red–purple. Subjects were asked to estimate the colour of their after-image using a 9 point scale with yellow (= 1) and purple (= 9) at the two poles. After several trials with the confederate actually present, five further trials were run with the confederate absent. Again, the after-image colours were recorded. The results were truly remarkable. Those who had been exposed to the confederate whom they thought was from a majority showed little or no shift in their after-image colours, but those who believed that the confederate was a minority person reported after-image colours which were significantly further towards the *purple* end of the scale (see figure 4.7). Since this after-image colour is more complementary of green than blue, it suggests that they had undergone some internal shift in their perceptual system as a result of the experience of minority influence. This shift persisted even when the confederate was absent. What gives these findings particular significance is that the after-image colours were different from the colours called out by the confederates and so there can be no question that the subjects simply 'copied' his/her response, especially since the relationship between stimulus colour and chromatic after-image is not a well-known one. Furthermore, Moscovici and Personnaz report that subjects seemed quite unaware that any change had taken place. Indeed, very few of them ever responded 'green' themselves in their public responses.

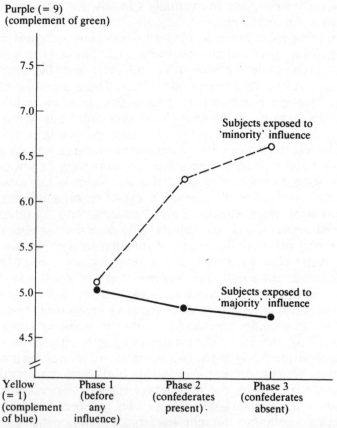

Purple (= 9)
(complement of green)

7.5

7.0

Subjects exposed to
'minority' influence

6.5

6.0

5.5

5.0

Subjects exposed to
'majority' influence

4.5

Yellow   Phase 1   Phase 2   Phase 3
(= 1)   (before   (confederates   (confederates
(complement   any   present).   absent)
of blue)   influence)

Figure 4.7 Changes in chromatic after-image as a result of majority and minority influence (from Moscovici and Personnaz, 1980, experiment 2)

Although Moscovici and Personnaz have now obtained similar results in four separate experiments, attempts to replicate these startling findings outside their laboratory have been less successful. In two close replications of their procedure, Doms and van Avermaet (1980) also found evidence of the changed after-image colour after exposure to minority influence. However, and problematically for the 'different processes' argument, they found equivalent changes in the majority influence condition also. Sorrentino et al. (1980) also attempted to replicate Moscovici and Personnaz's results using just the minority influence condition and some control conditions. They failed to find any reliable shift towards the red/purple after-image as a result of minority influence. However, an internal analysis of their data revealed that subjects who expressed most suspicion about the procedure showed the shift towards purple, while the less suspicious subjects did not.

Notwithstanding these conflicting findings (for which no really satisfactory explanation has yet been found), there does seem to be at least prima-facie support for those who argue that minorities and majorities exert their influence in different ways and with different effects. What of the rival hypothesis that minority and majority influence are but two sides of the same coin, differing only in the strength of their effects?

The clearest statement of this view has come from Latane and Wolf (1981). Drawing on Latane's (1981) social impact theory, they argue that the primary difference between majority and minority influence lies in the fact that in the former there are more sources of influence than in the latter. The importance of the number of sources stems from the basic proposition of social impact theory which is that the impact of any social stimuli increases with their number, but in a negatively accelerating fashion. That is, the first stimulus has a large impact on a person; adding a second will increase the impact but by not quite as much as the first; and subsequent stimuli will have only marginal additional effects.[5] In formulating this theory in this way, Latane draws a direct parallel with the experience of various physical stimuli where, since Stevens (1957), it has been reliably established that the subjective intensity of a sensation caused by a stimulus is a power function of the objective strength of the stimulus. If one plots the sensation against the magnitude or number of stimuli present then one typically gets a curve which resembles that shown in figure 4.8. This can be easily demonstrated. In a completely dark room the addition of one light source makes a large difference to the level of illumination. A second light increases the illumination still further, but the addition of nine more light bulbs does not make the room seem ten times brighter. By analogy, in Latane and Wolf's (1981) model of social influence, the 'light bulbs' are other people exerting influence on the experimental subject. The magnitude of their influence (or impact), as measured by the conformity shown, will thus depend on the number of them present. Because majorities contain more people than minorities they should exert greater influence.

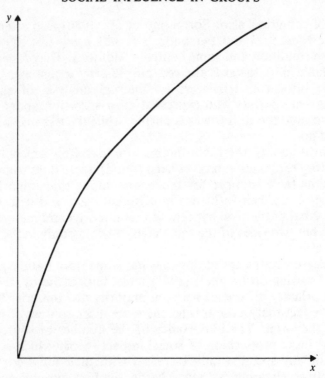

Figure 4.8   A typical negatively accelerating power function between two variables

In support of their theory, Latane and Wolf (1981) have re-examined a number of studies which have looked at the effects of varying the size of the majority on the level of conformity (see above). As predicted by their model, increasing the size of the majority does increase conformity but in a diminishing fashion. A comparison between figures 4.1 and 4.8 illustrates the resemblance between the observed relationships and the hypothetical one predicted by a mathematical power function. Extensive meta-analyses have also been performed by Mullen (1983) and Tanford and Penrod (1984). Though using different models from Latane and Wolf (1981), they came to essentially similar conclusions: increasing the number of source persons relative to recipients reliably increases the amount of influence exerted, though not in a linear fashion. Tanford and Penrod's (1984) analysis was significant in that it also examined the effects of varying the size of the minority (in more than twenty experiments). As we might have suspected from the studies of Moscovici and Lage (1976) and Bray et al. (1982) discussed earlier, Tanford and Penrod found that large minorities do have a greater quantitative impact than small ones.

Crucial to Latane and Wolf's model is the idea that social influence - whether emanating from a minority or a majority - is a unitary process. Support for this was obtained by Wolf (1985) in an extension of her earlier study of minority influence in a simulated jury (Wolf, 1979). Using the same paradigm, she created mock juries in which participants thought they were either in a majority of three (against the deviate) or in a minority of one (against a majority of three). The participants' legal judgements were clearly affected in both conditions, but much more strongly in the latter. Since these judgements were always made in private - and hence should favour the operation of *minority* influence processes, according to Moscovici - Wolf argued that her findings supported the view that the two forms of influence differ in degree but not in kind.

What can we say by way of a conclusion to this controversy? Supporters of the 'single process' hypothesis have amassed an impressive volume of evidence in support of their contention that the *quantitative size* of both minority and majority influence effects - particularly in the domain of overt public responses - *are* predictable from the same variable: namely, the number of those being influenced relative to the number doing the influencing. However, the 'single process' model is much less compelling when it comes to explaining the *qualitative nature* of majority and minority influence effects. In particular (and this is admitted by Latane and Wolf, at least), the unitary process model cannot explain the consistent finding that majorities tend to have their strongest effects at the level of overt or public compliance, whilst minorities seem to be more effective in changing people's internal constructs. In addition, the idea that the primary causal factor at work is simply the size of the influence source is not readily compatible with the discovery of Maass et al. (1982), and others since, that changing the nature of the influence task, or the perceived category membership of the influence source, can radically affect the extent of conformity. In these cases, the arithmetical ratios of influencers to influenced remain constant yet the outcomes are dramatically different. All this leads to the conclusion that whilst the numerical relationship between the minority and majority is clearly a significant feature of the group context which must not be ignored, a proper understanding of when and how group members are able to influence each other will not be reached until we know a great deal more than we do about their various *social* relationships also.

Summary

1 The most easily observed kind of social influence is when individuals conform to the attitudes and behaviour of the majority. This can occur to the extent that individuals are apparently willing to deny the evidence of their own senses in order to go along with the majority view. Such conformity is remarkably widespread and has been observed experimentally in many different countries.

2 The main explanations for this conformity to the majority (by Festinger and others) suggest that three main motivations are at work: the need to depend on others for information about the world and to test the validity of our own opinions; the achievement of group goals which is facilitated by a uniformity of purpose; and the need for approval arising out of not wishing to seem different.

3 These pressures towards uniformity are most visible when reactions to deviates in the group are studied. Deviates attract the most attention from the majority as attempts are made to make them change their mind. They are also liked less than other members of the group.

4 However, deviates, especially when they are not completely isolated and when they act in a consistent fashion, can be shown to influence the majority. This is most evident in the internal or private domain which suggests that the minority has its effect by generating socio-cognitive conflicts in the minds of the majority.

5 A controversy exists as to whether minority and majority influences are two separate processes with different effects or a single process with effects different only in magnitude. Moscovici argues for the former, pointing to the different outcomes obtained in public and private. On the other hand, Latane and Wolf hypothesize a unitary process, citing as evidence the consistent effects of group size (of both majority and minority) on the magnitude of influence.

Further reading

Allen, V. L. (1965) Situational factors in conformity, in Berkowitz, L. (ed.) *Advances in Experimental Social Psychology*, vol. 2. New York: Academic Press.

Cartwright, D. and Zander, A. (eds) (1969) *Group Dynamics*, 3rd edn, ch. 11. New York: Harper and Row.

Maass, A. and Clark, R. D. (1984) Hidden impact of minorities: fifteen years of minority influence research, *Psychological Bulletin*, 95, 428–50.
Moscovici, S., Mugny, G. and van Avermaet, E. (1985) (eds.) *Perspectives on Minority Influence*. Cambridge: Cambridge University Press.

CHAPTER 5

Individuals versus Groups

Are 'two heads better than one' or do 'too many cooks spoil the broth'? Do 'many hands make light work' or should you, in order to do something well, do it yourself? Is there really 'strength in unity' or should individuals best look out for themselves? These various (and conflicting) adages reveal our society's long interest in the question of whether people work harder, think more clearly, learn more effectively and are more creative in the company of others or on their own. This interest is hardly surprising in view of the close interdependence between people that is one of the hallmarks of human existence; today, as they have for millennia, people work together, play together and make crucial life and death decisions together. It has thus been of no little practical importance to have known how best to organize ourselves to perform these tasks effectively and harmoniously. Reflecting these concerns, group psychologists have long argued about the respective merits of group and individual performance. Indeed, the earliest recorded social psychological experiments addressed just these issues (Triplett, 1898, Ringelmann, 1913). This chapter will examine some of these debates and review the enormous fund of empirical research which they have generated.

The first section concerns some aspects of productivity. In other words, on tasks where there is some measurable index of performance, how do individuals and groups compare? As we shall see, there are a number of ways of answering this question and the outcome of the comparison very much depends on the method chosen. Nevertheless, across a wide range of tasks one finding seems to crop up quite regularly: groups often fail to operate as efficiently as one might have predicted from a knowledge of the attributes of their individual members. Such findings have led some theorists to propose that the group is inherently unlikely to maximize its full potential, either because it fails to utilize and coordinate its resources in an optimal fashion or because factors within the group lower people's motivation to perform well. As I hope to show, although much available data support these contentions, there are grounds for believing that they are unduly pessimistic about the capacity of groups to excel their potential productivity. Sometimes a group may, indeed, be more than the sum (or other combination) of its parts.

The second section considers the nature of group decisions and judgements on issues where there is no right or wrong answer, no larger or smaller outcome, but merely differences of opinion. What relationship does the group's collective voice have to its constituents' original views? Here the empirical conclusion is unequivocal: groups are typically more extreme in their views and behaviour than are their members considered individually. If the data are clear, the explanation for them remains controversial. As we shall see, a number of plausible theories have been proposed. One stresses the dynamics within the group which are generated by social comparisons among the members. Another places prime emphasis on the exchange of information and arguments which the group interaction facilitates. Still a third draws on social identity processes for its explanation. Deciding between these viewpoints turns out to be a far from simple matter. Finally, the factors which affect the quality of collective decision-making are discussed, and a theory which suggests that such decisions are prone to a detrimental set of symptoms known as 'groupthink' is examined.

Group productivity

Are two heads really better than one?

Towards the end of the nineteenth century, a French agricultural engineer called Max Ringelmann conducted a series of experiments designed to investigate the efficiency of various pulling techniques used in farming (Ringelmann, 1913; of which a detailed account is given in Kravitz and Martin, 1986). In one of these experiments he asked agricultural students to pull horizontally on a rope which was connected to a dynamometer to record the force exerted. The students either pulled alone or in groups of various sizes. What Ringelmann discovered was that although, of course, the more people who pulled the greater the force exerted, that force did not increase proportionately with the size of the group. Pulling on their own, the students managed a pull of around 85 kg. But when pulling in groups of seven they did not achieve anything like seven times that figure. In fact, they exerted a pull of around 450 kg, which is only about five times their average individual effort. Similarly, a fourteen-man group was able to achieve only just over ten times the individual pull. Looked at another way, the groups appeared to be pulling at only 75 per cent of their full capacity. Somewhere along the line some of the individuals' combined strength seemed to have been dissipated.

This simple little experiment illustrates a number of the issues that crop up in research on group performance. How, for example, should one make the comparisons between individuals and groups? A straightforward comparison between the performance of individuals on their own and the combined product of a group of individuals will often yield the wholly unsurprising result that groups do better than individuals: Ringelmann's seven-man team pulled 450 kg; on average, an individual could manage less than 90 kg. Alternatively, one could hypothetically combine the performances of isolated individuals in some way (as if they were acting as a group), and compare that pooled performance with the product of the real interacting group. This is what I did when I stated that Ringelmann's groups were only 75 per cent efficient: I computed what seven men *ought* to have been able to achieve (595 kg) and compared that to their *actual* performance (450 kg). This type of comparison between 'statisticized' and real groups is one of the most commonly used methods (Lorge, et al., 1958; Hill, 1982). A third type of comparison is to take not the whole output from such statisticized groups, but merely the performance of their best members. For some kinds of tasks this test yields some interesting results, as we shall see. Finally, one may compute some measure of individual productivity, much as the owner of a capitalist enterprise might do in calculating labour costs: how much output per worker per unit time is being generated? In Ringelmann's experiment, as we saw, this appeared to decline as the size of the group increased.

Of all the kinds of tasks on which social psychologists have attempted to assess the relative performance of individuals and groups, those which involve some kind of logical problem-solving have been the most popular. One of the earliest experiments was by Marjorie Shaw (1932). She set her subjects a number of reasoning problems to solve. Here is one of them:

> Three Missionaries (M_1, M_2, M_3) and three Cannibals (C_1, C_2, RC) are on the A-side of a river. Get them across to the B-side by means of a boat which holds only two at one time. All the Missionaries and one Cannibal (RC) can row. Never under any circumstances or at any time may the Missionaries be outnumbered by the Cannibals (except, of course, when there are no missionaries present). (Problem 2, from Shaw, 1932, p. 492)

Half the subjects worked on the problems individually, and half were allocated at random to four-person groups. Shaw observed whether or not the individuals and groups were able to solve the problems and how long they took. Her results from the first three problems are shown in table 5.1. Of the proportion of individuals and groups able to solve the problems, the groups were superior (see the first row in each half of table 5.1). On two of the problems, three of the five groups were successful and on the third, two. This compares to three, zero and two individuals, respectively. However, the groups took a little longer on the task ('time taken' includes both successful and unsuccessful attempts). This difference, when translated into person-minutes, becomes quite substantial. In other words, if Shaw had been paying her subjects by the minute to solve the problems, the group method of working would have proved much more expensive. But it is worth emphasizing again that, particularly on problem 2, at least for that extra money she would have obtained some correct solutions; none of the people working on their own on that problem were able to come up with the answer.

Table 5.1 Problem-solving by individuals and groups

	Problem 1	Problem 2	Problem 3
Individuals (n = 21)			
Proportion solving	0.14	0.00	0.095
Mean time taken (min)	4.50	9.90	15.50
Productivity (person-minutes)	4.50	9.90	15.50
Groups (n = 5 groups of 4)			
Proportion solving	0.60	0.60	0.40
Mean time taken (min)	6.50	16.90	18.30
Productivity (person-minutes)	26.00	67.60	73.20

Source: Shaw (1932)

Shaw (1932) did not compare her real groups with statisticized aggregates made up from combining individual performances. This was left to Marquart (1955), using very similar problems to those used by Shaw. As usual, half the subjects worked on the puzzles on their own, whilst the other half worked in groups (this time of three persons). Just as Shaw had found, the groups were more likely to solve the problems although they took a little longer to do so. However, when Marquart randomly combined the individuals into hypothetical groups of three and examined how many of these statisticized groups would have solved the problems (i.e. how many contained a successful individual), she found no difference between their performance and that of the real interacting groups. The same technique was used in two experiments by Faust (1959), who set real and statisticized groups a series of seven problems to solve, four of which were spatial and the remainder verbal. On the spatial problems there was little difference between them, but on the verbal problems the real groups did better: significantly so in one experiment and marginally in the other.

These experiments suggest that having a single person in the group who can solve the problem is enough to persuade the others to accept the solution also. This may not always happen, however, as Maier and Solem (1952) demonstrated with the horse-trading problem.[1] Individuals first attempted the problem on their own and only 45 per cent obtained the correct answer. They were then formed into groups of five or six to discuss the problem. These groups contained either a clear leader whose job was to encourage the participation of all the members, or they contained only a passive observer. After the group discussion, the individuals had to try to solve the problem again. All but four of the sixty-seven groups contained at least one person who had correctly solved the problem in the pretest. Yet despite this, many of the subjects failed to be convinced by this person and still gave incorrect answers in the post-test. This was particularly so in the 'observer' groups where 28 per cent of the subjects failed the problem in the post-test, but even in the 'leader' groups there was a sizeable incorrect minority (16 per cent).

A rather different kind of task was used by Taylor and Faust (1952). They modified the well-known 'Twenty Questions' game in which a person or a group has to deduce the identity of a hidden object or person by means of questions which require a yes/no answer. Individuals were compared to groups of two and four. On a number of criteria the groups were more successful. They asked fewer questions per problem, took less time to solve it and made fewer errors. However, except on the last measure (where the groups of four made fewer errors than the groups of two), there was no difference between the performance of the differently sized groups. Also, the groups were less efficient: the individuals required around five person-minutes per problem, the pairs 7.4, and the larger groups 12.6. Once again, groups were better but not twice or four times better as might have been predicted from their size.

The same conclusion seems to be true for tasks involving the recall of some previously learned material. Perlmutter and de Montmollin (1952) asked their subjects to learn some nonsense syllables and then tested their memory for these. Half of them did this task as individuals first and then in groups of three; for the other half, the sequence was reversed. The straight forward individual versus group comparison revealed that the groups recalled almost twice as much as the individuals although, at least on the early trials, they took a little longer about it. Such results do not seem to be confined to the learning of nonsense syllables. Yuker (1955) tested people's memory for items in a short story and found not only that groups were superior to individuals on average, but also that the group recall exceeded the initial recall of the 'best' individual in each group. Using the same short story, two studies by Stephenson and his colleagues confirmed these findings (Stephenson et al., 1983, 1986). They found that two- and four-person groups could remember more of the story than individuals. The groups were also more confident about the correctness of their answers, and this was true even when they got the answers wrong!

All the tasks considered so far have been of a convergent type where there has been an objectively right answer. How do groups fare on more open-ended activities which call for creativity and imagination? One such task is 'brainstorming', an ideas-generating technique which is often used in business and advertising (Osborn, 1957). The essence of this technique is that people try to think up as many solutions as possible to the problem at hand. There should be no attempt at criticism or evaluation of the quality of these ideas; rather, participants are encouraged to free associate in response to previous suggestions. This sort of activity can be very useful at the early stages in a project where one wants to explore the widest possible range of options before focusing more critically on one or two preferred choices. Intuitively, one might imagine that interacting groups ought to do very well at this kind of thing since they have a larger pool of original ideas to draw on coupled with the mutual stimulation which group members should be able to generate. In fact, this turns out to be far from the case. Taylor et al. (1958) set individuals and groups (of four) to work on three brainstorming problems. My favourite of these is the problem which asks one to imagine all the benefits or difficulties arising from the hypothetical event of everyone being born after 1960 having an extra thumb on each hand. While the interacting groups easily outshone the average individual in the number of ideas generated (by roughly 2:1), when those individuals were randomly formed into statisticized aggregates and the redundant ideas discarded, these statistical groups did far better than the real groups. On average, they produced around 68 novel ideas as compared to only 37 for the interacting groups. Furthermore, there was some evidence from a subsequent content analysis that this greater quantity was paralleled by superior quality also. These findings have been confirmed in other studies which leads to the somewhat surprising conclusion that brainstorming is actually most beneficial when carried out initially in *private*, the interacting group then being used as a forum for combining and evaluating these individually produced ideas (Lamm and Trommsdorff, 1973).

Potential and actual productivity: theories of group deficit

These findings on group performance present a rather confusing picture. Although groups seem to be generally superior in the simplest comparisons (i.e. groups versus average individual), when the performance of 'best' individuals or of statisticized groups is examined, the result often seems to go the other way, the extent of the deficit varying from task to task. One of the most influential attempts to bring some order to this complexity has been Steiner's (1972) theory of group process and productivity.

Steiner begins by proposing that a group's observed performance on a task will be determined by three factors: 'task demands', the 'resources' of the group and the 'process' by which the group interacts to accomplish the task. To understand what he means by these terms it may be helpful to use and extend the culinary analogy which he himself suggests. Imagine I am about to embark on the cooking of an elaborate dish. This is the *task* confronting me. Like as not, I will consult a recipe book and there on the appropriate page I will find a description of the kind and quantity of ingredients needed, the various procedures required for their combination, and perhaps (if I am consulting a book guided by a particular culinary or nutritional philosophy) various rules to be followed in their preparation and cooking. All these together constitute the *task demands*.

Steiner suggests that the various kinds of tasks which groups have to undertake can be usefully classified according to a number of criteria. At the most basic level they may be *divisible* or *unitary*, that is, they can be divided into subtasks each of which may be undertaken by a different person or they are holistic tasks whose accomplishment is an all or none affair. An example of a divisible task would be the manufacture of motor cars where, since Henry Ford, the making of the finished vehicle is broken down into thousands of simple tasks performed on the assembly line. Another might be a collaborative learning exercise where students are allocated to different tasks with a view to combining their efforts in some jointly produced project (see, for example, Aronson et al., 1978). We have already met examples of unitary tasks in Shaw's (1932) experiment where the reasoning problems required some flash of insight for the answer and could not usefully be broken down into components. The second criterion for classifying tasks is whether they are *maximizing* or *optimizing*. Does the task goal involve more quantity or speed (maximizing) or does it require the matching to some predetermined standard (optimizing)? Ringelmann's rope-pulling studies involved a maximizing task since the goal was to pull as hard as possible, whereas in Taylor and Faust's (1952) experiment the goal was to identify the mystery object (albeit as quickly as possible). Finally, the way the group members can combine their efforts can vary. Tasks may be *additive* (the contributions are simply added together as in brainstorming), *disjunctive* (where an either–or decision between different contributions is called for, e.g. reasoning problems), *conjunctive* (where everyone must complete the task, e.g. a group of mountaineers attempting a team conquest of a new peak) or *discretionary* (where groups can decide as they like how to accomplish the task).

If task demands constitute the recipe then, to continue the analogy, *resources* are represented by the contents of my larder and my pretensions as a cook. As with task demands, resources will vary from task to task. In a tug-of-war presumably physical strength is at a premium, whereas for learning tasks people's short-term memory capacities are much more relevant. In a perfect world, the resources of the group would always be exactly matched to the task demands so that, in fact, the task can be successfully accomplished. Steiner proposes that this idealized scenario represents the maximum or *potential productivity* of the group. In our analogy it is, if you like, the glossy photograph in the recipe book which shows me how the dish I am cooking should turn out.

The method of determining potential productivity depends on the nature of the task. Let us consider two simple cases, additive tasks and disjunctive tasks. With additive tasks, as we have seen, the group members' contributions are simply aggregated. Thus the potential productivity of a group undertaking tasks like these is simply the sum of their maximum *individual* contributions. In the Ringelmann study with which we began, the potential productivity of the seven-person team was around seven times the average individual person's pull capacity, i.e. 595 kg. Similarly, in Taylor et al.'s (1958) brainstorming study, since each individual could generate around twenty novel ideas, a four-person group could theoretically produce eighty (assuming no redundancy between people).

For disjunctive tasks, the calculation of potential productivity is slightly more complex. Here, the solution is an all-or-none affair and Steiner suggests that it will be solved simply when one member of the group comes up with the answer. Hence, he proposes that the potential productivity for a disjunctive problem is equivalent to the probability of finding someone in the group who is able to solve it. To compute this one needs some idea of the prevalence of such people in the population from which your group is made up. Let us call that proportion, P_i. From elementary probability theory it follows that the proportion of people in the population who *cannot* solve the problem is $1 - P_i$. Let us call that value, Q. Knowing Q, as Lorge and Solomon (1955) pointed out, it is then possible to calculate the predicted probability that groups of any given size (n) will be able to solve the problem. Obviously, the larger the group, the more likely it is that it will contain someone who can solve the problem, and mathematically this can be expressed as $P_g = 1 - Q^n$. P_g is the expected proportion of groups able to solve the problem and represents their potential productivity for that task. Let us quickly compute the potential productivity of Shaw's (1932) groups working on the first of her three problems. The proportion of individuals able to solve the problem was 0.14 (see table 5.1). Hence Q, the proportion *unable* to solve the problem, is 0.86. It is then simple to work out that the potential productivity of her four-person groups is, $1 - (0.86)^4 = 0.46$ (see Lorge and Solomon, 1955).[2] For the other tasks, the potential productivity figures are 0.0 and 0.33.

We now come to the crux of Steiner's theory. Just as the fruits of my labour in the kitchen almost always fail to match up to the picture in the recipe book, so Steiner proposes that a group's *actual productivity* (how it actually performs on the task) usually falls short of its potential productivity. This is, he says, because groups are seldom able to utilize their resources to the full; there are often losses due to processes within the group which impede the group's maximum attainment: 'Actual Productivity = Potential Productivity minus losses due to faulty process' (Steiner, 1972, p. 9). From this equation it is apparent that Steiner believes that though groups can approach potential productivity in their performance, they can never actually exceed it.

What kinds of 'faulty process' are responsible for this failure of groups to achieve their potential? Some are straightforward to identify. In a tug-of-war, group members will find it difficult to synchronize their pulls perfectly and to pull along exactly the same line.

Steiner calls this a problem of coordination and, as we saw from Ringelmann's results, these do appear to be real enough. Another source of faulty group process may be the social dynamics among the group members. Take the drastic losses which occurred in Taylor et al.'s (1958) brainstorming groups. It is likely that members of the real groups were affected by social influence processes (see chapter 4) and hence may have got 'stuck' on one perhaps unproductive chain of thought. They may also have felt inhibited from expressing some of their more bizarre or antisocial ideas out of embarrassment. Such social processes do not inhibit creative performance only. Recall Maier and Solem's (1952) experiment with the horse-trading problem. Despite the fact that 94 per cent of the groups contained at least one person who could solve the problem, there were still over one-fifth of the subjects who gave incorrect answers after the group attempt to solve it. Most of these came from the leaderless groups where those with incorrect opinions may have been able to dominate the other group members. Merely having a single person with the correct answer in the group is not always enough to guarantee that others will also obtain it. As a further illustration of their group deficit phenomenon, Stephenson et al.'s (1986) memory experiment is a case in point. As already noted, groups of two and four could remember more than individuals. However, using Lorge and Solomon's (1955) probabilistic calculations, it is possible to predict how many correct answers the groups *should* have obtained, based on the average recall scores from the individuals working on their own. For instance, a group of two should have been able to get over 70 per cent of the questionnaire correct (they managed only 60 per cent), and a group of four should have achieved over 90 per cent (compared to their actual score of 76 per cent).

So far we have only considered examples of 'process loss' where the group has fallen well short of what it might have been expected to achieve. However, some of the studies considered earlier actually indicate that these losses can sometimes be minimal. In Marquart's (1955) and Faust's (1959) studies of problem-solving, for example, there was little difference between real and statisticized groups, suggesting that once the correct answer became available in the group it was instantly recognized by the others. In Perlmutter and de Montmollin's (1952) memory experiment also, there were negligible process losses. Hoppe (1962) re-analysed their results by comparing their obtained group recall scores with those predicted by the Lorge-Solomon formula. He also ran a replication study of his own. In both sets of data the fit between the predicted and observed results was very close indeed, indicating that a group *is* sometimes able to utilize the pooled memories of its members efficiently.

Steiner's (1972) theory mainly emphasizes process losses due to problems which the group members may have in coordinating their activities or which arise from social influence processes within the group. There is another source of decrement which he identifies and that concerns motivation; perhaps people do not try as hard in a group as they do alone. Such a conclusion is suggested by some research by Ingham et al. (1974) which is the only published replication of Ringelmann's (1913) rope-pulling study. Having first replicated Ringelmann's results that groups do not pull as hard as the sum of their individual constituents, they modified the procedure slightly. Instead of using real groups to pull on the rope on each trial, they employed one naive subject and a number of confederates. Unknown to the real subject, who was always in the first position on the rope, the confederates had been instructed only to *pretend* to pull on the rope whilst making realistic grunts indicating physical exertion. In this way, Ingham et al. were able to construct 'pseudo-groups' of different sizes. Any decrement in pull from the real subject could only be attributable to motivation losses since no coordination losses could possibly exist. The results indicated that such a drop in motivation did indeed seem to occur (see figure 5.1).

A similar drop in effort on another kind of additive task was observed by Latane et al. (1979). They asked individuals and groups of different sizes to shout as loudly as they could and recorded the amount of noise which was produced. In line with Steiner's theory, they found that actual productivity did not match potential productivity. Groups of two performed at only 71 per cent of their individual capacity, while a six-person group could only manage 40 per cent of their potential. Then, borrowing from Ingham et al. (1974), Latane et al. (1979) created 'pseudo-groups' to eliminate coordination losses. Their subjects were blindfolded and wore headphones playing constant 'white noise' so that they could neither see nor hear the others who they were alleged to be shouting with. When told they were shouting with other people, their subjects still shouted less than when they believed they were on their own (at 82 per cent capacity for the 'groups' of two, 74 per cent for the 'groups' of six). These figures are an improvement on the real groups but still fall short of the potential productivity figure, indicating once again a lack of effort simply as a function of believing that one is doing a task with others. Similar results have been found with other tasks (e.g. Kerr and Bruun, 1981; Harkins and Petty, 1982).

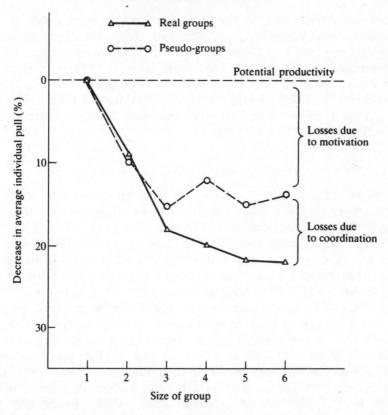

Figure 5.1 Coordination and motivation losses in group rope-pulling (from Ingham et al., 1974)

Latane et al. (1979) dubbed this apparent slackening of effort in groups 'social loafing' and explained it in terms of Latane's (1981) social impact theory, described in chapter 4. They argue that the major source of influence in group performance experiments is the experimenter's instructions. When these are directed solely towards an individual then they will have maximum impact. With groups, on the other hand, the theory suggests that the impact of the instructions is 'divided' between the group members with corresponding reductions in output. According to the theory, as group size increases so impact *decreases*, corresponding to some power function (as discussed in chapter 4). Consistent with this account, most of the group size effects on productivity do seem to conform to the typical negatively accelerating power function curve (see Steiner, 1972; and figure 5.1, for example).[3] Although 'social loafing' can be reduced by making people's contributions to the group task more identifiable or by increasing the complexity of the task (and thereby increasing involvement), none of the research within the social impact theory framework has recorded any *increase* in effort in the group (Harkins and Petty, 1982; Jackson and Williams, 1985; Brickner et al., 1986). Like Steiner's (1972) theory, therefore, social impact theory is essentially a theory of group *deficits* in performance. Some criticisms of this view are presented in a later section.

Modelling group process: social decision schemes theory

In several of the above comparisons between actual and potential productivity we have made use of a simple mathematical model to predict the potential productivity (e.g. assume group can solve problem if at least one member can; calculate the probability of finding such a person in the group). When actual productivity fails to match this, the presumption is that some factor has interfered with the operation of this 'ideal' model. Usually we are only able to hazard a guess at what that factor might be and hence speculate about the actual process by which the group arrived at its answer. This imprecision, though undesirable, is for a good reason. Direct observation of groups at work can be difficult and, as seen in chapter 2, often produces quite complex data which may be difficult to interpret. A way round this difficulty has been proposed by Davis and a number of others (Davis, 1969, 1973; Laughlin, 1980; Stasser et al., 1980). Essentially, the method used by these theorists is to conduct a number of 'thought experiments' in which one imagines all the various ways groups might work on a particular task. These are formulated mathematically as different 'decision rule' models. One then feeds into these models some assumptions about the abilities of people to complete the task or part of the task. These may be hypothetical or they may be based on some previously collected data on the distribution of individual abilities. Through the application of some quite complex mathematical techniques, one then computes the probable outcomes from the different models. These hypothetical outcomes are compared to the actual results from some real sample of groups. The decision model which best 'fits' the observed pattern of data is then presumed to be the one which the groups used.

A very simple example will help to illustrate how this modelling paradigm works. The actual models and techniques used by social decision scheme theorists are actually far more complex than this, but the basic principles are not too dissimilar. Imagine a three-person

Table 5.2 Hypothetical possibilities of group solution under different decision rules

Type of decision rule	Type of group composition										Theoretical probabilities of reaching correct solution
	Y_1	Y_1	Y_1	Y_1	Y_1	Y_1	Y_2	Y_2	Y_2	Y_3	
	Y_1	Y_1	Y_1	Y_2	Y_2	Y_3	Y_2	Y_2	Y_3	Y_3	
	Y_1	Y_2	Y_3	Y_2	Y_3	Y_3	Y_2	Y_3	Y_3	Y_3	
Truth wins (TW)	+	+	+	+	+	+	−	−	−	−	0.6
Majority rule (M)	+	+	+	+	+	−	−	−	−	−	0.5
Unanimous verdict (UV)	+	+	−	+	−	−	−	−	−	−	0.3

+ , Group solves problem.
− , Group fails to solve problem.

group attempting to solve a problem with a right/wrong answer. Suppose, for the sake of argument, there are three types of person in the population: people who are able to solve the problem (Y_1), people who cannot solve it but who can recognize the correct solution when they see it (Y_2), and people who can neither solve it nor recognize the correct solution (Y_3). There are, of course, many other types of person imaginable. What are the various combinations of these three types of person that could occur in a three-person group? There are ten in all, as shown in the column headings to table 5.2. Now think of various ways that the group might come to a decision about the solution of the problem. Let us take three common rules which operate in groups (again, many others are possible): truth wins (TW) (i.e., a demonstrably correct solution will always prevail), majority rule (M) (i.e., a majority has to agree on the solution) and unanimous verdict (UV) (i.e., everyone must agree on the solution). Then determine whether each of the ten permutations of group members could or could not solve the problem under each of the three decision rules which we have supposed might be operating. These are indicated by a plus or minus sign in table 5.2. We then have to make some assumptions about the distribution of our three types of people in the population, and also about the likely composition of our groups. To keep matters simple, I have assumed for this example that the three types are equally distributed throughout the population and also that the groups have been randomly formed. This implies that each of the ten group compositions will occur equally often. Again, we do not need to make such (probably rather unrealistic) assumptions, but other hypothetical distributions would complicate the example undesirably. It is now a simple matter to compute the theoretically predicted probabilities of reaching a solution under each of the decision rules. (For TW six out of the ten permutations solve the problem so the probability is 0.6, and so on.) Notice that at this stage we have not actually observed a single live group in action. All the work has been done on paper or, rather, in a computer. It is only now that we go out and conduct the experiment with randomly formed groups of three persons. Suppose we employ 100 groups and observe that fifty-nine of them are able to solve the problem. This gives us an 'observed' probability of solution of 0.59. The decision rule which produced the hypothetical probability closest to this figure was truth wins (= 0.6), and so we conclude that this is the group process which governs the solution to this particular problem.

One of the first attempts to use this modelling approach was by Davis and Restle (1963). They were interested to discover how groups went about solving logical problems which contained a number of steps. The two most likely models, they believed, were a *hierarchical* one in which the most able and efficient members dominate the group and the less competent ones are excluded, and an *equalitarian* model in which all members interact more or less equally, whether or not they are contributing effectively. The results from the experiment strongly supported the second model: the observed results were very close to those predicted mathematically by the equalitarian process model, and the observational and sociometric data which were also collected seemed to support this too. What this experiment seemed to show, therefore, was that reason and logic do not always prevail in problem-solving groups.

This conclusion is reinforced by a series of modelling experiments by Laughlin and his associates (see Laughlin, 1980). In these experiments, usually six or more hypothetical decision schemes are tested against the results from actual problem-solving groups. For the kind of intellectual tasks we have been considering, one decision scheme consistently seems to provide the closest fit with the observed data. That is what Laughlin calls the 'truth supported wins' model. In other words, the right answer will prevail in a group only if at least two members advocate it. In the three-person group of our very simple example in table 5.2 this also corresponds to the majority rule model. A single person suggesting the right answer (truth wins) is markedly less effective. The only exceptions to this conclusion seem to be for rather small groups (of two or three people) tackling difficult problems. Here, the truth wins model seems to apply rather better (Egerbladh, 1981).

The possibility of process gains in a group

In concluding this discussion of group productivity I want to raise two questions about the theories of group deficit outlined earlier. The first concerns the determination of a group's potential productivity. In both Steiner's (1972) and Latane et al.'s (1979) theories, as we saw, the group's potential performance was calculated by combining the individual group members' prior capabilities in some appropriate way, according to the nature of the task. This approach assumes, therefore, that the resources which individuals bring to the group task can be accurately ascertained and, once ascertained, remain more or less fixed. There are, however, grounds for questioning this assumption. What, for example, constitutes an 'individual' performance capability? At first sight it might be suggested that this is simply a person's ability to perform a task (or sub-task) in complete isolation. But assessing that ability under such conditions is practically very difficult. There will nearly always be another person physically present (i.e. the experimenter) and it is well known that the mere presence of another person can have significant effects on various kinds of task performance – sometimes enhancing it, sometimes depressing it – particularly if that person is seen to be evaluating the individual in some way (e.g. Cottrell, 1972; Zajonc, 1980; Harkins, 1987). Even if such social facilitation/inhibition effects could be controlled in the prior assessment of individual capabilities, they would presumably still operate once the person joined the group to undertake the collective task. If so, individual capabilities, far from remaining constant, are actually highly likely to undergo change.

It is not just the immediate situation that can affect individual performance. As we saw in chapter 4, Nemeth and Kwan (1985) showed that a *prior* experience of being exposed to different kinds of social influence can have a dramatic effect on the creativity of individual subjects. Those who had been in a condition of minority influence produced, when tested individually, a greater number of and more original word associations than those in the condition of majority influence or those control subjects who had received no influence at all. Such findings clearly have implications for the experiments comparing individual and group brainstorming discussed earlier.

Another factor that can influence individual performance concern people's beliefs about the nature of the testing situation. This was illustrated in an experiment by Brown and Abrams (1986) which was actually designed for quite another purpose (see chapter 8). During this experiment we arranged for school children to take an individual reasoning ability test under conditions *either* where they thought that their school was competing with another school *or* where they believed that their school and the other school were linked cooperatively. Although we were not originally interested in the children's individual test scores, when these were analysed we discovered that these had been reliably influenced by whether or not they believed they were in competition or cooperation with this other school: on average the latter subjects scored two more correct answers (out of 32) than the former. Here, then, we see the influence of an intergroup variable on a purely individual measure of task performance.[4] Which of the average levels of individual ability should be used to compute the resources of an interacting group?

If there are grounds for doubting whether the resources of the group are static, then this raises a second question: are process losses inevitable in groups as the group deficit theories suggest? Some authors have suggested not. Shaw (1976), for example, suggests that Steiner's (1972) equation linking actual and potential productivity should be amended to include 'process gains'. With such a formulation, if the gains outweighed the losses then a group might actually exceed its potential performance. Hackman and Morris (1975, 1978) make a similar point, arguing that the group deficit theories are based on research which has made no real effort to provide *facilitatory* process within the group. Instead, the groups have been left to work on the experimental tasks 'spontaneously', and hence probably rather inefficiently. With appropriate interventions to counteract process losses, Hackman and Morris believe that net gains might accrue from group interaction. These ideas seem intuitively appealing. Surely there are circumstances when a group is so well organized or is so significant to its members that they will work better or harder in it than they ever would on their own?

It is one thing to assert something, quite another to demonstrate it, and it must be admitted that the evidence for net process gains is rather fragmentary at present. Nevertheless, there are some scattered examples where groups seem to have exceeded theoretical expectations which persuade me that the phenomenon is not entirely illusory. Let us begin with two studies we have already discussed in some detail: the experiments by Shaw (1932) and Faust (1959). In Shaw's experiment, the proportions of groups actually solving the three problems were 0.60, 0.60 and 0.40 (see table 5.1). As we then saw, the potential group productivity figures for these same three problems – based on the number of successful individuals – were 0.46, 0.0 and 0.33, respectively. In other words, on all three problems the *actual* proportions exceeded the theoretical maxima. Lorge and Solomon (1955) calculate that the first and last differences were not significant but that the second *was*. Here, then, is one example of groups exceeding their potential productivity: on their own, no single individual could solve problem 2; yet three of the groups were successful. Similarly, Faust (1959) found that in one of his experiments his real groups out-performed his 'nominal' groups on a series of verbal problems. Shaw and Ashton (1976) found further evidence for what they called 'assembly bonus effects' using a crossword puzzle task. On a simple puzzles there was no difference between the observed and predicted performances, but in one experiment, using a more difficult puzzle, the groups did significantly better than expected from the individual performance data. In all these experiments, there seems to have been some process in the group whereby group members have been able to facilitate each other's performance.

As a last instance of process gain let us return to the rope-pulling task with which we began. As we noted, Ringelmann (1913), followed by Ingham et al. (1974), observed that in general the pull per person was less in a group than when people pulled on their own. However, in both these studies, and in the subsequent 'social loafing' research, the groups used were purely *ad hoc* affairs. Subjects were asked to pull on a rope (or shout at a sound meter) in twos, fours or other-sized units with no real group goal in mind. Nor could they have had any identity as a group since interaction amongst the members was minimal and the 'group' was disbanded as soon as the trial was over. In other words, psychologically speaking, these studies were concerned with the performance of physical aggregates rather than meaningful social groups (see chapter 1). With these thoughts in mind, Holt (1987) conducted a replication of Ringelmann's experiment. Arguing that members of mere aggregates would have no real reason to exert any extra effort collectively, Holt gave all his groups (of three) an opportunity of several minutes social interaction before the rope-pulling task. Some of his groups were given an additional opportunity to heighten their identity by devising a name for themselves, whilst others were made up from pre-existing groups (of flatmates). Although there were no reliable differences between these various types of group, one finding emerged with startling clarity: out of the total of thirty groups in the experiment only *four* pulled below their potential productivity! On average, the group pulls *exceeded* the sum of the individual pulls by 19 per cent, a statistically significant result. This evidence of process gain is all the more remarkable when one considers that it must have been achieved *despite* the inevitable coordination losses incurred in a rope-pulling task. Holt's provocative conclusion is that people will show motivation decrements in groups only to the extent that those groups are psychologically insignificant. Thus, he suggests, Latane et al.'s (1979) so called 'social loafing' phenomenon should more properly be named '*individual* loafing'. When groups matter to their members, he believes they show evidence of 'social *labouring*'.

Group decision-making

Most of the tasks with which we have been concerned so far in this chapter have been ones for which there is some well-defined outcome; performance can be measured as the ability to solve some logical puzzle, correctly recall some material or produce as large an output as possible. But many tasks which groups undertake in everyday life are not at all like this. Consider a family deciding where to go on holiday this year, a group of students trying to choose a topic for a cooperative learning project, a jury attempting to reach a verdict in a court case, a trade union deliberating over the best tactics to pursue in an industrial dispute or a government cabinet considering some political or military course of action. In all these (and countless other) examples of collective decision-making there is no one objectively verifiable answer or unequivocal optimum performance. Rather, what the groups are faced with is making a choice amongst various options, each of which may have some subjectively perceived merit. Thus, in studying group judgements of this kind the question is not, as it was in the last section, 'are individuals or groups superior?', but the more general problem, 'what is the relationship between individual opinions and the consensual view expressed by the group?' Having once established that relationship, we can go on to investigate the social psychological processes that might underlie it.

Do individual and group decisions differ?

Until about 1960 the conventional wisdom was that a group opinion corresponded roughly to the average of the opinions of its constituent members. This commonsense view was undoubtedly influenced by the theory and research on conformity processes (in their heyday in the 1950s) which, as we saw in chapter 4, strongly suggested that group members are liable to converge on some agreed or normative position when asked to make a collective judgement. Thus, it was thought, a board of directors comprised of a number of people with varying views on the future direction of their company would compromise around the 'middle road'. Some even argued that such compromises usually resulted in rather cautious and unadventurous business decisions (Whyte, 1956).

Given this climate of opinion, perhaps it is not surprising that a series of experiments claiming that just the opposite was the case should have had such an impact on the field of group dynamics. The first of these – probably one of the most famous unpublished experiments in the history of social psychology – was by Stoner (1961) and, ironically enough, in view of Whyte's (1956) conclusions about the health of American corporations, it involved business students. Stoner asked his subjects individually to make some judgements about a number of hypothetical social dilemmas. Each of these dilemmas involved someone having to make a choice between two courses of action, one of which (with the more desirable outcome) involved a higher degree of risk than the other. One of the dilemmas used was as follows: 'An electrical engineer may stick with his present job at a modest but adequate salary, or may take a new job offering considerably more money but no long-term security.' The subjects were asked to judge the lowest acceptable level of risk for them to advise the main character in the scenario to give the riskier alternative a try. (Two other examples are given in table 5.3.)

The subjects were then randomly formed into groups and asked to reach a unanimous decision on each of the dilemmas they had considered individually. Stoner found to his surprise that these group decisions were nearly always riskier than the average of the individual group member pre-discussion decisions. These results were quickly replicated by Wallach et al. (1962), who also established that these shifts in group opinion became internalized because they reappeared when the subjects were asked once more for their individual opinions *after* the group discussion. It was clear that group decisions (at least in these laboratory groups and on this kind of task) were *not* simply the average or compromise of the individual group members' initial positions; apparently, groups were willing to entertain greater risks collectively than they would as individuals.

In the several hundred studies which followed these two experiments, three other factors also became clear. The first was that the so-called 'shift to risk' which had been identified should more properly be called a 'shift to extremity'. Several experiments found that on some dilemmas groups regularly made more cautious or conservative choices than individuals (e.g. Stoner, 1968; Fraser et al., 1971). In other words, groups seem to shift away from the 'neutral' point of the

Table 5.3 Group polarization in decision-making: results from 89 groups participating in University of Kent practical classes, 1979–87

Item	Mean individual level of risk before group discussion (scale 1–11)	Mean level of risk adopted by groups (scale 1–11)	Shift
1 Chess-player	4.4	2.8	– 1.6*
2 Psychologist	4.6	3.7	– 0.9*
3 Rugby player	4.8	4.2	– 0.6*
4 Engineer	5.6	4.9	– 0.7*
5 Holiday/illness	7.4	7.5	+ 0.1
6 Marriage	8.3	9.4	+ 1.1*

* Statistically significant shift.

Sample items:

1   G, a competent chess-player, is participating in a national chess tournament. In an early match she draws the top-favoured player in the tournament as her opponent. G has been given a relatively low ranking in view of her performance in previous tournaments. During the course of her play with the top-favoured player, G notes the possibility of a deceptive though risky manoeuvre which might bring her a quick victory. At the same time, if the attempted manoeuvre should fail, G would be left in an exposed position and defeat would almost certainly follow. Imagine that you are advising G. Listed below are several probabilities or odds that G's deceptive play would succeed.

6   J and her boyfriend have been planning to get married. However, some recent arguments between them suggest some sharp differences of opinion over a number of important issues and, although still wanting to marry, she is no longer so sure. Discussions with friends and a counsellor indicate that a happy marriage, while possible, would not be by any means certain. Imagine that you are advising J. Listed below are several probabilities or odds that her marriage will be happy.

scale towards the pole which was initially favoured by the average of the individual choices. This polarization phenomenon (as it is now known) has proved to be remarkably general and robust, having been obtained in a wide variety of subject populations (Myers and Lamm, 1976). I have personally conducted the same group decision-making experiment for nine successive years, using some of the materials from the original studies. The cumulative results from these eighty-nine groups are presented in table 5.3. Polarization is clearly visible. On the first four items, where the mean of the pre-discussion individual decisions is to the left of the notional midpoint of the scale (= 6), the groups shift further to the left; where the individuals are initially cautious, the groups shift even further in that direction. There are some small year-by-year fluctuations but the overall pattern shown in table 5.3 is remarkably consistent.

The second conclusion to emerge from the explosion of group decision-making research set off by Stoner was that the size of the group polarization shift was correlated with the average individual initial position on the scale (Teger and Pruitt, 1967). This can also be seen in table 5.3. Note that items 1 and 6 (the two most extreme items) also show the largest shifts (though in opposite directions), whilst those in the middle of the scale show smaller shifts. In fact, the correlation between initial position and magnitude of shift in table 5.3 is very high indeed: +0.94. In other words, far from being constrained either statistically (by 'floor' or 'ceiling' effects) or psychologically (by wishing to appear moderate), the more extreme a group is to begin with the more extreme it seems to become.

The third important finding was that polarization effects are by no means limited to the choice dilemmas devised by Wallach et al. (1962). Moscovici and Zavalloni (1969) asked French school students to state individually their attitudes towards President de Gaulle and the United States. They were then formed into groups and the resulting consensually agreed attitudes showed evidence of polarization. Beforehand, their attitudes had been favourable towards de Gaulle and negative to the USA; in the groups they became even more pro-Gaullist and, somewhat less strongly, rather more anti-American. A similar polarization effect was found by Doise (1969) using attitudes to one's own college as the discussion topic, and by Stephenson and Brotherton (1975) who studied attitudes towards organizational roles amongst colliery supervisors. Polarization has also been observed in a variety of other domains including, as we shall see shortly, jury decision-making, gambling decisions, judgements of autokinetic movements and judgements of physical attractiveness (Myers and Lamm, 1976; Isenberg, 1986). All in all, therefore, there are ample grounds for believing that polarization is a pervasive consequence of group interaction.

There is one cautionary qualification that needs to be added, however. This is that almost all the studies on which these conclusions are based were conducted in laboratory settings with *ad hoc* groups in which the decision-making task was a novel one and – even more important – in which the outcome was almost always hypothetical. The decisions seldom had any real consequences, either for those making them or for some other party. On those rare occasions when real decision-making groups have been studied, polarization has not always been much in evidence. Semin and Glendon (1973), for example, gained access to a job evaluation committee in a medium-sized business. The purpose of this committee was to decide on the grading of different jobs in the firm which had direct implications for the status and pay of the incumbents of those jobs. Before the committee met each member was required to allocate points to the jobs under consideration along a number of dimensions. During the committee deliberations the individual ratings were made known to the other committee members and, after discussion, a committee recommendation was made on the point grading of each job. The procedure was thus almost an exact replica of the standard decision-making experimental procedure. However, unlike groups in the laboratory, Semin and Glendon (1973) observed no polarization whatsoever in their decisions. After twenty-eight decisions over a year, the average job evaluation made by the committee was virtually identical to the mean evaluations of the individual committee members. Similar findings were obtained by Fraser (1974) in studies of three real decision-making bodies: a students' union finance committee, a team of child psychiatrists and university examiners. In none of these three types of groups was there any consistent evidence of polarization.

On the other hand, Walker and Main (1973) analysed the judgements of American Federal judges, made alone or on a bench of three judges, and found that the collective and individual decisions differed markedly. Of the 400 or so cases tried by trios of judges, 65 per cent could be classified as libertarian, whereas only 30 per cent of the 1500 cases tried by single judges could be so classified. Clement and Sullivan (1970) also observed polarization amongst seminar groups of students trying to decide on what method of assessment should be used to evaluate their performance on a psychology course. Initially, they had a preference for a relatively conservative method, a tendency which became exaggerated after discussion with their fellow students.

An explanation for these discrepancies has been suggested by Semin and Glendon (1973). They point out that what distinguishes most real decision-making bodies from *ad hoc* laboratory groups is that the former are usually much more permanent affairs; they have a history and a future while laboratory groups have only a transient existence. This means that they are much more likely to develop an internal structure (e.g. designated officers), adopt conventional procedures (e.g. written agendas) and to establish norms about the decision issues, all of which might inhibit any 'natural' polarization from appearing. In this respect the judges in Walker and Main's (1973) study, although they were certainly real-life groups, actually were rather more like laboratory groups in that they came together for only a single case and then disbanded. It may also be the case that polarization is more likely to occur in the early stages of a group's life or when it is confronted with a relatively novel or unusual situation. The groups in the studies which found no polarization had been extant for some time and also had considerable experience of the issues that they were deliberating. The same can hardly be said for a group of subjects participating in a typical group decision-making experiment! Whatever the explanation for these anomalies between 'natural' and 'laboratory' groups, one thing is clear: group dynamics badly needs further research in which field and experimental methodologies are pursued in parallel, as noted earlier.

Explanations of group polarization

Pushing the caveat about the possible unrepresentativeness of most group decision-making research to the back of our minds for the moment, how are polarization phenomena best explained? There are currently four main approaches to this question.

The first is a familiar one to us from the earlier discussion of group performance; it is Davis's (1973) social decision schemes theory. The essence of this perspective, as we have seen, is to try to capture (by means of various mathematical combination rules) the nature of the group process which gives rise to the observed outcomes. The hypothetical decision scheme which comes closest to predicting the obtained findings is presumed to be the one which the group actually used. Davis et al. (1974) adopted this approach in their study of people's gambling dicisions. Individuals and groups were asked to rate the attractiveness of various monetary bets in which the probability of winning was varied systematically. As usual, polarization occurred: for gambles in which there was a good chance of winning, individuals' initial positive ratings were exaggerated in the group, whilst poor odds bets elicited less favourable individual ratings and even more negative ratings by the groups. However, despite the fact that groups had been instructed to reach a *unanimous* decision (and many of the groups believed that this was what they had actually done), the hypothetical decision scheme which best fitted the actual data was some form of *majority verdict* model, i.e. the group went along with the alternative advocated by most of the group. This pre-eminence of the majority in determining the decision in judgemental tasks has been confirmed in a number of studies (Laughlin, 1980). However, on discussion items where the initial tendency is very clearly in one direction or another, extreme members become especially influential, providing that they have at least one supporter. Laughlin and Early (1982) found that a risk (or caution) supported wins model fitted their data best for clearly risky (or cautious) items (e.g. item 3 in table 5.3) whilst for less-polarized issues some sort of majority process seemed to be in play.

One of the major applications of this modelling approach has been to understand how juries reach their verdicts. Although real juries are (by law) very difficult to study empirically, researchers have been able to create very realistic mock trials (often based on actual trial transcripts) and then study the kinds of verdicts the mock juries reach. Here, again, majority rule seems to be the order of the day (e.g. Davis et al., 1975). In one of the most elaborate of these simulated trial experiments, Hastie et al. (1983) found that there was virtually no difference between the kinds of verdicts reached on the same case by juries operating under three different instructions: unanimity, 10 v. 2 majority, or 8 v. 4 majority. There were some differences in the time and process by which the verdicts in the three different conditions were arrived at, but the net result was the same. This suggests that the change which was introduced in Britain, the USA and elsewhere some years ago to relax the unanimity requirement for jury verdicts did little more than to make explicit what was probably happening in practice anyway. Whether or not the quality of the decision-making process has been improved as a consequence is a matter of some debate (see Hastie et al., 1983; Brown, 1986).

The mathematical modelling approach taken by social decision schemes theorists can help to discover how the individual opinions in the group are typically combined to form the collective decision. However, it is less informative about the social psychological processes that give rise to that combination rule. Once we have identified majority verdict as the most frequent decision rule, the question is 'why?' One answer is provided by an extension of Festinger's (1954) social comparison theory (see chapters 3 and 4) and this is the second of the explanations for polarization we shall consider. Two prominent advocates of this approach have been Sanders and Baron (1977). According to them, polarization occurs in the following way: associated with any issue on which a group must reach a decision are likely to be a number of social values (e.g. caring for others, being adventurous, not taking risks with one's health, and so on). Taken together, these values will result in an initial social preference towards one decision outcome rather than another. Each individual, before the group discussion, will probably perceive him/herself as being somewhat further towards this socially desirable outcome than his/her peers (Codol, 1975). Once the group discussion gets under way – thereby heightening the salience of the relevant social values – some of these individuals discover that this was a misperception because there are others who endorse positions further towards the socially valued pole than they. The outcome of this social comparison is that they will then shift further in this direction in order to present themselves in a more favourable light. This is rather akin to the 'unidirectional drive upward' process which Festinger suggested occurs in people's ability comparisons (see chapter 3). There will, of course, be some who find themselves already further towards the socially desirable extreme than most others in the group but, although conformity pressures may modify their opinion somewhat, they will have less reason to shift than their colleagues who are on the other ('wrong') side of the modal position. The net result is that the collective decision will be slightly more extreme than the average of individual positions and will come to represent more nearly the majority viewpoint in the group, as suggested by social decision scheme analyses.

The key factor in this social comparison explanation is people's knowledge of other group members' positions relative to the dominant social value(s) in question. It follows, then, that actually discussing the issues with those other group members may not be necessary to produce polarization, if one could provide the social comparison information in some other way. This is the rationale behind a number of experiments which have examined the effect of 'mere knowledge' on people's opinions. One of the first of these was by Teger and Pruitt (1967) who modified the original Wallach et al. (1962) paradigm to include a 'no discussion' condition, where group members were permitted only to hold up signs indicating their individual pre-discussion positions on each item. Sure enough, their subsequent decisions became more polarized after receiving this information, although not as strongly as those who had had the benefit of discussion as well. This polarizing effect of being exposed to other people's opinions was confirmed by Myers (1978). He found that simply presenting subjects with either the mean or the distribution of responses of apparently similar others was enough to shift their choices further in the initially preferred direction. Something similar has been observed in studies of gambling behaviour. Blascovich et al. (1973) found that people playing blackjack in groups made riskier bets than when playing as individuals, even when no discussion of bets was permitted. This was subsequently replicated even when subjects used their own money to play with (Blascovich et al., 1975, 1976).

More direct evidence for the importance of social comparison processes has come from studies which have varied the salience of a social value directly. If it is, indeed, a movement towards a positively valued pole which underlies polarization then one should expect greater shifts as the value becomes more explicit. This is exactly what Baron and Roper (1976) found. Adapting Sherif's (1936) autokinetic effect paradigm, they suggested to their subjects that large estimates of movement of the light were indicative of superior intelligence. This, then, was the relevant social value. Upon hearing the responses of other subjects in the 'public' trials of the experiment, people's estimates became significantly larger than those subjects who always responded privately and were thus deprived of social comparison information.

A similar idea lay behind Goethals and Zanna's (1979) experiment. They argued that for social comparisons to be effective in producing opinion shifts, they must convey information not just about the issue in question (i.e. people's opinions on the acceptable level of risk on each item), but also on some related attribute, for example, intelligence (Goethals and Darley, 1977; see chapter 3). Accordingly, they extended Teger and Pruitt's (1967) idea of having subjects simply hold up cards to indicate their opinions on choice dilemma items. In one condition, they asked subjects also to display a card which contained information about their self ratings of 'overall talent, creativity and ability'. They found that the shifts of opinion in this condition were as marked as those obtained with a full group discussion, and much more so than those produced, as in Teger and Pruitt's procedure, after revelation of opinions only on the items themselves. Once again, we find that simply learning something about others in the group is sufficient to generate polarization, even when one never actually engages in direct discussion with them.

The emphasis in the social comparison explanation is on the self-presentational or self-enhancement motives which are stimulated by comparisons with others. The focus is very much on relations among the group members; the actual *content* of the group discussion leading to the group decision is seen as irrelevant except as it affects these. In the third approach to be considered this order of priorities is reversed. According to this view, the main causal factor – and in some strong versions of the theory, the *only* causal factor – underlying group polarization is the exchange of information and arguments which precedes the collective decision. The champions of this 'persuasive arguments' theory (as it is known) have been Burnstein and Vinokur (1977), and they have accumulated an impressive array of evidence in its support. Before examining that evidence I need to explain why Burnstein and Vinokur believe that exchange of arguments is so crucial. They begin by assuming, reasonably enough, that on any issue under deliberation it is unlikely that in the group there is a precisely equal balance of arguments and evidence for and against. Usually there will be a preponderance in one direction, presumably not unrelated to the dominant social values which are thought so critical for the social comparison explanation. Of course, each individual will not at first have access to all these arguments and nor will all the individuals in the group be aware of the same arguments. Once the discussion gets under way, all this different information comes out into the open; each person becomes acquainted with more of the arguments supporting the dominant view and perhaps one or two extra arguments against, although probably not as many. Burnstein and Vinokur (1977) suggest that the group members then act as rational 'information processors' and respond to the additional arguments and evidence supporting their initially preferred view by shifting their opinion further in that direction.

This idea that group decisions result from the pooling of individual contributions is, of course, strongly reminiscent of Steiner's (1972) theory of group productivity discussed earlier. It has received considerable support from studies which have either analysed or manipulated the argumentative content of group discussions. Vinokur and Burnstein (1974), for instance, counted up the number of pro-risk and pro-caution arguments that were generated over typically 'risky' or 'cautious' choice dilemma items. As they expected, the pro-risk arguments outweighed the pro-caution arguments on 'risky' items by about 6 : 4, and for 'cautious' items the ratio was reversed. When those arguments were subsequently rated for persuasiveness by independent judges, the arguments from the larger set on any item were also found to be more persuasive. Finally, Vinokur and Burnstein (1974) ran a small experiment in which subjects were simply provided with prototypical arguments produced on different items, with no opportunity for discussion. The usual shifts occurred. These findings were confirmed by Ebbesen and Bowers (1974). Like Vinokur and Burnstein (1974), they found a correlation between the proportion of risky to cautious arguments produced and the average degree of polarization. They then went one step further and asked subjects to listen to tape-recorded group discussions in which the proportion of risky to cautious arguments expressed was systematically varied. Irrespective of the particular items heard, the subjects' changes in opinion were clearly related to the proportion of risky to cautious arguments in the discussion (see figure 5.2).

Not content with demonstrating the validity of their persuasive arguments theory, Burnstein and Vinokur (1973) have also attempted to show the *in*validity of the rival social comparison approach. They reasoned that if it is the persuasive content of arguments which causes polarization rather than comparisons between oneself and others,

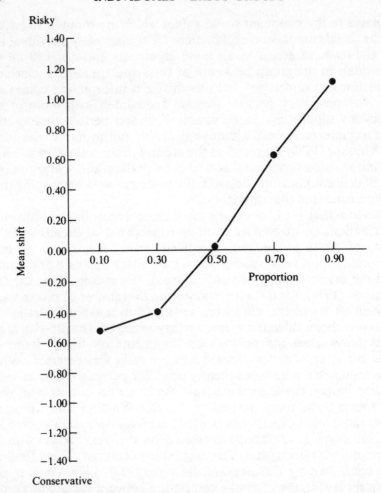

Figure 5.2 Average shift in opinion as a function of the proportion of risky arguments heard (from Ebbesen and Bowers, 1974. Copyright (1974) by the American Psychological Association. Reprinted by permission of the author)

then it should be possible to produce shifts in opinion even when people are unable to infer the views of others, provided that the relevant arguments which emerge are sufficiently persuasive. On the other hand, even if people know where others stand on an issue, unless they are exposed to enough varied and convincing arguments, they should not polarize. They then designed two ingenious experiments to put these hypotheses to the test. Both were based on the traditional Wallach et al. (1962) procedure: subjects initially answered choice dilemmas individually, discussed these same items in a group and then recorded their subsequent individual opinion. However, instead of the usual situation where everyone simply argued their own point of view, the experimenters announced that each person would be asked to argue a point of view provided by the experimenter. This might be the same as their own or it might differ and people would not know what others had been asked to do. In this way social comparisons became impossible to make since other people's true opinions would be occluded. Each subject was then given his instructions privately. In half the groups people were all told to argue *for* their own point of view; the other half had to advocate a position directly contrary to what they really believed. The purpose of this manipulation was to vary the number and persuasiveness of the arguments generated in the groups. Burnstein and Vinokur (1973) assumed that people would have less to say and be much less convincing when arguing for something they did not really believe in. In the second experiment, Burnstein and Vinokur used the same technique only this time they informed the subjects that everyone had actually been instructed to argue directly against their true views (and this was indeed what subjects were asked to do). Now social comparisons were possible again since people could infer each other's true positions simply by inverting whatever they said. However, the arguments generated here should not be very plentiful or persuasive since, as in half the groups in the first experiment, people were being asked to play a devil's advocate role.

Table 5.4 Shifts in opinion resulting from persuasive arguments and social comparisons

	Social comparisons?	Persuasive arguments?	Items	Mean shift
Experiment 1				
Condition 1	No (Others' positions not known)	Yes (Everyone arguing *for* own position)	Risky	− 0.59*
			Cautious	+ 0.44*
Condition 2	No (Others' positions not known)	No (Everyone arguing *against* own position)	Risky	− 0.03
			Cautious	+ 0.06
Experiment 2	Yes (Others' positions could be inferred)	No (Everyone arguing *against* own position)	Risky	− 0.25
			Cautious	− 0.46*

* Statistically significant shift.

Source: Burnstein and Vinokur (1973)

The main results from these two experiments are presented together in table 5.4 and, on the whole, they provide a rather strong – not to say persuasive – argument for the validity of Burnstein and Vinokur's (1973) account. Notice, first of all, the clear polarization which occurred in condition 1 of the first experiment where comparisons were impossible but where group members could be persuasive arguing for their own opinions. As usual, the polarization was negative on risky items and positive on cautious items. In condition 2, on the other hand, where people's arguments were presumably less persuasive, the polarization all but disappears. The same is true for the risky items in the second experiment where social comparisons were possible yet little polarization occurred. The only fly in Burnstein and Vinokur's ointment was the result from the cautious items in experiment 2. Unexpectedly, there was a significant shift in opinion here in the *risky* direction. In other words, despite starting out at around 8 (well to the cautious end of the 10-point scale), the groups regressed back to finish nearly a half scale point riskier. Although this should not have occurred according to Burnstein and Vinokur's theory, it is equally inexplicable from the social comparison point of view since, if anything, the shift should have been in just the other direction.

For the persuasive arguments explanation, the actual discussion in the group is more important than the person who puts forward the argument; the information content – and hence persuasiveness – of the arguments expressed is presumed to be a property of the arguments themselves and is independent of their source. But is this plausible? Are we really as receptive to arguments from people we see as our opponents as we are to those from our friends? This brings us to the fourth of our explanations of group polarization, an explanation which invokes social identification with the group as the key process (Wetherell, 1987). Drawing on Turner's (1987) self-categorization theory, outlined in the last chapter, Wetherell argues that what is happening when a group polarizes is that the group members are attempting to conform more closely to the normative position which they see as prototypical for their ingroup. When the situation makes their ingroup identity more important – say, for example, when an intergroup relationship comes particularly to the fore – then the relevant ingroup norms are likely to become more extreme so as to be more clearly differentiated from outgroup norms, and the within group polarization will be enhanced. Wetherell (1987) conducted a simple experiment to test this idea. She asked subjects to listen to a tape-recording which purported to be of a previous group discussion from a series of intergroup debates, and the subjects believed that they themselves would shortly be taking part in one of these debates. They were told that the recording was either of an *ingroup* discussion – one which they expected to join later – or of an *outgroup* discussion. In fact, of course, the same tape was played to all subjects and hence the number and quality of arguments was held constant. When the subjects' own opinions on the items under discussion were elicited, there were some signs that they had been influenced by the identity of the tape. Once corrected for the degree of extremity in initial opinion, the degree of polarization was higher in the 'ingroup' tape condition than in the 'outgroup' condition.

Even more convincing evidence was provided by Mackie and Cooper (1984) using the same paradigm but introducing a stronger element of intergroup competition and more relevant attitudes. They found that students' attitudes towards the use of standardized tests for university entry could be dramatically altered after hearing a taped 'ingroup' arguing for the retention (or abolition) of these tests, but were much less affected when the tape was alleged to be of an outgroup (see figure 5.3). Notice that initially the student subjects were mildly in favour of retaining the entrance tests, a tendency which was exaggerated after hearing the pro-retention 'ingroup' tape. But on hearing the pro-*abolition* 'ingroup' tape their attitudes switched completely and actually fell below the mid-point of the 31-point scale. The changes after hearing the same arguments attributed to an 'outgroup' were much smaller and were generally in the reverse direction. In subsequent experiments, Mackie (1986) found that the same effects could be obtained even without the element of intergroup competition; it was sufficient to maintain one of the tapes to be from a collection of individuals (and not an outgroup) to eliminate the polarization. In line with Turner's (1987) theory, Mackie also found that people's estimates of what the taped group's normative position was were more extreme when they believed they would be joining it – and hence might have identified with it – than when they believed it was irrelevant to them.

An anticipation of an intergroup encounter may not always lead to greater polarization however, as Reid and Sumiga (1984) found. They devised an experiment in which social science students participated in the group discussion over four issues (two important, two less so), which they believed was a rehearsal for a forthcoming debate. This debate was to be either within a tutorial group in their faculty (*intra*group condition) or was to be between students from different faculties (*inter*group condition). Although both of these experimental conditions would be expected to highlight social identity concerns – and

hence encourage group polarization – Reid and Sumiga (1984) hypothesized that this polarization should be greatest in the intergroup
condition, especially on the important issues. In fact, on the important
issues it was in the *intra*group condition where polarization was most
evident, and only on the less important items did the expected intergroup effects occur. Reid and Sumiga speculate that the polarizing
effects of increased group identification which Turner (1987) predicts
may sometimes be counterbalanced by interpersonal considerations of
impression management: trying to present oneself more favourably
compared to those whom one expects to meet in a forthcoming
encounter.

Let me now summarize these four approaches and assess their competing merits. The first approach simply tries to map how individual
preferences are combined into a collective opinion. The dominant

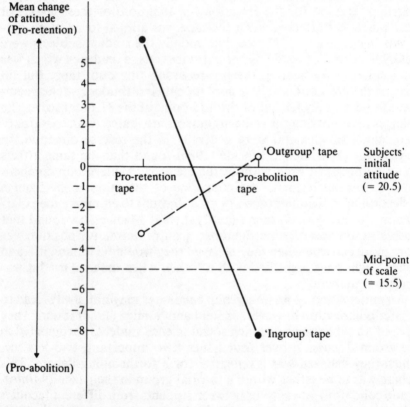

Figure 5.3 Intergroup effects on attitude polarization (from Mackie and
Cooper, 1984)

decision scheme, at least for tasks with no unequivocally correct solution, is some kind of majority rule: the views of more than half the group – or, in some cases, the largest single subgroup – largely determine the group decision. Although methodologically sophisticated, this approach is not very informative about the processes underlying the transformation from individual opinions to a group voice. The other approaches address precisely this question. The social comparison explanation is at its strongest in explaining polarization in domains where there is little opportunity either to engage in or exchange arguments but where, nevertheless, there is some information available as to the socially preferred way of behaving and as to how others actually are behaving. Decisions in blackjack gambling or estimates of autokinetic movement do not seem readily amenable to the very cognitive information processing approach advocated by the persuasive arguments theorists and yet, as we have seen, polarization can be observed as clearly here as with more verbal discussion tasks. On the other hand, in the latter situations, the persuasive arguments approach convincingly shows that it is the content of the messages which are exchanged during the group discussion that determines the extent of polarization (and *not* the positions taken up by the message senders). Both the social comparison and persuasive argument approaches seem most applicable when one initially knows little about one's fellow group members or where the decision taken is a novel one. After all, if one knows everybody's views about an issue and one is well acquainted with all the relevant arguments it is hard to see why either process should come into play. Perhaps that is why polarization has not been so easy to observe in real-life groups which have been in existence for some time. The essence of the fourth approach is that group members have some knowledge of their group's main attributes and characteristic normative attitudes, and then shift towards these as their group membership becomes salient or threatened in some way.

It seems difficult to explain the differential polarization caused by exposure to 'ingroup' or 'outgroup' arguments in any better way than by such a social identity perspective. Certainly, such findings are especially difficult to reconcile with the persuasive argument approach since the actual information content of the messages is always held constant. However, powerful though these intergroup effects are, it is less easy to imagine how they would come into play in (say) a jury where there is not an obvious outgroup against which to define the prototypical ingroup norm.

We are left, then, with the theoretically inelegant but nevertheless probably correct conclusion that all three types of process are present to some degree in most decision-making situations in the real world. Their relative weights may vary from situation to situation but it seems unlikely that any one operates to the complete exclusion of the others.

The quality of decision-making process: 'groupthink' and how to avoid it

So far I have said little about the *quality* of group decisions. This is because if we think simply in terms of outcomes we usually do not have any straightforward criteria against which to measure quality. Who knows whether an appointment committee offered the job to the best candidate or whether the jury returned the 'true' verdict? However, if outcomes are difficult to assess, perhaps it is possible to evaluate the decision-making process which led to those outcomes. According to one influential theorist, it is (Janis, 1972). Janis (1972) has analysed a number of American foreign-policy decisions made between 1940 and 1970 and has come to the conclusion that where these turned out 'badly' for the decision-makers (i.e. where American interests were damaged), the decision process was marked by five features. First, the group making the decision was very cohesive. Secondly, it was also typically insulated from information outside the group. Thirdly, the decision-makers rarely searched systematically through alternative policy options to appraise their relative merits. Fourthly, the group was often under some stress caused by the need to reach a decision urgently. And last, but by no means least, the group was nearly always dominated by a very directive leader. These five conditions, Janis believes, generate strong conformity pressures in a group and it is these 'concurrence seeking tendencies' which lead to defective decision-making, or what Janis calls 'groupthink'.

What are the symptoms of 'groupthink'? Janis lists several, some of which will be familiar from our earlier discussions of social influence (chapter 4) and group performance (this chapter), and some of which we will explore more fully in later chapters. First, a very cohesive group is likely to exert pressures on dissenters to conform to the consensus view. Some of this pressure may be implicit, but often the leader or other members of the group will take it upon themselves to bring the deviates into line and reject them if they do not do so. Arising out of this pressure towards uniformity is the second 'groupthink' symptom: an illusion of unanimity and correctness. As seen in chapter 4, other people often provide very powerful sources of reality construction. If they all give the appearance of total agreement on some issue, then we may be led to the conclusion that this view is the only valid one. Such a state of mind is likely to inhibit any creative search for other opinions and even to lead to a positive rejection of those opinions and a ridiculing of their sources. Since some of these may emanate from outside the group, a third symptom of 'groupthink' is a negative stereotyping of outgroups. This is particularly likely to occur in political decision-making which is nearly always conducted in a conflictual intergroup context. As we shall see in chapter 7, a common consequence of intergroup conflict is derogation of the outgroup and a glorification of the ingroup.

The picture which Janis (1972) paints, therefore, is of a tightly knit group, isolated from outside influences, converging rapidly onto a normatively 'correct' point of view and thereafter being convinced both of its own rectitude and of the inferiority of all other competing opinions (or groups). He argues that such a set of symptoms is almost exactly the opposite of what should characterize good decision-making process (namely, the rational weighing of possible options in the light of all the available evidence) and hence where they occur one should expect the outcomes to be less than ideal (Janis and Mann, 1977).

Janis believes that the link between process and outcome may not be a perfect one since other factors may intervene to rescue a 'faulty' decision or abort a 'good' one. Nevertheless, other things being equal, poor decisions are likely to lead to poor results and he presents convincing evidence from such American misadventures as the attempted invasion of Cuba at the Bay of Pigs in 1961, the bombing of North Vietnam in 1965 and the lack of defence of Pearl Harbour in 1941 which indicates that in each of these events 'groupthink' probably occurred amongst key decision-makers. Nor is it just American governments who are liable to 'groupthink'. Consider the following descriptions of decision-making in the British Cabinet during Mrs Thatcher's period as Prime Minister:

> It is January 1984. The place is No. 10. The forum is the Cabinet's Overseas and Defence Committee. The subject is the possibility of an attempt to normalize relations with Argentina . . . Sir Geoffrey Howe is four minutes into the Foreign Office paper on the need to open exploratory talks with the Alfonsin Government. Mrs Thatcher cuts in, 'Geoffrey, I know what you're going to recommend. And the answer is "No!".'
> End of item: nobody argues with the boss. (Anonymous source quoted in Hennessy, 1986, p. 99)

> I don't think it was ever as good as a debating forum again. There was more and more control by the Prime Minister. To that extent there was

greater cohesion in the Cabinet, because there were a lot of new faces who owed their promotion much more to her than to their record in the party. (James Prior, former Cabinet Minister, quoted in Hennessy, 1986, p. 95)

If true, these accounts bear more than a passing correspondence to Janis's list of antecedent conditions of 'groupthink'.

If 'groupthink' is a potential hazard in collective decision-making, how can it be avoided? Janis notes that the answer is *not* simply to have all important decisions made by a single individual. Leaving aside the ethical and political difficulties in delegating such powers to one person, there are several practical disadvantages to such a solution. First, as seen chapter 3, any problem of even moderate complexity is likely to prove more than one person's cognitive capacity can readily handle; some division of labour is essential in most important decisions. Allied to this are the advantages which accrue from the pooling of ideas and experience which, as we saw earlier in this chapter, lend the group an unassailable advantage. The pooling of individual ideas may also lead to a cancelling out of idiosyncratic biases and prejudices which, if left unchecked in any individual decision-maker, must surely be detrimental. Finally, there are potential motivational gains from the cohesion and identification provided by a group which may not be available to a lone individual. The question is not, therefore, how can we dispense with group decision-making, but how can we capitalize on its advantages while circumventing its defects?

Janis suggests a number of antidotes to 'groupthink', all of which are aimed at combating the undesirable effects of concurrence seeking. Perhaps the most important of these concerns the role of the leader. According to Janis, the likelihood of 'groupthink' will be reduced if leaders adopt a more neutral role and avoid stating their preferences too explicitly. This helps to avoid the problems which stem from ingratiaton to the leader. In addition, it is helpful if the leader encourages the expression of minority and deviant viewpoints in discussion so that a wider range of options is considered. It may even be desirable to institutionalize such dissent and criticism by the appointment of independent experts or 'devil's advocates', whose role is to provide a critical appraisal of the group's currently preferred decision. However, Janis reminds us that it is important that such people are not relegated to token status and used by the group to legitimate their decision by providing an official record of dissent.

When these remedies are adopted, policy-makers may be able to act more effectively. One of the best examples of this, in Janis's view, is the Cuban missile crisis of 1962 where President Kennedy and his advisors engaged in some brinkmanship diplomacy with the Soviet Union over the siting of missiles in Cuba. This was a particularly interesting case since it involved the same group of officials which had perpetrated the Bay of Pigs fiasco a year earlier. But from published accounts of the second crisis it seems that Kennedy took active steps to avoid the blinkered vision which had led to the earlier disaster. He encouraged his Executive Committee to debate policy options freely, even absenting himself from some meetings to encourage greater dissent. His brother Robert Kennedy, the Attorney General at the time, was unofficially assigned the 'devil's advocate' role and apparently spent most of his time ruthlessly criticizing other people's ideas. Although decisions taken during the thirteen-day crisis came perilously close to initiating a major military conflict between the USA and the USSR (hardly a 'successful outcome'), the *way* the decisions were reached was markedly superior to the other incidents documented by Janis.

For his evidence, Janis relies almost exclusively on historical material, usually eye-witness accounts by participants. Such evidence inevitably has its limitations. Participants in events can only ever give partial – and sometimes deliberately censored – descriptions of them, and the over-reliance on historical case studies may, in any case, lead to a kind of 'hindsight wisdom', as Fischhoff and Beyth-Marom (1976) have noted. Still, there is some evidence from field and experimental studies which support at least part of Janis's theory.

Recall, first of all, the experiment by Maier and Solem (1952), described above, in which groups attempted to solve the horse-trading problem. Despite the fact that nearly every group contained a successful 'solver', that person was not always able to convince the others of the correct solution. For our present purposes, however, the key finding of that study was that the presence of a leader who encouraged maximum participation by all group members led to improved problem-solving, as compared to a 'laissez-faire' observer. The importance of leadership style in reducing 'groupthink' was confirmed by Flowers (1977). She created groups of high and low cohesiveness with leaders who had been trained to use either a non-directive participative style or a directive and task-orientated approach. The groups were asked to role play a committee of school administrators facing a delicate but urgent personnel problem. An analysis of committee deliberations showed that, contrary to Janis's hypothesis, the level of cohesiveness had no effect on either the number of different solutions proposed or the number of facts considered in reaching a decision. The leadership style, on the other hand, *was* influential. More solutions were produced and more information was considered with the open, non-directive leaders than with the more directive kind.

The importance of the leader and the relative *un*importance of cohesiveness was confirmed in a field study by Vinokur et al. (1985). They studied the process and outcome of National Institute of Health conferences in which a panel of experts and consumers meet to evaluate new medical technologies. From the participants of six such conferences, Vinokur et al. (1985) obtained various measures of the decision-making process, ratings of the chairperson, assessments of the amount and quality of information exchanged and, lastly, the outcome measure: an evaluation of the quality of the final policy statements. Consistent with Janis's theory, Vinokur et al. found that one of the variables most highly correlated with the quality of outcome was that dealing with the facilitative role played by the chairperson in encouraging full participation amongst the experts. Other important predictors of the quality of decision were the process during the conference and the content of the information discussed. However, contrary to Janis's theory, cohesiveness was a much less predictive variable and, if anything, was also *positively* correlated with the quality of decision (where Janis predicts the reverse).

These studies provide evidence for some of the main elements of Janis's theory, particularly those which refer to the tendency for groups not to process all the available information in the most sensible or systematic fashion. However, the absence, of any consistently deleterious effects for cohesiveness suggests that Janis's emphasis on this variable as a cause of 'groupthink' may be misplaced. Apparently, tightly knit groups are just as able to make effective decisions as fragmented ones, so long as their decision-making procedures still permit a proper appraisal of all the relevant ideas. If cohesiveness plays a role perhaps it is, as Steiner (1982) has suggested, more in the *desire* for it than in its actual presence. Perhaps it is only when groups are desperately seeking to manufacture unity that they become prey to the concurrence seeking defects which Janis has identified; having once achieved it, the pressure for the illusion of unanimity may be less intense.

Summary

1 The question of the relative superiority of individual or group performance depends entirely on the mode of comparison. In the simplest contrast – between groups and the average individual – groups invariably

outperform individuals. However, if the comparison is made with statisticized groups – formed by pooling individuals' performances statistically –
then real interacting groups usually, but not invariably, perform less well
on a range of physical and intellectual tasks.

2 Two influential theories which have tried to explain this apparent deficit
are Steiner's theory of group productivity and Latane's social impact
theory. In Steiner's theory, actual productivity is thought never to exceed
potential productivity because groups usually fail to utilize their resources
in the optimum way for a given task. Tasks can be classified according to
whether they are divisible or unitary; maximizing or optimizing; disjunctive, conjunctive or discretionary. The particular type of task determines
the nature of the resources required and their best method of combination.
In Latane's theory, the deficits are attributed to a lack of motivation which
is thought to occur in groups. This happens, it is supposed, because the
impact of the experimental instructions is 'diluted' amongst the group
members.

3 Social decision schemes theory is a mathematical modelling approach
which attempts to simulate various possible methods of combining
individual contributions to the group product. The hypothetical combination rule which generates predictions closest to observed patterns of group
performance is assumed to be the one which is operative. For a number of
intellectual tasks it appears that a truth supported wins model is the best
'fit' with the data. That is, a group will arrive at the right answer if at least
two people in it are able to do so.

4 Although much of the available group performance data supports the
group deficit theories, occasionally group interaction can lead to process
gains. There are several studies in which the collective performance is
actually higher than one would have predicted from a knowledge of
individual attributes. These findings are problematic for Steiner's and
Latane's theories.

5 When groups make judgements on tasks in which there is no one correct
answer they nearly always exhibit polarization; the collective decision is
more extreme than the average of individual opinions in the same direction. This has been found in a great many laboratory experiments although
less consistently in naturalistic studies.

6 There are four main current explanations of this group polarization
phenomenon: social decision schemes theory, social comparison theory,
persuasive arguments theory and social identity theory. In the first, the
best fitting model is a majority decision rule, and this has been found to
apply to mock juries, even when instructed to reach a *unanimous* decision.
Social comparison theory proposes that polarization is caused by group

members competing with one another to endorse the socially most desirable viewpoints. Persuasive arguments theory, on the other hand, emphasizes the role of information exchange. Polarization occurs, according to this view, because new arguments and evidence come to light during the discussion. The social identity approach proposes that polarization is due to group members' conforming to ingroup norms in contrast to outgroup norms. Each perspective finds much supportive evidence and it is probable that more than one of the processes underlies polarization.

7 Groups can sometimes make bad decisions by not considering all the relevant information and not appraising the full range of options available. Janis calls this 'groupthink' and believes that it is caused by an overcohesive group being led by an overdirective leader. Several historical examples support his analysis, although more controlled research points particularly to the role of the leader. In these studies, cohesiveness generally seems to have little effect on decision-making.

Further reading

Performance

Davis, J.H. (1969) *Group Performance*, ch. 3. New York: Addison Wesley.
Shaw, Marvin (1976) *Group Dynamics*, 2nd edn, chs 3, 9. New York: McGraw Hill.
Steiner, I.D. (1972) *Group Process and Productivity*, chs 1-3. New York: Academic Press.

Decision-making

Brandstätter, H., Davis, J.H. and Stocher-Kreichganer, G. (eds) (1982) *Contemporary Problems in Group Decision Making*. New York: Academic Press.
Brown, Roger (1986) *Social Psychology*, 2nd edn, chs 6, 8. New York: The Free Press.
Janis, I.L. and Mann, L. (1977) *Decision-Making*. New York: The Free Press.

CHAPTER 6

Prejudice and Discontent

Thus far I have been concerned mainly with processes *within* the group: the way people behave towards and influence other members of the ingroup. In this and the next two chapters the focus shifts to the *inter*group domain: to the factors which govern people's behaviour and attitudes towards members of outgroups. However, this change of emphasis is not complete. Just as we saw that in various aspects of intragroup dynamics intergroup relations could not be ignored, so too we will discover that intergroup phenomena cannot easily be separated from what goes on inside the group.

This chapter is about prejudice, that is, the expression of derogatory attitudes or discriminatory behaviour towards most or all of the members of an outgroup (or number of outgroups). Other names for prejudice are racism (the belief that members of another ethnic or national group are inherently inferior), sexism (an ideology asserting the superiority of one gender), ageism (discrimination by chronological age) and so on. In seeking to understand the origins of prejudice, this chapter will concentrate on various explanations which locate its cause in the psychological make-up and functioning of the individual, beginning with a well-known psychoanalytic theory which proposes that prejudice is a symptom of a particular personality type which in turn is thought to be the product of a certain familial history. A particular upbringing, so this theory claims, produces someone who is predisposed to be receptive to right-wing and fascist propaganda alleging the moral and intellectual pre-eminence of the ingroup. This idea is extended in the second of the theories considered. According to this view, prejudice is not confined to right-wing personalities but is characteristic of dogmatic thinkers of right *and* left. In this same theory another idea is put forward: that prejudice is not really directed towards members of outgroups as such, but towards those whose beliefs are seen to be different from our own. In these theories the origin of prejudice is seen as residing in the personality dynamics of the individual, a view which runs into a number of difficulties which are outlined. Further criticisms of this individualistic approach are offered in the following two chapters where other, more social, perspectives are developed.

In the third approach examined prejudice is linked to the more general phenomenon of social discontent. In this explanation discontent is traced to frustrating events, either in the individual's past or as currently experienced. This frustration, the theory proposes, leads inexorably to various forms of aggression which are directed either towards the actual source of the frustration or, more commonly, onto some scapegoat target such as a minority group. In the final perspective under discussion this frustration–aggression hypothesis is modified. Instead of viewing frustration as an absolute deprivation of basic needs (e.g. food, money), it conceives of it as a state of *relative* deprivation. In other words, it believes people are discontented not because they are hungry or poor, but because they are hung*rier* or poo*rer* than they believe they should be.

The prejudiced person

Look here, in South Africa you get some good types of natives, but others steal, never wash, are always asking for something. I think it has to do with their upbringing. Some of them have good discipline. The other day my car broke down. All the whites drove past, but this native crossed the road and gave me a push.

I don't know any blacks of my age, and have never spoken to any. I don't think it is a good idea that black and white should know each other. I would just hate to live with them. I don't know anything about them. I don't know if our maid has any children. I never speak to her. I have never been into a Bantu location and don't want to.

(Two white South African teenagers quoted in the *Sunday Times*, 5 December 1976)

In South Africa the apartheid system provides a supportive milieu for the expression of prejudice, but it is doubtful whether, outside South Africa, most people would reveal their bigotry quite so blatantly and offensively as this. Nevertheless, however well disguised, there is ample evidence that prejudice is alive and well in many countries throughout the world (see, for example, Berry et al., 1977; Bagley and Verma, 1979; Pettigrew, in press). And, whether hidden beneath the veneer of liberal tolerance or displayed with the arrogance of the oppressor, the central question to be answered is the same: where do such prejudiced attitudes come from?

One view which has enjoyed considerable currency both within and outside psychology is that prejudice is primarily a personality problem. The theory which did most of popularize this idea within social psychology was that proposed by Adorno et al. (1950). Their starting hypothesis was that an individual's political and social attitudes form a coherent pattern and that this pattern is 'an expression of deep lying trends in personality' (Adorno et al., 1950, p. 1). Working from a Freudian perspective, they believed that most people's personality development involves the repression and redirection of various instinctive needs by the constraints of social existence. The parents, of course, were considered to be the main agents of this socialization process and in 'normal' development they usually struck a healthy balance between discipline and allowing the child self-expression. The problem with the bigot, argued Adorno et al., was that this balance was upset by the parents adopting an excessively harsh disciplinary regime and by being over-anxious about the child's conformity to social mores. The effect of this, they believed, was that the child's natural aggression towards the parents (an inevitable consequence of being subjected to constraints) was displaced onto alternative targets because of the fear of the consequences of displaying it directly. The likely choice of targets would be those seen as weaker or inferior to oneself, for example, members of deviant groups or ethnic minorities. The end result, therefore, was someone over-deferential towards authority figures (since these symbolize the parents) and overtly hostile towards non-ingroup members, the so-called 'authoritarian personality'.

In the post-war era this theory stimulated a massive research effort into the nature and origins of racial prejudice. Adorno et al. themselves developed a personality inventory – the F-scale – which was designed to distinguish between those with potentially fascist/racist tendencies and those with more 'democratic' leanings. By a combination of psychometric, projective and clinical methods, they were able to show that high scoring adults on this F-scale did seem to have had rather different childhoods and to have more dogmatic and conservative attitudes than low scorers. The latter also seemed to have a tendency to see the world in rather more complex terms and be more tolerant of ambiguity than the former.

In the 1950s authoritarianism became widely used as an explanatory concept. Countless experiments and surveys were conducted in which the F-scale was correlated with just about every variable imaginable (see Christie and Jahoda, 1954; Titus and Hollander, 1957). Even today, more than thirty years after the book's publication, the concept of the 'authoritarian personality' is still attracting interest. Bray and Noble (1978) employed it in a simulated jury study. High-scoring subjects on the F-scale (authoritarians) tended to propose harsher verdicts, and polarized still further in that direction when reaching a collective decision as a 'jury'. Tetlock (1981, 1983), in a series of archival studies of politicians' rhetoric, has repeatedly found that extreme conservatives tend to argue in a less complex fashion than their more liberal counterparts, thus supporting Adorno et al.'s notion of the authoritarian seeing the world in simple black and white terms. However, less comfortably for the original theory, he has also found that the cognitive style of politicians' arguments also varies with whether they are in opposition or government. In opposition, they tend to make speeches which are less qualified and circumspect than when in power (Tetlock et al., 1984). Still more problematic for the idea that an authoritarian style of thinking is confined to the right of the political spectrum, he has also found that left-wing politicians show less integrative complexity in their speeches than those of the political centre (Tetlock, 1984). This finding is of relevance to the theory considered in the next section.

Ironically, the early popularity of Adorno et al.'s (1950) theory and measuring instruments almost proved to be their undoing. With such extensive usage, the F-scale inevitably came under close scrutiny and it soon became apparent that as a psychometric device it was flawed in several respects. Roger Brown (1965) has provided a masterly summary of its shortcomings and I will do no more here than note two of his most damning criticisms. One of the most obvious problems with the F-scale was that all the items were so worded that agreement with them indicated an authoritarian attitude. In other words, authoritarianism (as measured) was confounded with acquiescence. A second problem was that the technique for validating the instrument (conducting in-depth interviews with high and low scorers) was contaminated by the fact that the interviewers knew *in advance* the score of each respondent. This opened up the worrying possibility that they could have influenced (whether unconsciously or otherwise) those respondents to produce the theoretically 'correct' replies (see Rosenthal, 1966).

However, perhaps more important than these methodological problems are the more general limitations to any 'individual differences' perspective of this kind (see also Billig, 1976, for a more extended critique). First, by locating prejudice in the dynamics of the individual personality, they tend to neglect situational and socio-cultural factors which are often much more powerful determinants. Pettigrew (1958) demonstrated this clearly in his cross-cultural study of prejudice in South Africa and the United States. Not surprisingly, he found that white South Africans – like the two quoted at the beginning of this section – showed very high levels of anti-black prejudice, as did respondents from the Southern United States. However, he also found that they did not appear to have particularly high levels of authoritarianism as measured by the F-scale. In other words, in terms of personality type they were rather similar to 'normal' populations, despite their overtly racist attitudes. With these and other findings, Pettigrew argued convincingly that the origin of this racism lay much more in the prevailing societal norms in which his respondents lived than in any personality dysfunction. A similar conclusion is reached by Minard (1952) in his study of a Virginian mining community in the USA. He observed that the rigid segregation and prejudice which existed in the mining town disappeared almost completely once the miners were at work underground. This strongly suggests that situational norms were a much more critical influence than any enduring personality dispositions. Further evidence to this effect was provided by Stephan and Rosenfield (1978) in their study of changes in racial attitudes following school desegregation. Of a number of predictors of positive change, the most powerful was the increase in inter-ethnic contact. Much less significant was the authoritarian nature of the children's parental background, although this did have some slight effect. Once again, a situational factor (amount of contact) seems to override a personality variable.

A second problem, closely related to the first, is the inability of the personality approach to explain the widespread uniformity of prejudice in certain societies or subgroups within societies. If prejudice is to be explained via individual *differences* amongst people, how can it then be manifested in a whole population or at least in a vast majority? In pre-war Nazi Germany, and in many other places since, consistently racist attitudes and behaviour were shown by hundreds of thousands of people who must have differed on most other psychological characteristics. As a contemporary illustration of the pervasiveness of prejudice, albeit in a milder form, we can turn to a recent developmental study in England by Davey (1983). In one of the tasks he devised, the children were asked to share out some sweets between members of different ethnic groups who were identified in photographs. Of the 500 or so children who took part in the study, fully 50 per cent of them were ethnocentric in their distribution of the sweets.

That is to say, the majority gave more to the ingroup person than to other group members. This prejudice was particularly evident amongst the white children, of whom nearly 60 per cent showed such discrimination. In a follow-up task designed to elicit trait stereotypes of different ethnic groups, positive traits assigned to the ingroup always outnumbered those associated with outgroups, whilst for negative traits this pattern was reversed. Again, these invidious intergroup distinctions were particularly evident amongst the white (majority group) children.

A third problem concerns the historical specificity of prejudice. At the same time that uniformities of attitude are difficult to explain with the personality approach, it is equally hard for it to account for the sudden rises and falls of prejudice. Again, the example of Germany springs to mind. The growth of antisemitism under Hitler took place over the space of a decade or so, much too short a time for a whole generation of German families to have adopted new forms of child-rearing practices giving rise to authoritarian and prejudiced children. An even more dramatic example is provided by attitudes of Americans towards the Japanese which underwent a rapid change after the bombing of Pearl Harbour. And, just to complete the picture, after the war the USA and Japan became close economic and political allies with considerable cultural and tourist traffic between them. Examples such as these strongly suggest that the attitudes held by members of different groups towards each other have more to do with the objective relations between the groups – relations of political conflict or alliance, economic interdependence and so on – than with the familial relations in which they grew up (see chapter 7).

Adorno and his colleagues set out to discover why large numbers of people were so susceptible to racist propaganda, asking the question: 'Why are they so easily fooled?' (Adorno et al., 1950, p. 10). They believed that the answer lay in the personality structure and dynamics of the individual: children exposed to a particular upbringing would grow up to be narrow-minded, deferential towards authority and, above all, hostile towards deviant and minority groups. But, as we have seen, such a personalistic approach runs into difficulties in accounting for both the pervasiveness of prejudice in some times and places, and its virtual absence in others. If personality factors do play a role, as it seems likely that they do, then it is much more plausible to suggest that they are important for the minorities at the two extremes of the distribution of prejudice, the perpetually tolerant and the unremitting bigots. For the remaining large majority it seems that their enduring personality dispositions, diverse though they must be, are much less potent causes of prejudice than the many and varied *situational* influences on their behaviour. Or, if I may rephrase a famous saying from that early opponent of racial oppression, Abraham Lincoln: a few of the people never get fooled; a few of the people get fooled all of the time; but – and probably for quite different reasons – most of the people get fooled some of the time.

Prejudiced beliefs or 'belief prejudice'?

At about the same time that *The Authoritarian Personality* was published, another personality theory of prejudice was being developed by Rokeach (1948, 1960). Like Adorno et al., Rokeach believed that prejudice was marked by an oversimplified and rigid style of thinking. However, Rokeach claimed that this mental rigidity was prevalent not just in those with very conservative views but characterized the extreme left also. The authoritarianism measured by the F-scale, Rokeach believed, was merely a special case of a more generalized syndrome of intolerance, what he called the 'closed mind' or dogmatic personality. The critical features of the 'closed mind' were, according to Rokeach, an isolation of different belief systems from one another so that mutually contradictory opinions could be tolerated, a resistance to change in those beliefs in the light of new information and the use of appeals to authority to justify the correctness of the beliefs. Rokeach devised two personality inventories – the dogmatism and opinionation scales – to measure this syndrome and, as he expected, people's scores on these correlated well with authoritarianism and also seemed to stand up well to the usual tests for reliability and validity (Rokeach, 1960).

   Like the authoritarian personality approach, Rokeach's personality theory has attracted a good deal of controversy. Much of this debate is quite technical and need not detain us here, especially since the general criticisms made of the personality approach to prejudice apply as well here as they did to the authoritarian personality (for detailed evaluations see Brown, 1965; Billig, 1976; Billig and Cochrane, 1979). What is more worth while to discuss is Rokeach's other theory of prejudice which, to some extent, cuts across his earlier personality account (Rokeach, 1960). In this theory Rokeach proposes that the critical determinant of one person's attitude towards another is the degree of similarity or 'congruence' of their two belief systems. Like Festinger (1954), Rokeach believes that similarity of opinion will lead to mutual attraction because of the validation that such agreement provides (see chapter 4). Conversely, dissimilarity results in rejection and dislike because of the threat to the individuals' belief systems. Rokeach then makes the radical suggestion that ethnic, religious and national prejudices have little to do with people's memberships of those various social groups, their associated norms and intergroup relationships. Instead, he argues that such prejudices are a result of 'belief congruence', a perception that those other people possess belief systems which are incompatible with our own. In his view, blacks (or any other minority group) are discriminated against not because they belong to a particular social category, but because they are assumed to have different beliefs from the discriminators. In short, 'belief is more important than ethnic or racial membership as a determinant of social discrimination' (Rokeach, 1960, p. 135).

To test this hypothesis, Rokeach et al. (1960) devised an experimental paradigm (much used since) in which ethnic group membership and belief congruence are systematically varied. Typically, subjects are asked for their attitudes towards a number of (usually hypothetical) stimulus persons who belong to either the same or a different group from themselves, and who are seen to possess similar or dissimilar beliefs. These stimuli are represented as verbal descriptions, in photographic form or, occasionally, by real people. In a large number of studies it has been found that using this technique belief seems to be a more important determinant of attitude than race, although the latter does have an effect. For example, white subjects usually say that they find a black person with similar beliefs more attractive than a white person with dissimilar beliefs (e.g. Rokeach et al., 1960; Byrne and Wong, 1962; Rokeach and Mezei, 1966; Hendrick et al., 1971). The exceptions to this general finding seem to be for measures relating to rather more intimate behaviours (e.g. potential close friendship or marriage), where several investigations have found that race seems to outweigh belief as a casual factor (Stein et al., 1965; Triandis and Davis, 1965; Insko et al., 1983). These troublesome findings apart, Rokeach's theory is apparently well supported empirically.

Has, then, Rokeach succeeded in solving the problem of prejudice? Is it really, as he suggests, just a matter of those two South Africans whom we quoted at the start of the chapter thinking that blacks believe different things from themselves? If so, the strategy for reducing their prejudice would seem to be clear: re-educate them so that they understand that these perceptions are often *mis*perceptions; once they realize that the targets of their prejudice believe in roughly the same things as they do, then the bigotry should soon disappear. Unfortunately, matters are not so simple. We shall deal with the complexities involved in programmes to reduce prejudice in chapter 7; for now, though, let us probe Rokeach's theory and methodology a little more deeply.

First, we should note that Rokeach hedges his theory with one important qualification. He wishes to exempt from the belief congruence explanation those instances where prejudice has become institutionalized (e.g. by law, as in South Africa), or where there exists significant social support for its expression (e.g. in the Southern States of the USA). In these cases, he concedes, people's respective ethnic group memberships will supersede belief congruence as a determinant of prejudice (Rokeach, 1960, p. 164). But, in the language of insurance policies, is this not rather too large an 'exclusion clause'? For many social commentators, prejudice is the problem it is precisely because it *is* institutionalized and socially sanctioned in so many societies. If one rules out of court so much of the phenomenon in question, how useful is the theory as a tool for its understanding and prevention?

A second, and perhaps even more critical, problem concerns the relevance of the findings from the race–belief experimental paradigm for intergroup prejudice (see Brown and Turner, 1981). Recall the procedure which is typically used in these studies. People are presented with someone who happens to be of the same colour (or religion) as them and who also happens to profess to hold similar or different beliefs. There is little information about how others in their group (or the outgroup) might react to the stimulus, nor about how representative the latter is of his/her group. Indeed, the 'repeated measures' design which is frequently used in these studies, i.e. where subjects rate several members of the ingroup and outgroup, leads to the clear inference that there is little homogeneity within the groups (since the members of them appear to disagree amongst themselves). In other words, the social situation which Rokeach and others have employed is one in which there is ambiguity about the degree of uniformity of response within the ingroup and clear evidence of a *lack* of intragroup homogeneity in the distribution of various attributes (e.g. opinions). Now, in chapter 1, I outlined three criteria which are necessary for a social encounter to be regarded as an intergroup situation. The first was the presence of at least two social categories; the second was the existence of some intragroup uniformity of behaviour; and the third was an individual's perception of homogeneity within the ingroup and the outgroup. I think it is fairly clear that in the race–belief paradigm only one of these three criteria is properly satisfied. My conclusion is, therefore, that it is more appropriate to consider this particular experimental context as one in which *interpersonal* considerations are uppermost. If so, then as we note elsewhere, 'The importance of belief in these experiments suggest to us not that Rokeach has an adequate theory of ethnic prejudice, but simply that it is an effective determinant of *interpersonal* attraction' (Brown and Turner, 1981, p. 53). If this conclusion is valid, then one might expect that where ingroup uniformity is heightened, i.e. where the appropriate norms are more clearly understood, or as the perceived homogeneity of the groups is enhanced, then the situation becomes more of an intergroup one and the importance of group membership (as opposed to belief congruence) should be increased. The first of these conditions would account for those few anomalous findings in the race–belief literature which found race to be a more powerful influence than belief (e.g. Triandis and Davis, 1965). Where these occurred, as I have already noted, it was usually for behaviours which are much more likely to be subject to ingroup normative constraints, for example, dating, marriage and so on.

For the second set of conditions we must turn to those few studies which have deliberately sought to emphasize the group-like nature of the situation. The first of these was by Billig and Tajfel (1973). Employing the 'minimal group situation' (described more fully in chapter 8), they examined how children's reward allocations to anonymous recipients were affected by different methods of group formation. In one condition the children were informed merely that some recipients were more similar to them than others because they had preferred the same kind of paintings in a pretest. No mention was made of groups. This was the 'similarity' condition. In a second condition no mention was made of any belief similarity, but the children were told that everyone had been randomly allocated to two meaningless groups (X and Y) by the toss of a coin. This was the 'categorization' condition. In a third variant, these two conditions were combined by making the group allocations appear to be based on their pretest picture preferences; those liking the same paintings were informed that they had been assigned to the same group. Finally, there was a control condition in which neither similarity nor group memberships were referred to. If Rokeach is correct, one would expect discrimination in the first and third conditions, since there is some basis for inferring belief similarity. On the other hand, if group membership is the key factor, then the *second* and third conditions should reveal most discrimination. The results clearly supported this second interpretation as can be seen in table 6.1. In the two conditions where a social categorization was present, clear-cut ingroup favouritism was

Table 6.1 Categorization and similarity as determinants of intergroup discrimination and reward allocations

	No categorization	Categorization
No similarity	– 0.2	+ 2.0*
Similarity	+ 1.0	+ 3.9*

Discrimination scores could range from – 12 to + 12, with positive scores indicating favour-itism towards the ingroup.

* Statistically significant score.

Source: Billig and Tajfel (1973) figure 1

shown in the reward allocations. The effect of the similarity variable, though statistically significant overall, was dwarfed by the size of the categorization effect.

This experiment was followed by another, this time by Allen and Wilder (1975), again using minimal groups. They independently var-ied the similarity of the ingroup and the outgroup to the subject, apparently on the basis of some artistic and political beliefs, and then examined people's reward allocations. Directly contrary to what Rokeach would have predicted, varying the apparent belief similarity of the outgroup had absolutely no effect on the level of intergroup discrimination; subjects were as strongly biased against the 'dissimilar' outgroup as they were against the 'similar' outgroup. On the other hand, increasing the similarity of the ingroup *did* have some effect; those in an ingroup seen to be similar to themselves were more biased against the outgroup than those in 'dissimilar' ingroups.

These consistent findings are slightly undermined by two further experiments which also heightened 'groupness' cues but which, at the same time, provided evidence more consistent with Rokeach's theory. Taylor and Guimond (1978) exploited the conflictual situation in Quebec between French- and English-speaking Canadians. In both studies Taylor and Guimond modified the traditional race–belief paradigm so as to vary the salience of the intergroup situation. In one variant, subjects responded alone; in another, they responded individ-ually but amongst a group of fellow French or English Canadians and across the room from their English or French counterparts; to heighten the sociolinguistic division still further, in a third condition they first discussed their responses with ingroup members. Despite these variations, only the conventional belief congruence effect was found with any consistency; no matter how salient the ingroup/outgroup division was made, stimulus persons of either group per-ceived to have similar beliefs were rated more positively than those with dissimilar beliefs. These results can be reconciled to the previous two studies only if we assume that, in spite of their efforts, Taylor and Guimond's situation still retained some interpersonal characteristics. For instance, similarity was manipulated relative to each individual (and not to the group), and the usual 'repeated measures' format (five stimulus persons were rated) may have worked against Taylor and Guimond's efforts to create group homogeneity.

Even with the inconsistency introduced by Taylor and Guimond's (1978) findings, there are arguably enough theoretical and empirical grounds for questioning the adequacy of Rokeach's theory as a *comprehensive* account of prejudice. Like the personality explanation considered earlier, it seems plausible to suppose that in *some* contexts – particularly those where in which intergroup situation is overlaid with various interpersonal relationships – people's evaluative and affiliative attitudes *are* affected by their perceptions of others' similarity. But as situations shift towards the group pole of the interpersonal-group continuum, considerations of interpersonal belief congruence give way to the stark fact of differential group membership.

Frustration, prejudice and discontent

We saw earlier that one of the difficulties of the 'authoritarian personality' explanation of prejudice was its inability to account for the historical fluctuations in prejudice. A few years before its appearance another theory had been published which offered the promise of explaining exactly this variation. Along with the 'authoritarian personality', this theory quickly established itself as one of the major landmarks in the study of prejudice. It was the frustration-aggression theory and was proposed by Dollard et al. (1939).

One of its attractions is its simplicity. In one hypothesis, stated on the very first page of their book, Dollard et al. attempt to provide a single explanation for aggression in individuals, aggression within groups and aggression between groups in the wider society. That hypothesis was as follows: 'the occurrence of aggressive behaviour always presupposes the existence of frustration and, contrariwise . . . the existence of frustration always leads to some form of aggression' (Dollard et al., 1939, p. 1). In a unique integration of psychoanalytic and learning theories, Dollard et al. supposed that frustration – by which they meant some interference with a goal response, usually one associated with the satisfaction of some basic need (e.g. hunger, thirst) – gave rise to the build up of some 'psychic energy' in people.

This they termed an instigation to aggress. This energy had then to be expended in removing the source of the interference. If it could not be immediately expended, the aggressive energy was not simply dissipated but remained within the system, ready to burst out at the slightest opportunity.

Dollard et al. (1939) then incorporated two further psychoanalytic concepts into their theory. The first was the notion of 'catharsis'. If the instigation to aggress, once created by frustration, would not decline spontaneously then perhaps it could be reduced by providing outlets for the expression of aggression. If it could be channelled, for example, into sporting activities then there would be less energy within the system for more harmful displays of anger. The second and closely related concept was that of 'displacement'. Sometimes, Dollard et al. observed, the aggression resulting from frustration is not directed at the real source of the frustration. On those occasions when I remonstrate with one of my children over some misdemeanour, they will often not express their annoyance at me directly but by slamming a door behind them or kicking a football violently into a neighbour's garden. Such redirected or displaced aggression, as Dollard et al. call it, occurs, either because the person suffering the frustration may have learned some inhibitions against attacking a more powerful target (parents are usually bigger and stronger than children after all!), or because the true source of the frustration is not immediately obvious. To the poor or dispossessed, the real perpetrators of their condition may not always be visible or accessible. Whatever the reason for its diversion, the aggression must still find an outlet and so it is displaced onto substitute targets, usually those for whom there are fewer associated inhibitions because they are seen as weaker or less able to retaliate.

From these few ideas, Dollard et al. developed their theory of prejudice, a theory which attempted to explain not only why prejudice seems to be so pervasive in many countries, but also why it rises to particularly virulent heights at certain times in history. The *generality* of ethnocentrism comes about, they believed, because of the frustrations endemic in social existence. Whether it is a child having to adapt to the inevitable constraints of family life, or adults confined by the informal and formal conventions of society, one way or another human beings are seldom free to gratify their every desire. In a word, they are frustrated. Because frustration is thought inevitably to lead to aggression, there will therefore always be a baseline level of aggressive behaviour. Most often that aggression is displaced onto convenient scapegoats in the form of prejudice against deviants and minority groups because of the severe sanctions that are nearly always imposed for its direct expression (e.g. towards the parents or against the state).

From this baseline level, Dollard et al. hypothesized that prejudice may rise because of particular social and economic circumstances. Thus, if a society experiences a severe economic recession, people will become more frustrated due to the poverty and hardship that it brings. This frustration causes an upsurge in prejudice which is often patterned along national or ethnic lines. The classic illustration of this, which Dollard et al. cite, is the antisemitism which was so rife in Germany between the two world wars. That Hitler was able to find such a receptive audience for his racist ideas was due, they argue, to the previous decade of frustrations caused by the collapse of the German economy in the 1920s. One study which supported this hypothesis was an archival analysis by Hovland and Sears (1940). Concentrating on the Southern States in the USA, they correlated an economic index (the price of cotton) with an index of racial aggression (the number of lynchings of blacks) over a fifty-year period. As expected, the two indices were negatively related: as the economy declined and times got hard so the number of lynchings increased.[1]

Frustration–aggression theory stimulated an enormous amount of research in the three decades following its publication, and that research established beyond doubt that frustration was certainly an important cause of aggression, if not the only cause as we shall see. Unfortunately for our present purposes, the bulk of that work was directed towards examining aggressive behaviour between individuals and relatively little towards prejudice and intergroup aggression. The most relevant studies are those which have examined the concept of displacement. The earliest of these was by Miller and Bugelski (1948), conducted with a group of young men at a summer camp. On the evening when the men were eagerly anticipating a night out on the town the camp authorities suddenly announced that they would be required to stay on at the camp to take some uninteresting and difficult tests. This constituted the frustrating experience since the men's 'goal response' (going out for the night) had been blocked. Before and after this experience they were also asked for their attitudes towards two minority groups. Analysis of these intergroup attitudes revealed that after the frustration their stereotypes of the outgroups became less favourable; a control group experiencing no frustration showed little such change. This seemed like a classic demonstration of displacement. Although, understandably, the men were angry at the real agents of their frustration (the camp authorities), this anger also appeared to have 'spilled over' onto the minority groups who could have had no conceivable responsibility for the men's plight.

However, this scapegoat version of prejudice based on displace-ment has not always been easy to verify. Stagner and Congdon (1955), for instance, found no evidence for increases in prejudice in students following the frustration of failing in some academic tests. On the other hand, Cowen et al. (1958), using a similar methodology, *did* find some increase in anti-black feeling after failing some puzzles, although on a more general measure of ethnocentrism against all minorities there was little change. Finally, just to add to the complex-ity, Burnstein and McRae (1962) found that doing badly in an experi-mental task had just the opposite effects on the evaluation of a black team member. Far from displacing their anger at performing poorly onto him, the white subjects actually saw the black confederate *more* favourably, and this was especially evident in highly prejudiced sub-jects who should have been the most eager to derogate him!

Moving away from the laboratory, Tanter (1966) has tried to test the displacement hypothesis at a societal level by examining the asso-ciation between internal strife in a country and its conflictual relations with other countries. From frustration–aggression theory one would predict that the two variables should be negatively correlated since one consequence of the displacement process is thought to be a shift of aggression away from the ingroup to targets *outside* the group. One might, on the other hand, argue that a temporal analysis would reveal a positive relationship since the pre-occurrence of intragroup conflict should eventually transfer to belligerance towards outgroups. Tanter (1966) found only partial support for these predictions. Examining data from eighty-three nations, he found that the correlation between intra- and intergroup conflict at the *same* time was virtually non-existent. However, there was a small positive correlation between external conflict and the degree of internal conflict three years earlier. However, the overall association was rather weak and subsequent research cast further doubt on it. In his analysis of American involvement in the Vietnam war, Tanter (1969) found that the simul-taneous correlation between internal and external conflict was actu-ally *positive*: as the war overseas escalated so the protests at home intensified.

One of the problems with the displacement explanation is that it is difficult to predict with any certainty which target will be chosen as the scapegoat. Miller (1948), one of the authors of the original theory, suggested that targets which are neither too similar nor too dissimilar to the real source of frustration would be selected. He derived this hypothesis from considering how the contradictory processes of 'generalization' (the association of a learned response to a new stimulus similar to the original conditioned stimulus) and 'inhibition' (the suppression of a response to a stimulus due to its association with punishment) would combine. Because the processes operate in opposite directions – one tending to elicit aggression in direct proportion to the similarity of the stimulus, the other tending to prevent it, also as a function of similarity – the situation producing the highest likelihood of aggression is when stimuli are of intermediate similarity (see Brewer and Campbell, 1976; Brown, 1984c). However, this analysis often proves rather difficult to apply outside the confines of the laboratory. For instance, Horowitz (1973) has identified a number of examples of civil unrest where the violence has been directed not against the original cause of the strife, but against some third party. One of these took place in Burma in 1938, a country which was at that time under British colonial rule. After the break-up of a demonstration by British police, there was extensive rioting. This uprising, however, was not directed against their colonial oppressors but against Muslim Indians; Hindu Indians were much less affected. Although this looks like a prime example of displaced aggression, as Horowitz (1973) points out, simply from the point of view of 'stimulus similarity', the Hindus should have been as good a displacement target as the Muslims. And yet, in the event, they escaped quite lightly. In discussing several other historical examples, Horowitz points out that although *after the event* it is usually possible to suggest that the conflicts were a result of displaced aggression, the specific choice of outgroup in each case is as well explained by historical and cultural factors as by any single psychological motivation like frustration.

In addition to these difficulties with the idea of displaced aggression, frustration–aggression theory ran into some other obstacles. Perhaps the most fundamental of these was the discovery that frustration was neither necessary nor sufficient to cause aggression; several studies reported that aggression had occurred with no prior frustration or, alternatively, where frustration had been experienced and no overt aggression had resulted (see Berkowitz, 1962; Bandura, 1973). These findings led Berkowitz (1962) to propose a major reformulation of the theory. The first important change he suggested was to stress the importance of situational cues to release the aggression which had been engendered by frustration. These cues were stimuli in the social environment which had been associated with aggression in the past. Applying this idea to the scapegoat theory of prejudice, Berkowitz reasoned that the likely choice for a scapegoat is an outgroup with prior associations of conflict or dislike for ingroup members. The second modification Berkowitz made was to redefine the concept of frustration. Dollard et al. (1939), true to their behaviouristic epistemology, tried to define frustration in objectively observable terms, 'an interference with a goal response'. But it soon became apparent that this was inadequate. The same frustrating event can lead to aggression or not, depending on how it is interpreted (Pastore, 1952). Accordingly, Berkowitz widened the meaning of frustration to include a subjective or cognitive element: frustration, he believed, is not just some state of objective deprivation, it is also the thwarting of people's expectations – whether they *think* they're deprived. But this was not all. Berkowitz had also found that a whole range of other things seemed to give rise to aggression – for example, pain, extreme heat or cold, and other noxious stimuli – even though, strictly speaking, they were not interferences with goal responses. This led him to propose that the general cause of aggression was not frustration itself, but 'aversive events'. For Berkowitz, frustration was just one of a number of unpleasant experiences which were likely to give rise to anger and aggression.

This revamped frustration–aggression theory proved to be almost as influential as its predecessor. Scores of experiments successfully demonstrated the importance of environmental cues and cognitive mediators in controlling the amount and direction of aggression (Berkowitz, 1974; Konecni, 1979). The theory was given additional support by studies which linked collective violence to adverse meteorological conditions. Baron and Ransberger (1978), followed by Carlsmith and Anderson (1979), showed that riots in American cities were much more likely to occur in very hot weather (i.e. more than 29 °C) than when the temperatures were more moderate (i.e. less than 20 °C). In Berkowitz's terms, the extreme heat (probably coupled with high humidity) was an aversive stimulus which increased city dwellers' arousal levels, and hence their propensity to violence.[2]

But whether this arousal factor is the only or even the major cause of prejudice and other forms of intergroup aggression is another matter (see Billig, 1976 for an extended critique). First, there is the problem of translating the separate individual states of frustration into collective acts of aggression. Frustration–aggression theory assumes that whenever there is an outbreak of prejudice or discontent then several hundred (or thousand) people are simultaneously in roughly the same emotional state of anger arousal and coincidentally select the same targets for the discharge of that anger. Elsewhere, I have used a cafeteria analogy to show the implausibility of this assumption (Brown and Turner, 1981). Imagine a student cafeteria at

1 p.m. during term time. It is probably crowded with a hundred or more customers. Are they all there at the same time and in the same place because, and only because, they are all hungry, as a simple arousal explanation would have us believe? Of course, there is an element of truth there. People do eat because they are hungry! But the simultaneous choice of time and location must also surely have at least something to do with such social factors as patterns of mutual influence ('are you coming for lunch then?'), the availability of other places to eat and the scheduling of classes in the institution concerned. So it is with aggression. The patterning and selectivity of intergroup antagonism suggest that over and above the mere anger of the individuals involved, factors like social norms and collective goals must also be involved. (This point is explored more fully in chapter 7.)

A second problem with the idea that prejudice is simply the aggregation of individual emotional states is that it implies that conflict between groups is seldom guided by any deliberate strategy on the part of the group members involved, but is rather an irrational affair. Again, such a conclusion seems unwarranted. Fogelson (1970), in his analysis of the American race riots of the 1960s, observed that one noteworthy feature of these riots was that the violence, though widespread, was not completely arbitrary or directionless. Particular stores and houses were selected for looting and arson; others were left virtually untouched. The rioting was also confined to particular geographical areas – usually the home territory of the rioters. All this led Fogelson to suggest that the rioting, though it gave some appearance of irrationality, was actually consciously directed towards particular ends – namely, the publicizing of the rioters' state of deprivation and the defence of their neighbourhood. As we saw in chapter 1, exactly the same conclusion was reached by Reicher (1984a) in his study of a small disturbance in Britain in 1980. Such observations suggest a degree of cognitive control by the participants which is inconsistent with the idea in frustration–aggression theory that such events are caused simply by the welling up of anger in individuals. If this is true for the extreme behavioural manifestations of discontent which occurred in these riots, then it is plausible to suppose that milder forms of prejudice might also contain similar 'rational' elements such as the perception of some intergroup competition over jobs or housing, or the attempted preservation of deeply held cultural values and practices. In chapters 7 and 8 these possibilities will be discussed in more detail.

Relative deprivation and social unrest

> Talking once with a miner I asked him when the housing shortage first
> became acute in his district; he answered, 'When we were told about it',
> meaning that 'till recently people's standards were so low that they
> took almost any degree of overcrowding for granted. (Orwell, 1962,
> p. 57)

This excerpt from Orwell's brilliant essay on the condition of the
British working class in the 1930s, *The Road to Wigan Pier*, makes an
important point about the origins of discontent. Deprivation, he
implies, is not an absolute condition but is always relative to some
norm of what is considered acceptable. This is the idea that lies at the
heart of several explanations of social unrest, known collectively as
relative deprivation theory.

The central proposition in relative deprivation theory is that people
become discontented and rebellious when they perceive a discrepancy
between the standard of living they are currently enjoying and the
standard they believe they *should* be enjoying. For Gurr (1970), who
has done much to formalize the theory and test out its implications
empirically, it is precisely this gap between attainments and expectations, or 'relative deprivation', that is the motor force for collective
violence. The bigger the gap, and the more widely it is felt, the greater
the likelihood of unrest.

Gurr's version of relative deprivation theory, as he knowledges, is a
direct descendant of the frustration–aggression theory discussed in the
previous section, particularly the amended version of Berkowitz
(1962). Probably because of this, Gurr places much emphasis on the
individual's direct experience of relative deprivation: what person X is
experiencing relative to what person X expects. However, others have
pointed out that there is another kind of deprivation, a deprivation
derived from people's perception of the fortunes of their group. The
most prominent of these is Runciman (1966), who suggests that in
collective movements the most important factor is a sense that the
ingroup is deprived relative to some desired standard. Runciman
labels this 'fraternalistic deprivation' to distinguish it from the other
form, 'egoistic deprivation'. Of the many lines of evidence which
Runciman draws on to support this distinction, perhaps the most
telling is his observation that participants in uprisings are seldom the
most deprived *individuals*. Caplan (1970), for instance, has noted how
supporters of Black Power during the American race riots of the 1960s
were drawn mainly from middle and upper income blacks and rather

less from the poorest (and most egoistically deprived) blacks. However, slightly privileged though they may be relative to others in their (black) ingroup, as members of that disadvantaged *group* they experienced relative deprivation just as keenly as the most destitute of their fellows (see also Walker and Pettigrew, 1984, for an interesting further development of Runciman's theory).

What gives rise to a perception of relative deprivation? At the most general level, as noted above, relative deprivation is caused simply by a gap between expectations and achievements. Cantril (1965) conducted a large cross-national survey in which, amongst other things, he asked respondents to indicate how they valued their past, present and future life as compared to their 'ideal' good life. The difference between each respondent's actual rating and their ideal aspiration represents a direct measure of relative deprivation. Gurr (1970) correlated the mean relative deprivation scores from each of the thirteen nations in Cantril's study with indices of 'turmoil' derived from archival records of incidents of civil unrest in these same countries. Just as the theory predicted, the correlation between relative deprivation and internal turmoil was strongly positive. Crawford and Naditch (1970) used exactly the same measure of relative deprivation in a survey of black residents in Detroit shortly after a large-scale riot in the city. The respondents' attitudes towards the rioting, Black Power and militant political action generally were strongly influenced by their level of relative deprivation, as can be seen in table 6.2. Those indicating a large discrepancy between their present and ideal lives were much more likely to endorse support for violent protest.

So, people's expectations are clearly implicated in their support for social change. The next obvious question is what governs people's

Table 6.2   Black militancy and relative deprivation

Attitude item		Relative deprivation* %	
		Low	High
Do you think that riots help or hurt the Negro	Help	28	54
cause?	Hurt	60	38
Do you approve or disapprove of Black Power?	Approve	38	64
	Disapprove	36	22
Will force or persuasion be necessary to change	Force	40	51
white attitudes?	Persuasion	52	35

* Perceived discrepancy between 'actual' and 'ideal' life.

Source: Crawford and Naditch (1970), table 1 ('don't knows' omitted)

expectations? One possibility is past experience. Davies (1969) has suggested that people tend to extrapolate from their own recent experiences of affluence or poverty and expect the future to be similar. If, for example, their standard of living has risen steadily over previous years this will generate an expectation of future gains. Starting from this assumption, Davies (1969) proposed his famous J-curve hypothesis. This states that rebellions are most likely to occur not after a period of prolonged deprivation, but after a period in which the general standard of living has risen for a number of years and then taken a sudden downturn. This sharp decline after a period of relative prosperity produces the requisite gap between actual and desired living standards for the arousal of relative deprivation. This sequence is depicted hypothetically in figure 6.1, where the shape of the solid curve which gives the theory its name can be seen. From the figure, one of Davies's counter-intuitive predictions becomes clear: unrest is actually more likely at some points in history (t_2) when people are better off in absolute terms than at some previous and objectively more impoverished time (t_1).

In support of his theory, Davies (1969) cites mainly historical evidence. Pointing to major upheavals such as the French and Russian revolutions, the American civil war, the rise of Nazism in Germany in

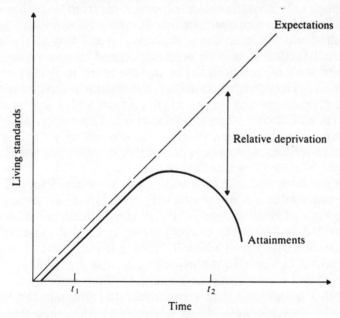

Figure 6.1 The J-curve hypothesis (from Davies, 1969)

the 1930s and the growth of Black Power in the 1960s, he argues that before each of these events there had been a period of 20–30 years gradually increasing prosperity followed by a steep economic recession. Arguing from such historical evidence is necessarily always somewhat speculative, mainly because we seldom have access to records of people's subjective expectations at the times in question. Unfortunately for Davies, attempts to verify his theory more directly have not always proved successful. A good example is a recent study by Taylor (1982) which tested the two key ideas in the J-curve hypothesis: that people's immediately past experience predicts their expectations for the future, and that their satisfaction is related to a failure of the present to match up to expectations. For her data Taylor turned to a longitudinal survey of American social and political attitudes conducted in 1956, 1958 and 1960. Three of the questions in this survey were of particular interest: one asked whether people's recent financial circumstances were improving or declining; a second enquired in similar terms about their expected future financial circumstances; and a third asked how satisfied they were with their present condition. If Davies is correct, people's recent experiences should correlate positively with their expectations for the future. Taylor found that they did, but only weakly: the overall correlations were not high enough to be able to predict 'expectations' from 'experience' with any certainty. Even more problematic for the J-curve hypothesis were the results from the satisfaction measures. According to the theory, present satisfaction should be *inversely* related to past expectations: the higher one's expectations in the past the more likely they are to be disappointed. However, when she correlated present satisfaction levels with expectations two years previously, Taylor could find absolutely no evidence of such a negative association. The major, and hardly surprising, determinant of satisfaction was actually one's *present* financial condition: those who reported this as improving were happier than those who said it was declining.

If comparisons with the past seem to be poor predictors of disappointed expectations, comparisons with other groups are a much more potent source of relative deprivation. A classic demonstration of this was provided by Runciman's (1966) survey of English class attitudes. The basic class distinction which Runciman investigated was between those working in manual (or blue-collar) occupations and those in the better-paid and higher-status non-manual (white-collar) jobs. One of Runciman's questions asked respondents to nominate the sorts of people who they felt were 'doing noticeably better' than them. This was followed by a question to elicit their approval or disapproval of this state of affairs. Most of the answers to the first question cited other people who were similar in some way to the respondent, either similar individuals or other *groups* of workers in similar occupations. However, a sizeable number of the better-off white-collar workers actually mentioned the less well paid manual workers as doing better, and in answer to the second question it was these respondents who were most likely of all to indicate disapproval. This was an important finding because it showed that members of a 'superior' group could experience relative deprivation. Up until then, most relative deprivation research had concentrated on more obviously deprived subordinate groups.

Runciman's discovery that intergroup comparisons could lead to relative deprivation has been confirmed in several other studies. Vanneman and Pettigrew (1972), for instance, found that amongst whites in the USA the holding of racist attitudes and support for conservative political candidates was related to the respondents' feelings of relative deprivation. Once again, observe that relative deprivation is occurring in a dominant group. Also, and in support of Runciman's distinction between 'fraternalistic' and 'egoistic' deprivation, they found that the most racist attitudes were to be found amongst those who were fraternally deprived, i.e. those who thought that whites *as a group* were doing worse economically than blacks as a group. Abeles (1976), on the other side of the coin, discovered that black militancy in the USA was correlated with 'fraternalistic' deprivation. Also, and consistent with Caplan's (1970) findings, the levels of militancy appeared to be higher amongst blacks of higher socioeconomic and educational status, groups who were less deprived in an objective or absolute sense than poorer and less well educated blacks. Gaskell and Smith (1984) also found that relative deprivation was associated with discontent amongst black and white young men in London. However, the correlations were not strong and the discontent was focused on the school system and the job market. More generalized negative attitudes about British society were not related to relative deprivation. It is perhaps significant that this study, unlike the previous two, used a measure of 'egoistic' deprivation as the main independent variable. As Guimond and Dubé-Simard (1983) observed amongst some French Canadians in Quebec, measures of 'egoistic' relative deprivation were not well correlated with support for French nationalism, whilst 'fraternalistic' deprivation was.

The importance of intergroup (as compared to individual) deprivation was further underlined in a study of unemployed workers in Australia (Walker and Mann, 1987). Of course, being unemployed itself constitutes deprivation in both an absolute and a relative sense, but Walker and Mann were able to show that it was principally those people who felt a strong sense of 'fraternalistic' deprivation who were prepared to contemplate militant protest activities, such as participating in demonstrations, breaking the law and destroying public and private property. Those who felt 'egoistically' deprived, on the other hand, tended to report more symptoms of individual stress such as headaches, indigestion and sleeplessness. Walker and Mann conclude, correctly I believe, that while both 'fraternalistic' and 'egoistic' deprivation are important determinants of people's behaviour, they are important in different ways: the former leading to social or collective outcomes, the latter to internal individualized responses.

The theory of relative deprivation has, therefore, been quite successful in helping us to understand when and where social discontent will arise, especially when compared to the rather mixed support for its predecessor, frustration–aggression theory. It owes its success to three important revisions which were made to that traditional approach. The first, for which the credit goes to Berkowitz (1962), is its emphasis on the subjective experience of deprivation rather than the objective fact of it. As Berkowitz suggests, people become frustrated and discontented when they *think* they are deprived, not necessarily when they *are* deprived. (The two, of course, can often go hand in hand.) Secondly, in formulating relative deprivation as the discrepancy between what 'is' and what 'ought to be', a crucial new variable is introduced, that of perceived legitimacy. In other words, the concept of relative deprivation contains within it notions of social justice. Now where do such ideas come from? They are, first and foremost, *socially* constructed. People's perceptions of what is fair or appropriate derive mainly, as we saw in chapter 2, from norms and values which evolve out of the dynamics of intra- and intergroup relations. This, then, helps to overcome one of the objections to frustration–aggression theory: the implausibility of whole groups of people being simultaneously in similar states of arousal. If what motivates discontent is not an individually experienced state of frustration but a socially shared sense of injustice, then the uniformity of behaviour within protest movements becomes easier to understand. The third crucial difference concerns the recognition that dominant groups can be discontented too! Frustration–aggression theory, not unnaturally, focused on the plight of subordinate and oppressed groups. But if deprivation is redefined as a *relative* matter, it follows that if a higher-status group sees its superior position being eroded then it, too, will be inclined to take action – to restore the status quo. Recent events in

South Africa, where we have seen the ruling white Nationalist party adopting even tougher and more repressive measures against the black majority, serve as a vivid illustration of this.

Relative deprivation theory, then, offers several advantages over other explanations of social discontent. However, there is one difficulty with the theory which should be mentioned (see Walker and Pettigrew, 1984). Social comparisons, as we have seen, are an important cause of relative deprivation since they often provide the means by which people assess their group's standing and progress in society. But whether the outcome of a comparison leads to a feeling of deprivation – or its converse, gratification – obviously depends entirely on which group we choose to compare with. If I, as a university lecturer, compare my lot to that of nurses then I can have no possible reason to feel deprived; the appallingly low pay of the nursing profession makes university salaries look positively exorbitant. But, of course, my colleagues and I seldom make this comparison. We are much more likely to point bitterly to engineers in industry, or lawyers at the bar, or scientists in the civil service to underline how poorly we are paid. Runciman (1966) and Gurr (1970) suggest that this is because people tend to use 'similar others' for purposes of comparison, an idea familiar to us from Festinger's (1954) theory (see chapter 3). This hypothesis certainly seems to fit my wage comparison example above, and several of the other studies considered earlier (e.g. Runciman, 1966; Abeles, 1976). However, it is not so easy to reconcile with more extreme cases of social unrest and rebellion where, it must be assumed, members of the subordinate group are actually making comparisons between themselves and a quite *different* dominant group. For example, what motivates supporters of the African National Congress in South Africa as they protest against the iniquities of apartheid are presumably *not* the minor differences amongst the black population, but the huge and glaring disparities in wealth, health and education between blacks and whites. Quite what precipitates comparisons between such manifestly dissimilar groups as these will be considered further in chapter 8.

Summary

1 Prejudice is the expression of derogatory behaviour or attitudes towards most or all of the members of an outgroup. One influential explanation for prejudice is that it is caused by personality disorder, a disorder with its origins in the childhood family of the prejudiced person. An excessively

strict upbringing, so it is thought, produces an 'authoritarian personality', someone overdeferential towards authority figures and conventional moral standards but hostile towards deviants and 'outsiders'. Although such a portrait fits some extreme bigots, this personality theory of prejudice has difficulty explaining widespread prevalence of intolerance at particular times and in particular places throughout history.

2 Another explanation of prejudice is in terms of belief congruence. On this view, prejudice arises not out of people's membership of different social groups but from a perception that others hold different beliefs. In apparent support of this theory, many studies have found that people will prefer an outgroup person with similar beliefs to themselves than an ingrouper who professes rather different opinions. However, most of these studies were concerned with interpersonal attitudes and hence may not be relevant to the inter*group* problem of prejudice. In studies where groups have been more significant for the participants, people's respective group memberships, rather than their beliefs, have usually been found to be the more important variable.

3 A third theory links prejudice and social discontent together by considering them both to be a product of frustration. According to this frustration-aggression theory, both kinds of phenomena are examples of displaced aggression caused by the frustrations endemic to social life. In times of economic depression these frustrations are intensified still further and the resulting aggression (or prejudice) is more violent and more widespread. This theory was subsequently modified by Berkowitz to incorporate cognitive factors and to attempt to predict which 'scapegoat' would be chosen as the target of prejudice. However, even in its revised form, frustration-aggression theory still posits individual anger arousal as the main cause of collective discontent. Such a view may be difficult to reconcile with the seemingly uniform and also goal-directed nature of much intergroup aggression.

4 A direct descendant of frustration–aggression theory is relative deprivation theory. The core idea of this theory is that people become discontented when they perceive a negative discrepancy between their current standard of living and the standard of living they believe they deserve. Relative deprivation is this gap between attainments and expectations and has been found to correlate with various societal indices of disorder. One of the most important causes of relative deprivation is a negative comparison between the ingroup and other groups. In various contexts these have been found to be associated with dissatisfaction in both high- and low-status groups. A crucial problem for relative deprivation theory is to be able to predict the choice of comparison groups. Often this is determined by similarity, but occasionally very dissimilar groups engage in mutual comparisons.

Further reading

Billig, M.G. (1976) *Social Psychology and Intergroup Relations*, chs 4–5. London: Academic Press.
Brown, Roger (1965) *Social Psychology*, 1st edition, ch. 10. New York: Macmillan.
Brown, R.J. and Turner, J.C. (1981) Interpersonal and intergroup behaviour, in Turner, J.C. and Giles, H. (eds) *Intergroup Behaviour*. Oxford: Blackwell.
Gurr, T.R. (1970) *Why Men Rebel*. Princeton, NJ: Princeton University Press.
Konecni, V.J. (1979) The role of aversive events in the development of intergroup conflict, in Austin, W.C. and Worchel, S. (eds) *The Social Psychology of Intergroup Relations*. Monterey: Brooks/Cole.

CHAPTER 7

Intergroup Conflict and Cooperation

Prejudice and discontent, the subjects of the previous chapter, are two special instances of the wider class of phenomena known as intergroup behaviour: the behaviour of members of one group towards the members of other groups. They happen also to be two instances which are most usually associated with conflict between groups. But obviously they do not encompass the whole range of possible intergroup behaviours; groups are as capable of friendly and cooperative orientations towards one another as they are of hostility and competition. In this chapter, therefore, I want to widen the discussion to consider both the positive and negative aspects of intergroup relations.

The discussion will be widened in another sense as well. In trying to explain the origins of prejudice in chapter 6, I concentrated mainly on theories which located the causal factors within the individual; prejudice was seen as a personality disposition, an outcome of perceived different beliefs or the result of accumulated frustrations. In this chapter I want to consider an alternative view: that intergroup behaviour – whether competitive or cooperative – is the response of ordinary people to their real or imagined group interests. Where these are incompatible with another group, so that what the outgroup is seeking will be at the expense of the ingroup, then the outcome is likely to be mutual antagonism and discrimination. An example of such conflicting interests would be the relationship between workers and their employers in a capitalist economy where one party's wages are at the expense of the other's profits. On the other hand, where the interests are concordant, so that both groups are working towards the same objective, a much more amicable relationship is probable. An example of concordant goals would be when minority political parties form coalitions to achieve political power: for example, the Communist and Socialist parties in France in the early 1980s.

The idea that goal relationships like these could be important determinants of people's behaviour towards members of their own and other groups crops up frequently within the social sciences and led Campbell (1965) to dub it the realistic group conflict theory. Within social psychology the best-known proponent of this approach is Muzafer Sherif, whom we have already encountered more than once in this book. It is Sherif's work, therefore, that serves as the point of departure for all the research discussed in this chapter. I begin by discussing the effects of conflicting group goals on people's intergroup attitudes and behaviour. The focus then shifts to inside the group where the effects of intergroup conflict on intragroup dynamics will be considered in some detail. From competition and conflict, I turn to their converse: cooperation and harmony. What situations promote collaboration between groups and how are such situations best engineered? In a final section this theme is continued in an examination of one of the best-known panaceas for the reduction of prejudice: the contact hypothesis.

Conflicting goals and intergroup competition

The very first Israelis I ever saw were soldiers. They came to my village and entered the school. I think there is nothing good to be said about them. When I see any soldiers, I think that those soldiers will be killed some day . . . There will be no peace. Some day there will be another war, and the Arabs will be successful. We will take back all of Palestine. (Najeh Hassan, 20-year-old Palestinian)

You have to understand the Jewish people. We are a small people; our identity in the past was as a persecuted people, a hated people. Young Israelis like me feel that it is about time Israel is not oppressed but a nation that is independent and controls its own destiny . . . [A Palestinian] is someone who is poor, weak physically and mentally. I don't mean stupid, but I wouldn't say brilliant either. A simple worker whose mentality is directed towards how to make a profit. (Yaacov Leviatan, 20-year-old Jew)

According to the newspaper report from which these comments were taken (*Observer*, 31 May 1987), Najeh Hassan and Yaacov Leviatan were born within days of each other and not many miles apart in June 1967. In the same week, the Israeli government launched a major military offensive against its Arab neighbours which resulted in the Israeli occupation of east Jerusalem, the West Bank and the Golan Heights. Why should these two young men living in the same country have such hostile attitudes, if not actually towards each other, then certainly towards the group to which the other belongs? One answer is to be found later in the same newspaper article in a remark by Yaacov's father, Shlomo Leviatan: 'There is a basic conflict of interest between the Palestinians and us: what is good for us is bad for them, and what is good for them is bad for us.' This, in a sentence, is Sherif's (1966) theory of intergroup conflict, a theory which has had a seminal influence on the whole field of intergroup relations since the war.

At the heart of Sherif's theory is the proposition that group members' intergroup attitudes and behaviour will tend to reflect the objective interests of their group *vis à vis* other groups. Where these interests conflict, then their group's cause is more likely to be furthered by a competitive orientation towards the rival group, which is often easily extended to include prejudiced attitudes and even overtly hostile behaviour. In the Israeli–Palestinian example above the conflict of interest is plain. The groups are disputing over an area of land, for which each claims sole historical, political and religious ownership and rights. At the same time, the ingroup's success in achieving the goal is likely to be furthered by very positive attitudes towards other ingroup members, thereby engendering high morale and cohesion. Where, on the other hand, the groups' interests coincide, then it is more functional for the group members to adopt a cooperative and friendly attitude towards the outgroup. If this is reciprocated then a positive joint outcome is more probable.

To demonstrate the validity of this perspective Sherif, together with his colleagues, conducted three famous field experiments which have come to be known as the 'summer camp' studies (Sherif and Sherif, 1953; Sherif et al., 1955, 1961). Although these experiments differed slightly from one another, they are similar enough in conception and outcome for us to be able to consider them together. They were longitudinal (lasting some three weeks) and were designed to show systematic changes in behaviour as a result of changing intergroup relations. The full design included three stages: group formation, intergroup conflict and conflict reduction.[1] To effect this design, Sherif and his colleagues arranged for the experiments to be conducted in the context of a boy's summer camp. In fact, as far as those participating in the experiments were concerned, that is exactly what it was since all the activities were exactly the kinds of things which went on in American summer camps in the 1950s (and probably still do!). The difference was, of course, that, unknown to the boys, the adults running the camp were all trained researchers making careful observations of all that went on. The boys themselves – all white, middle class and aged around twelve years – had been carefully screened before being invited to the camp, and only those who seemed to be psychologically well adjusted and from stable homes were accepted. In addition, none of the boys knew each other before coming to the camp. Although this was a highly select and unrepresentative sample, it did ensure that any behaviour they subsequently exhibited could not be attributed to a prior history of social or psychological deprivation, or to pre-existing personal relationships between the boys.

In the first stage of the experiments the large group of 22–24 children was split up into the two experimental groups of the study. Care was taken to match these two groups as carefully as possible. In the first two experiments, in addition to matching on various physical and psychological characteristics, it was also arranged to have the majority of each boy's best friends in the *out*group.[2] In the third experiment the boys never actually met each other before the groups were formed and initially were camped some distance from each other, unaware of the other group's presence. For some days the children engaged in various activities in these groups without, however, having much to do with the other group. Very quickly, the groups developed an internal structure and evolved mini-cultures of their own with their own group symbols and names, and norms of appropriate behaviour. Although the other group did not figure much in their thinking, it is interesting to note that in the first two experiments the observers did record some instances of comparisons between the groups and in these comparisons 'the edge was given to one's own group' (Sherif, 1966, p. 80). Furthermore, in the third study, where the groups did not know of each other's existence at this stage, on being informed of the presence of the other group several boys spontaneously suggested to the camp authorities that the other group be challenged to some sporting contest. As we shall see, it is significant that these expressions of ingroup favouritism occurred *before* the intergroup conflict phase of the experiment had actually been introduced.

The second stage then began. It was announced to the boys that a series of intergroup contests would take place (e.g. softball, tug-of-war etc.). The overall winner of these contests would receive a cup and each member of this successful group would be given a gleaming new penknife – just the kind of prize every 12-year-old boy covets. The losers would receive nothing. In this way, an objective conflict of interest was introduced between the groups. In technical terms, they had moved from being independent of one another to being negatively *interdependent* – what one group gained the other lost. With the advent of this conflict stage the boys' behaviour changed dramatically. Whereas in the first stage the two groups had coexisted more or less peaceably, they were now transformed into two hostile factions, never losing an opportunity to deride the outgroup and, in some instances, physically attack it.

In a variety of micro-experiments, disguised as games, Sherif and his associates were able to document systematic and consistent ingroup favouritism in judgements, attitudes and sociometric preferences. One of these experiments was designed as a bean-toss game in which a large number of beans was scattered over the grass. Each team member had a set time to pick up as many beans as possible. Each boy's pickings were then displayed onto a screen by means of a projector (or so it seemed to the children), and everyone estimated how many each had collected. In fact, through some sleight of hand, the experimenter contrived always to project the same number of beans onto the screen. Despite this constant 'stimulus', the boys' judgements showed remarkable and consistent bias in favour of their own group. These biases are shown in figure 7.1 where it can be seen that both groups over-estimated the performances of their own members as compared to those in the outgroup. Notice also that the winning group shows even more bias (or discrimination) than the losing group.

Changes took place *within* the groups too. They invariably became more cohesive and the leadership structure sometimes changed with a more aggressive boy assuming dominance. When asked to nominate their best friends, over 90 per cent of the children in both groups chose people in their own group. This was all the more remarkable when it is remembered that, in the first two studies at least, every boy's best friends had been placed in the *other* group. How fragile those initial interpersonal relationships proved to be in the face of the changing intergroup relationship!

On the face of it, these experiments seemed to provide strong support for Sherif's theory. The behaviour of these ordinary well-adjusted children was shown to vary systematically with the nature of the intergroup relation. These changes in the boys' behaviour were too widespread and too rapid to be attributable to any enduring personality disposition. Moreover, members of the winning group, who were presumably less frustrated than the losers, actually seemed to show *more* evidence of outgroup derogation than those who really had been frustrated by being denied the prizes. On both these counts, then, the theories considered in chapter 6 – the authoritarian personality and frustration–aggression – were shown up as deficient.

These deficiencies were underlined by later research inspired by the 'summer camp' studies. In a series of experiments by Blake and Mouton (1962) it was found that groups in competition with one

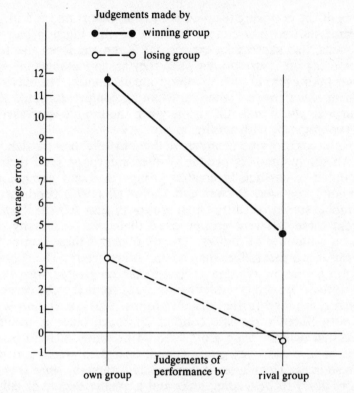

Figure 7.1 Ingroup bias in judgements after intergroup competition: errors in estimating a performance by victors and losers (from Sherif, 1966, p. 84, figure 5.2. Copyright © 1966 by Houghton Miffin Company, Boston. Used by permission)

another consistently over-evaluated their own group's product in comparison with that of the outgroup. In one of these experiments, forty-eight groups (mainly of managerial staff in organizations) were asked to solve an organizational problem. The groups were arranged in competitive pairs. Afterwards, each group evaluated both its own solution and that of its rival. Of the forty-eight possible group judgements, forty-six favoured the ingroup solution, two reckoned the solutions to be equal, and not one of them conceded any superiority to the outgroup! (Blake and Mouton, 1962). Similar results were obtained by Kahn and Ryen (1972) when they asked groups to engage in a simulated 'football' game in the laboratory. Despite the fact that members of their own team were unknown to them and could not even be seen throughout the session, they were rated more favourably than members of the opposing team. Also, just as Sherif had found, winning teams showed much more evidence of this ingroup bias than losing teams. In a subsequent experiment, Kahn and Ryen also found bias favouring the ingroup even when they asked members merely to *anticipate* taking part in such an intergroup encounter. The bias in this experiment was strongest when anticipating competition but, somewhat surprisingly, it was still visible when the groups were asked to imagine *cooperating* with another group.

The readiness of group members to demonstrate their partiality for their own group (and its products) over outgroups (and theirs) is not confined to artificially created groups in social psychological experiments, however. Brewer and Campbell (1976) conducted an ethnographic survey of thirty tribal groups in East Africa. Respondents from these different groups rated their own and many other groups on a number of indices. Twenty-seven of these groups gave higher ratings to themselves than to any other group. The degree of this ingroup bias in relation to particular outgroups was weakly related to their proximity: nearby outgroups seemed to be derogated somewhat more than further distant groups. This correlation is consistent with Sherif's realistic conflict approach since it would be expected that neighbouring groups would be more likely to become involved in disputes over grazing land, access to water and other scarce resources. The matter is complicated, though, since there are also more likely to be trading links and a greater degree of cultural similarity between nearby groups. Such relationships might be more likely to generate favourable attitudes towards the outgroup as, indeed, was shown in another of Brewer and Campbell's results: a positive association between proximity and liking for the outgroup. Both of these findings, based as they are on gross ratings across a number of groups, become easier to understand (and reconcile) once one analyses *specific* intergroup relationships amongst neighbouring groups which may vary from intense conflict to strong alliance in particular instances (Brewer, 1979a).

This was certainly the conclusion I reached after conducting a study of relations amongst workgroups in a large paper factory (Brown et al., 1986). As is often the case, when we asked people to judge their own and other groups' contributions to the running of the organization, they almost invariably favoured the ingroup (see table 7.1). Notice that the owngroup score (in the boxes) is always the highest or one of the highest in each row. These ratings favouring the ingroup were sometimes accompanied by mildly disparaging remarks about the performance of other groups: 'I think they damage too many [paper] reels down there' and 'some of the paper they turn out is a bit rubbishy' are just two of the several which we recorded. In addition to eliciting people's attitudes, we also asked them to characterize each intergroup relationship on a harmony–conflict dimension ('two teams pulling together' v. 'two groups on opposite sides working against each other'). It turned out that this index of conflict was strongly correlated with the amount of ingroup bias shown against each outgroup: those outgroups with whom a conflictual relationship was perceived were reckoned to contribute less to the organization than those who were seen to be working *with* the ingroup (see also Brown and Williams, 1984).

Table 7.1 Ingroup bias in a paper factory: mean ratings of each group's 'contribution to the running of the factory'

	Group being rated (scale 1–7)						
Respondents	Pap	Con	Fin	Sal	Wha	Man	Eng
Papermakers	6.3	5.3	6.0	4.8	5.5	4.7	5.8
Conversion	6.2	6.0	5.8	5.9	5.7	4.9	5.8
Finishing	6.1	4.7	6.0	4.6	5.3	4.4	5.0
Salle	5.8	6.1	5.2	6.4	5.4	5.2	5.4
Wharf	6.5	6.0	6.0	5.5	6.7ˈ	4.7	5.8

Respondents came from five departments in the factory. Papermakers prepared the initial pulp and produced the first crude paper. Finishing polished the paper. Conversion cut it to required sizes. The Salle was responsible for quality control and the Wharf for dispatch of the finished product.
Boxed figure is each group's rating of itself.
Man, management; Eng, engineering.

Source: Brown et al. (1986)

I began this section with one real-world intergroup conflict, let me finish with another. In 1984 British coal miners went on strike over the threatened closure of a number of mines. The strike lasted for twelve months during which time there were several violent confrontations between striking miners picketing pits and power stations and the police attempting to prevent them. Viewed in Sherif's terms we could describe this as a 'classic example of a 'realistic conflict'. In any specific incident we could regard the miners and the police as disputing the territory outside the pit gates but, more generally, we might say that they were engaged in a political 'win–lose' struggle over the conduct of industrial disputes. The dramatic effect which this conflict had on miners' attitudes towards the police is graphically described in this bitter comment from a South Wales miner during the strike: 'We've always been brought up to respect policemen but I've got no respect for any of them now. There was a time when if I saw a policeman have a hammering I'd go and help him. I'd walk past and spit in his eye now' (quoted in *Striking Back* by the Welsh Campaign for Civil Liberties, 1984, p. 182).

Intergroup conflict and intragroup dynamics

So far we have dealt with the effects of an intergroup conflict on attitudes and behaviour *between* the groups. Yet, as anyone who has ever participated in a team competition or been involved in an inter-group dispute will know, conflict often has effects *within* the group also. One of the most common of these is an increase in the solidarity and cohesion of the ingroup; the group and the people in it come to matter more to the group members. Many years ago the sociologist William Sumner, commenting on this phenomenon, suggested a direct and functional link between intergroup conflict and cohesion: 'The relation of comradeship and peace in the we-group and that of hostility and war towards others-groups are correlative of each other. The exigencies of war with outsiders are what make peace inside, lest internal discord should weaken the we-group for war' (Sumner, 1906, p. 12).

This is, of course, exactly what Sherif and his colleagues observed in the 'summer camp' studies, noted earlier. As the competition between the groups intensified so each group became more tightly knit. This connection between conflict and cohesion was confirmed by Julian et al. (1966) when they compared army squads training under a competi-tive team regime and squads under less-competitive conditions. On a number of measures they found that the competitive squads showed greater solidarity and morale than the control groups. This also reminds us of the work by Deutsch (1949b), discussed in chapter 2, which also found increased cohesiveness in groups working under conditions of intergroup competition. Further confirmation of the intragroup effects of conflict was provided by Stagner and Eflal (1982) in their study of American car workers. In 1976 workers at Ford plants went on strike whilst their colleagues at General Motors and Chrysler did not. Stagner and Eflal were able to compare those two groups (of strikers and non-strikers) on a number of indices. The strikers showed more militancy towards their employers, enhanced evaluation of their leadership and greater participation in the union (although only marginally greater cohesion) than the non-strikers.[3]

Another consequence of intergroup conflict, hinted at by Stagner and Eflal's (1982) findings, is a more differentiated intragroup structure as the group adapts to its new circumstances. Once again, some of the first evidence of this came from the Sherifs. Their observations of changing leadership structures, not only in the 'summer camp' groups but also in the urban youth gangs of a later study, support the idea that intragroup relationships change as a response to the changed *intergroup* environment (Sherif and Sherif, 1964; see chapter 3). A related finding has been reported by Lauderdale et al. (1984). They suggested that one way in which a group can increase its cohesion is to find an unpopular person in the group to act as a kind of 'scapegoat' for the remaining group members. They found that a legal discussion group whose continued existence was called into question by a high-status 'expert' (expressing disapproval towards them and implying criticism of the quality of their discussion), distinguished sharply between the least popular member in the group and the rest. Those groups not so threatened were much less rejecting of the unpopular member. If we equate the 'expert' in this study with an outgroup, then Lauderdale et al.'s results suggest that the increased cohesion resulting from intergroup conflict is sometimes bought at the expense of one or two unfortunates in the group.

If conflict generates intragroup cohesion then does the reverse also apply? Sumner (1906) thought that it did, but there is very little evidence to suggest that he was right. In one of the very few experiments to examine the effects of varying cohesiveness on intergroup behaviour, Dion (1973) found no obvious signs of increased outgroup rejection as a result of increased ingroup cohesiveness. He used the well-known prisoners' dilemma game for his experiment (Rapoport and Chammah, 1965). In this paradigm two individuals (or groups) each have to choose between two options in a pay-off matrix (see notes to table 7.2). Their monetary outcomes depend on the conjunction of their two choices. If both choose A then jointly they gain. However, if X chooses A and Y chooses B, then Y benefits at X's expense (and so on, for the other two combinations). Dion (1973) had his participants play a game like this with both ingroup and outgroup opponents. The cohesiveness of the ingroup was manipulated by leading its members to believe that it either comprised people with very similar personalities and values, or rather different people. As table 7.2 shows, this manipulation had a strong effect on their behaviour towards ingroup members; the percentage of cooperative A choices was considerably higher than in any other condition. However, the behaviour towards the outgroup was little affected by the cohesiveness of the ingroup. Similar results were also obtained on various sociometric trait ratings of the two groups.

Table 7.2 The effects of varying ingroup cohesiveness on intergroup game-playing strategies: percentage of 'cooperative' A choices

Opponent	Cohesiveness of ingroup	
	High	Low
Ingrouper	59.1	36.1
Outgrouper	30.0	36.7

Source: Dion (1973)

Prisoners' dilemma pay-off matrix used by Dion:

		Player X	
		A	B
Player Y	A	X gets 20 ¢ Y gets 20 ¢	X gets 25 ¢ Y gets 0 ¢
	B	X gets 0 ¢ Y gets 25 ¢	X gets 10 ¢ Y gets 10¢

What is it about a conflictual goal relationship which generates the increased intragroup cohesion? Does it stem from the fact of the goal incompatibility itself or does it arise out of the *interaction* consequent on that incompatibility? In the 'summer camp' and other studies these two factors could not be separated and it was left to Rabbie et al. (1974) to show what happens when they are. Rabbie and his colleagues were concerned with *anticipated* intergroup competition and cooperation, that is, what happens when a group perceives some goal relationship between itself and an outgroup but has not yet actually met it. They set up a union–management simulation in which groups of students had to pretend to play the role of union negotiators in a forthcoming bargaining session with management. The groups were given different briefs. Some were told to adopt a cooperative bargaining strategy and attempt to achieve a jointly agreeable outcome to the negotiations. A sum of money was promised if they were successful in this. Others were told to be more competitive and try to gain the best outcome for their group. Again, they would be rewarded financially if successful. Then, by varying the background materials describing the simulation exercise, the 'union' groups were led to believe that their bargaining position was either *strong* or *weak* in relation to management. The group then spent about ten minutes planning its negotiation strategy after which the dependent measures in the experiment were administered. Note that they never actually met the 'management' group. In line with Sherif's (1966) findings, inducing the competitive orientation led the groups to feel more hostile towards the outgroup than those given the cooperative instructions. However, of more interest here are the results for ingroup cohesiveness. Anticipated competition did not cause a *general* increase in cohesiveness. It was only for those groups who felt they were in a 'strong' bargaining position that competition had this effect; for those believing themselves to be in a 'weak' position, the competitive goal relationship led to a *decrease* in cohesion.

Rabbie et al.'s (1974) results suggest that the outcome of an intergroup competition may have important consequences for intragroup cohesion. Common sense suggests that when this is favourable for the ingroup, cohesion will increase; when the ingroup looks like losing there may be forces towards resentment and disintegration. An earlier study by Myers (1962) lent support to this idea. He compared over a four-week period the changes in morale of army cadet rifle teams who took part in either a competitive league (against one another) or a non-competitive league (against some absolute standard). As usual, intergroup competition had the effect of increasing group morale, but this greater cohesion was strongly qualified by how well the teams did in the rifle shooting events. In general, those who succeeded (whether in competition or not) showed higher morale; those who did badly reported less satisfaction with one another. A very similar result was obtained by Worchel et al. (1975) in a laboratory experiment. Those groups who had clearly won an intergroup competition, and even for those for whom the outcome was ambiguous, showed greater ingroup cohesiveness than those who had lost.

The conclusion from these studies seems clear: success breeds cohesion, failure lowers morale. But does defeat always result in such negative outcomes? Experience suggests not. Last season my son was playing for his school football team. They had a disastrous season, losing every match except one, sometimes by double-figure margins! And yet, despite this string of ignominious defeats the team remained remarkably bouyant and pleased with itself, after each match finding solace in the reduced size of the deficit, the number of goals they had scored or how hard they had tried. A similar phenomenon was observed (somewhat more systematically) by Taylor et al. (1983) in their longitudinal case study of a college ice-hockey team. Like my son's football side, this team did not have a very good year, winning only three of their twenty-five games and in one match going down by a full sixteen goals! Nevertheless, Taylor et al., who were able to obtain ratings from team members after every game, report that the overall level of cohesiveness and team spirit stayed high throughout the season. While there were consistent positive correlations between each match's outcome and the team members' levels of cohesion, the latter seldom dipped below the midpoint of the satisfaction scale, even after that crushing sixteen-goal defeat.[4]

How can this maintenance of cohesion in the face of repeated failure be explained? According to Turner et al. (1984), it may have to do with the group members' high level of identification with and commitment to the group which has been fostered by them choosing to belong to the group in the first place. Resurrecting an idea from cognitive dissonance theory (Festinger, 1957; see chapter 2), they argue that when people feel personally responsible for their behaviour – for example, when they have voluntarily chosen to join a group – then if that behaviour results in negative consequences for them (i.e. the group does badly) they will justify these negative consequences by increasing their identification with the group. Such reasoning might go as follows: 'I chose to enter this group because it seemed attractive to me. Nevertheless, the group failed in its objectives. Why, then, did I join this apparently not so good group? It must have been because it was even more important for me than I originally thought.' To test this hypothesis, Turner et al. designed an experiment in which schoolgirls took part in an intergroup problem-solving competition. The crucial variable manipulated was whether the girls believed they had chosen to belong to their group or, alternatively, whether it seemed to have been decided completely by the experimenters. The distinction was, in fact, illusory since nobody was really given any choice but in half the groups it was made to seem that they were by giving them a form to sign which stated that they agreed to stay in their present group. After the competition which, of course, one group had to lose, various scales measuring self-esteem and cohesiveness were administered. For those who had had 'no choice' about their group membership, the usual pattern emerged: winning groups showed greater cohesiveness and reported higher levels of self-esteem than losers. However, for the voluntary 'choice' groups this pattern was completely reversed, as can be seen from figure 7.2; losing groups had more cohesion (and higher self-esteem) than winning groups.

Superordinate goals and intergroup cooperation

Conflicting goals, as we have seen, lead quickly to the development of hostilities between groups, the arousal of competitive ingroup favour-ing biases and internal group cohesion. What about the other side of the coin? How may cooperation and friendliness between groups be induced? According to the realistic group conflict approach outlined at the start of this chapter, the solution is clear. A way must be found

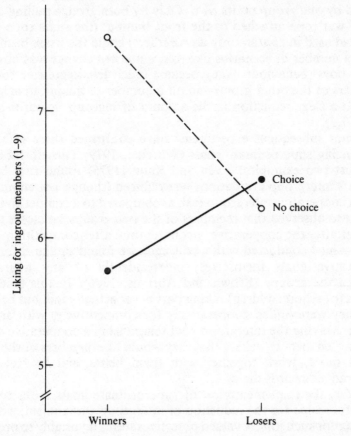

Figure 7.2 Group cohesiveness after victory and defeat (from Turner et al., 1984)

to replace the objectively conflictual relationship between the warring groups with one in which they are *positively* interdependent, each needing the other for the attainment of some desired objectives.

This, at least, was the strategy adopted by Sherif and his colleagues in the 'summer camp' studies. Having so easily generated such fierce competition between the boys, the researchers attempted to reduce the conflict by introducing a series of *superordinate goals* for the groups, that is, goals which both groups desired but which were unattainable by one group by its own efforts alone (Sherif, 1966). One such super-ordinate goal was engineered by arranging for the camp truck to break down some miles from the camp. Since it was nearly lunchtime, the children had a clear common interest in getting the truck started to return them to camp. However, the truck was too heavy to be push-started by one group on its own. Only by both groups pulling on the tug-of-war rope attached to the front bumper (the same rope which they had used in *contest* only days earlier!) could the truck be moved. After a number of scenarios like this, a marked change was observed in the boys' behaviour. They became much less aggressive towards members of the other group and on a number of quantitative indices showed a clear reduction in the amount of ingroup favouritism (see figure 7.3).

Several subsequent experiments have confirmed these effects of introducing superordinate goals (Worchel, 1979; Turner, 1981). To give just two examples: Ryen and Kahn (1975) found that bias in people's intergroup evaluations was reduced (though not eliminated) after a cooperative intergroup task as compared to a competitive task. They also observed that members of the two groups sat closer to one another after the cooperative encounter than after competition. In an experiment I conducted with a colleague we found similar effects for cooperative goals themselves, independently of any interaction between the groups (Brown and Abrams, 1986). In this study the groups (of schoolchildren) taking part never actually met but believed that they were linked cooperatively (or competitively) with another school. Making the intergroup goal relationship a cooperative one in this way led them to believe that they would like members of the other school more, work together with them better and to feel more cooperative towards them.

So far, the implementation of superordinate goals looks to be a powerful recipe for the reduction of intergroup antagonism; working together for such jointly valued objectives seems invariably to promote harmony and to reduce discrimination. But before leaping to that conclusion, we must look at some other research which has identified

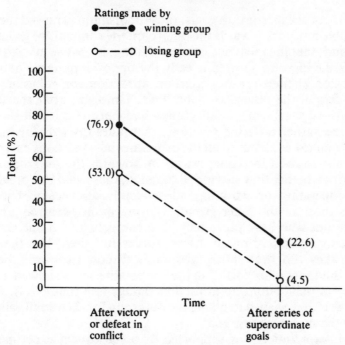

Figure 7.3 The reduction of outgroup prejudice after a series of super-ordinate goals: percentage of categorically unfavourable ratings of outgroup (from Sherif, 1966, p. 92, figure 5.4. Copyright © 1966 by Houghton Miffin Company, Boston. Used by permission)

some important limitations of the superordinate goals strategy. The first of these concerns the *outcome* of the cooperative endeavours and has been investigated extensively by Worchel and his colleagues. Noting that in the 'summer camp' studies the cooperative episodes between the groups were always successful, Worchel et al. (1977) reasoned that it may have been this successful outcome rather than the cooperation itself that led to the reduced hostilities. Accordingly, they designed an experiment in which they arranged for two groups working together on two tasks (e.g. the writing of a toothpaste advertisement slogan) either to succeed or to fail. This cooperative encounter was preceded by a period of interaction in which the groups had variously been competing or cooperating or working independently on two other tasks, the outcome of which was never made clear to them. Worchel et al. suggested that this prior 'history' of intergroup relations might have an important impact on the groups' subsequent reaction to failure in the later cooperative task. So it turned out. After the first phase of interaction, attitudes were predictably affected by the nature of the intergroup goals: those cooperating showed the most favourable attitudes towards the outgroup, the competitive groups the least, and the independent groups falling in between. Attitudes towards the ingroup showed exactly the opposite pattern. As usual, competition elicited greatest ingroup attraction (or cohesion) with slightly less in the other two conditions. However, after the second phase – where, remember, all groups had been cooperating – there were some rather different reactions. Attitudes towards the ingroup hardly changed at all but in all the experimental conditions except one the groups showed increased attraction towards the *outgroup*. Irrespective of whether they succeeded or failed, those who had previously been cooperating or working independently all became friendlier towards those in the other group. The exception occurred amongst those groups who have previously been competing with one another. If the cooperation in phase 2 was 'successful' then, like the other groups, they too were more favourably disposed towards the outgroup. But those who 'failed' in the cooperative tasks showed a sharp decrease in their outgroup attraction ratings (see figure 7.4). It was almost as if they wished to blame the outgroup for their joint failure to achieve the superordinate goal.

This interpretation was supported by a subsequent experiment by Worchel and Norvell (1980) in which, once again, a cooperative endeavour ended in apparent success or failure. This cooperative task was conducted in a laboratory which was made out to be either ideally suited for the task at hand or ill designed for and possibly detrimental to good performance at the task. This time all groups had had a prior experience of intergroup competition and Worchel and Norvell found that reactions to failure varied considerably under the two 'different' laboratory environments (in actuality, of course, the laboratory conditions were always the same). Where conditions were 'perfect' the groups who failed showed decreased liking for the outgroup, as they had in the earlier Worchel et al. (1977) experiment. However, where the poor environment could be blamed instead for their lack of success, liking for the outgroup showed the usual increase. Groups which succeeded invariably showed increased attraction towards the outgroup.

It is not just the outcome of the cooperation over superordinate goals which affects intergroup attitudes. Sometimes people seem to react adversely to the convergence or blurring of boundaries implied by that cooperation. Blake et al. (1964) report how in a chemical plant attempts to reduce interdepartmental rivalry by imposing company-wide superordinate goals were not always successful in eliminating friction. I made a similar observation in the course of a case study of

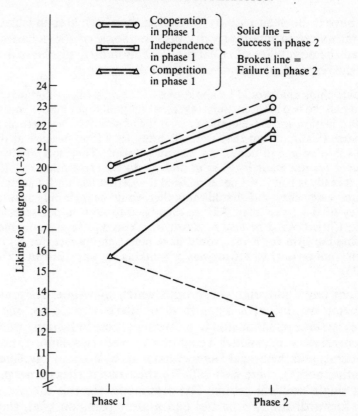

Figure 7.4 Reactions to success and failure in a cooperative task with a prior history of cooperation, competition or independence (from Worchel et al., 1977)

an aircraft engineering factory (Brown, 1978). I shall describe that study in more detail in chapter 8, but for our present purposes a finding from towards the end of my interviews with the shop stewards working in the factory is of interest. I asked the respondents to imagine a situation in which the management announced a 10 per cent redundancy programme across the whole factory. For active trade unionists, as these men were, such a situation represents a clear and common threat to all groups of workers in the factory, one which they could most effectively deal with by a concerted and joint programme of inter-union action. To my surprise, however, only one-fifth of my respondents reacted to this hypothetical situation by talking of developing a joint strategy and cooperative links between the different sections of the workforce.[5] Most seemed to see the threat as one which would have to be dealt with by defending their own area in isolation. The atmosphere of intense rivalry between some of the departments rendered the possibility of collaborative action difficult. Here is how one of the respondents summed up these difficulties:

> I should think that would be about one of the only things that maybe could pull the two main factions together that you've got here – you've got Production and Development . . . if they knew that they were all in the same boat and that they were all going to suffer. Because at the moment, I've got to admit, its 'us' and 'them'. They sort of [two-fingered gesture made by S] at us and we do the same thing . . . It's bad, it really is bad . . . I never realized it was that bad until I actually became a steward . . . I should think that would be their only answer. If they tried – I say 'they' – if we then tried to do it in our separate areas; Christ! We'd be lost wouldn't we? You'd have not only men fighting the firm for a job, you'd have men fighting men for a job, which is not on is it? Not to my way of thinking anyway. (Brown, 1978, p. 425)

It is not only industrial workgroups which sometimes resist closer cooperation in spite of it being in their interests to do so; one can observe the same phenomenon in political parties. In Britain, after the 1987 general election in which a coalition between two minority parties (the Liberals and the Social Democrats) had, by common agreement, done rather poorly, there were calls for these two parties to merge and form a single political group. The arguments for this merger were straightforward: the two parties had a clear common goal, that of defeating the newly elected Conservative government and of preventing the more left-wing Labour party from taking power in its place; this goal would be more easily achieved if the two parties in the coalition pooled their resources and presented a single united front to the electorate. Despite this clear superordinate goal, there was considerable opposition to the proposed merger amongst the Social Democrats who were, it should be added, the younger of the two parties (they had only been in existence for six years). According to one political commentator there were two reasons for this opposition: 'First, with on million fewer votes than the Liberals and with fewer than a third as many MPs, they [the SDP] fear they will simply be swamped in the new grouping. Second, they believe the SDP stands for something distinct from Liberalism' (Robert Harris, in *The Observer*, 21 June 1987). In other words, what was fuelling the resistance to the merger was a feeling on the part of the Social Democrats that their distinctive group identity would be lost in the new conglomerate.

I found evidence of similar reactions to a superordinate goal in two laboratory experiments (Deschamps and Brown, 1983; Brown and Wade, 1987). In both we created a cooperative situation in which two groups had to work together for a considerable financial reward. The task was to rework some factual material into a lively and interesting article suitable for a popular magazine. Their joint success at this would be judged by an expert journalist. However, we varied the manner in which the two groups worked together. In some conditions the two groups were given very *distinctive* roles to play: one had to concentrate on the text, the other on the figures, pictures and headlines. In other conditions they were given very *similar* roles: each was given roughly half the materials to work with. Finally, in the Brown and Wade (1987) study, we made the groups' roles still more similar or ambiguous in a third condition by not allocating any sub-tasks whatsoever. In both experiments we found that varying the distinctiveness of the groups' roles in this way had reliable effects on their friendliness towards the other group. Despite the fact that they were all cooperating towards the same superordinate goal, those with distinctive roles showed greater friendliness towards the outgroup than those whose group contributions were not so easily distinguishable.

These findings suggest that groups which have a common interest in uniting or even just working together more closely may be well advised to think carefully about how to allow each group to retain something of its identity in the joint operation. A good example of how this can be achieved is provided by Hartley et al. (1983) in their study of the 1980 national steel strike in Britain. In the steel industry there are at least six different trade unions representing various occupational groups. When the strike began, a joint trade union strike committee was set up in each area to coordinate the activities of the strikers. Hartley et al. (1983) report how the advent of the strike brought about close inter-union cooperation as they attempted to attain their superordinate goal of a better pay award from their employers. One of the ways in which this cooperation was achieved is interesting and confirms the experimental findings I have just presented. As Hartley et al. describe it:

Interunion cooperation was also the product of an emergent division of labour, especially on the Rotherham Strike Committee. URTU (the road haulage union) representatives were extremely knowledgeable about the local haulage industry (by contrast with ISTC – the main steel workers union) and their contributions concerning it were highly valued. By confining their contributions to this, and rarely participating in the major tactical debates, the URTU members adopted a specialist role on the Rotherham Strike Committee with was conducive to cooperation. (Hartley et al., 1983, pp. 130–1)

Reducing prejudice through intergroup contact

In 1954, in the case of *Brown* v. *Board of Education, Topeka*, the United States Supreme Court ruled that school systems which segregated black and white students violated important articles of the American constitution. That decision proved to be a historic one since it paved the way for the comprehensive desegregation of the American education system over the next three decades. An important ingredient of that legal judgment was the belief that the continued separation of white children from black (or Hispanic or Chicano) children was detrimental to the life chances of those minority groups and instrumental in perpetuating ethnic prejudice and intolerance. The corollary of this belief was that the increased contact between such groups brought about by school desegregation would reverse these harmful effects (Cook, 1979).

In the same year, there was another significant landmark in American race relations. This was the publication of a book called *The Nature of Prejudice* by Gordon Allport (1954). In that book Allport provided not only a seminal analysis of the origins of intergroup prejudice but also a series of influential policy recommendations for its elimination. Taken together, these recommendations have come to be known as the contact hypothesis since underlying all of them is the idea that bringing members of different groups into contact with one another in various ways is the best way of reducing any tension or hostility which might exist between them.

In Allport's view, however, it was not enough just for groups to see more of each other; contact alone would not guarantee intergroup harmony. This point was vividly borne out by some further findings from the 'summer camp' studies of Sherif and his colleagues. Before engineering the superordinate goal situations just discussed, the researchers attempt to reduce the friction between the groups by arranging for the boys to interact with each other in what would normally be pleasant and enjoyable surroundings. A big feast was organized for them on one day; an enormous firework display on another. However, apparently these events did little to ease the hostilities. Indeed, Sherif reports: 'Far from reducing conflict, these situations served as occasions for the rival groups to berate and attack each other' (Sherif, 1966, p. 88).

So, mere contact is not enough, and Allport provided a long list of conditions which he believed needed to be satisfied before one could expect it to have its desired effects. Of these, the most important are as follows: first, the contact between the groups should be prolonged and involve some cooperative activity rather than be casual and lack any real purpose. Without the incentive provided by the presence of a common objective, the interaction is unlikely to generate very much change in attitude. Once again, the 'summer camp' studies provide the key demonstrative findings. Recall that it was only after a series of encounters in pursuit of superordinate goals that the animosity between the groups showed signs of abating. Secondly, there should be a framework of official and institutional support for the new policy of integration. The establishment of Equal Opportunities Commissions or Race Relations Tribunals may not in themselves be effective in outlawing discrimination but they do help to create the kind of social climate in which more tolerant norms can emerge. Thus, the significance of that *Brown* v. *Board of Education* decision may have derived less from its immediate effect on other state education systems (many of whom resisted any change for several years) but more from the impact that it had on social attitudes, an effect which came to full fruition in the Civil Rights Movement of the 1960s. Thirdly, the contact should ideally involve people of equal social status. It is little good, Allport contended, having extensive contact between members of two groups if those groups are fundamentally unequal in status and power. Such encounters are only likely to reinforce prejudiced and derogatory attitudes in the dominant group. The relationship between slaves and their owners, often one involving a high degree of contact, is the obvious example here. On the other hand, if contact takes place between equal status groups then improved intergroup attitudes can result as Clore et al. (1978) found in their study of an inter-racial summer camp. Black and white children, mainly from economically deprived homes, showed evidence of more positive inter-racial attitudes and more generous inter-racial behaviour after only a week's camping together.

With these (and some other) qualifications, Allport argued that such policy interventions as the establishment of integrated housing schemes, the abolition of discriminatory and separatist employment practices, and the introduction of properly desegregated education and leisure facilities could all contribute effectively to the reduction of prejudice.

The thirty years since the publication of Allport's theory have seen much research aimed at testing and verifying its main tenets, most of which has had at least some measure of success; provided that the contact takes place under the favourable circumstances he specified, hostile intergroup attitudes and behaviour do seem to diminish (Amir,

1976). Nevertheless, despite its empirical support, the theory still continues to attract controversy as attempts are made to understand the processes by which contact has its positive effects, and the scope and limits of these effects (see, for example, Miller and Brewer, 1984; Hewstone and Brown, 1986). Three main issues dominate this debate.

The first of these concerns the role of intergroup contact in dispelling ignorance about the outgroup, and the possible effects which this increased knowledge and understanding might have on attitudes towards that outgroup. Stephan and Stephan (1984), for instance, argue that ignorance is an important element in prejudice and that programmes for improving intergroup relations should focus on providing information about the outgroup which highlights similarities between ingroup and outgroup. The rationale behind this is the belief that the discovery of such group similarities will lead to attraction between the respective group members, much as attitudinal agreement between individuals leads to interpersonal liking (Byrne, 1971). This idea has long formed part of the contact theory (see, for example, Pettigrew, 1971). Now, although Stephan and Stephan (1984) present some evidence which is supportive of a relationship - albeit a weak one - between knowledge of an outgroup and positive attitudes towards that group, there are grounds for doubting whether that relationship is central to the successful implementation of contact policies. To begin with, it is surely misguided to teach people that others are similar in all respects and to ignore obvious differences. This will only create more difficulties when these differences become apparent as, for example, when Muslim schoolgirls in Britain appear for physical education lessons wearing long trousers, whilst others are wearing shorts.

Furthermore, one of the presumed consequences of contact - i.e. the discovery of similarities between groups - may sometimes be rather unlikely to occur. For the groups concerned may often, in reality, turn out to have rather *dissimilar* values and attitudes. For instance, in Northern Ireland Catholics and Protestants differ fairly fundamentally in their religious beliefs, and in other respects also (see Trew, 1986). Contact in cases such as these is likely to reveal these differences and hence, according to the causal process alleged to underlie the contact hypothesis (i.e. similarity–attraction), should result in *less* intergroup liking not more.

Finally, there is now ample evidence to show that intergroup discrimination and hostility are caused by factors *other* than a mere lack of knowledge or inaccurate perceptions. Thus, as we saw earlier in this chapter, objective conflicts of interests are a potent source of mutual derogation. Alternatively, to anticipate chapter 8, the mere fact of categorization or factors which affect the identity of group members can be sufficient to trigger discrimination. All these factors, rooted as several of them are in objective features of the environment, are unlikely to be affected by any new knowledge resulting from contact between groups, even under the ideal conditions specified by Allport (1954).

The second problem which crops up persistently in discussion of the effects of contact is that of generalization: how far do the changes of attitude brought about by encounters with outgroup members generalize to other members of the group concerned, especially those whom one has not actually met? At first glance the outlook is gloomy. Time and again researchers have noted the very specific effects which contact experiences seem to have. Harding and Hogrefe (1952), for example, found that white department store workers showed more positive attitudes regarding working with blacks after contact with black employees, but that these changes did not extend to other social activities (e.g. eating together). Similarly, Cook (1978), who has conducted a massive programme of experimental work on inter-ethnic contact, reports how cooperative encounters between members of different groups frequently elicit more positive attitudes towards the actual *participants*, but very little change towards the outgroup as a whole (see also Amir, 1976). Why might this be? Perhaps it may have to do with the fact that often the contact in these studies takes place between individuals *as individuals*, rather than as group members. It is, in other words, interpersonal rather than genuinely intergroup contact (see chapter 1). If this is the case, then any increased attraction which results from the interaction would inevitably be confined to the individuals concerned; there would be no basis to extrapolate the positive attitudes associated with one person to the other members of his/her group. Somewhat paradoxically perhaps, the solution to this dilemma may be to make people's group affiliations *more* salient in the contact situation and not less, thereby ensuring that the participants see each other as representatives of their groups and not merely as 'exceptions to the rule' (Pettigrew, 1979).

Surprising though this idea may seem, there is some evidence to support it. The most relevant is an experiment by Wilder (1984b) in which the typicality of the outgroup member in an intergroup encounter was varied. In one set of conditions the outgroup member, who in this case belonged to a rival college, was made to fit some of the subjects' stereotypes of that college. In another set of conditions, the same person appeared to be rather atypical of the outgroup in question. The nature of the contact was also varied in line with Allport's theorizing on contact. Thus, the contact person behaved either in a pleasant and supportive way towards the real participants, or in a less pleasant and more critical fashion. The interaction took place over a cooperative task. Wilder (1984b) predicted that only where the interaction was pleasant *and* the partner could be seen as typical of her college would the ratings of the outgroup become more favourable. In the other conditions, either there would be no positive change or there would be no basis on which to extend the change from the particular individual to her colleagues at the college. As figure 7.5 shows, Wilder's results were exactly in line with his prediction. Only one condition showed a clear increase in the rating of the outgroup as a whole as compared to the no-contact control condition: this was the pleasant encounter with the typical outgrouper (see also Weber and Crocker, 1983; Rothbart and John, 1985).

A rather different solution to the problem of generalization is advocated by Miller et al. (1985). In contrast to the approach adopted here (and elsewhere, see Brown and Turner, 1981; Hewstone and Brown,

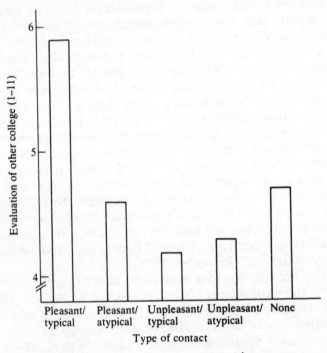

Figure 7.5 Evaluation of an outgroup after contact with a typical or atypical outgroup member (from Wilder, 1984b, table 1)

1986), Miller et al. (1985) argue that for contact to produce successful generalization to other outgroup members, the interaction must be structured so as to eliminate as far as possible any psychological salience of the groups concerned. The optimal arrangement, they believe, is when people interact on the basis of their unique personal attributes and adopt socio-emotional rather than task orientations (see chapter 2). They reason that any strategy that draws attention to existing category divisions is likely to interfere with the positive effects of contact through the arousal of categorization processes which may in themselves lead to intergroup discrimination (see chapter 8). In two quite complex experiments they found some evidence that attention to personal characteristics and socio-emotional concerns (rather than category labels and task issues) did sometimes seem to reduce the degree of bias against outgroup members they had not actually met. However, the fact that the researchers employed only *ad hoc* and criss-crossing experimental groups with minimal psychological significance for their members may have made it easier for the subjects to 'decategorize' the situation and think in interpersonal terms. In real intergroup settings, such as the multiracial classroom context Miller et al. set out to simulate in their experiment, it may not be so easy to distract people's attention from their ethnicity.

This brings us to the third controversial issue, one of particular relevance to those working in multicultural school settings. Should educational programmes draw explicit attention to ethnic differences amongst students or should they adopt an essentially 'colour blind' policy, eschewing all reference to group distinctions? This is not an easy question to resolve. On the one hand, the 'colour blind' policy seems the obvious one to pursue given that an often expressed goal of integrated schooling is the breaking down of ethnic barriers. What better way of doing this, one might ask, than to treat each child as an individual without regard to group affiliations? But, as Schofield (1986) points out, such an apparently progressive approach has its pitfalls. First, given that many schools still practise some form of ability streaming, a 'colour blind' policy can quickly lead to the virtual reestablishment of segregation as socially and educationally deprived minority group students end up in the lower streams and the white majority dominates the academically more prestigious streams. Secondly, such an approach appears to ignore the psychological reality of some intergroup differences, especially for minority group members. The Asian girl in a British school, forbidden by her parents to go swimming because of cultural taboos against the exposure of the female body, cannot simply be regarded as 'one of the others' when it comes to swimming lessons, a point made earlier. Thirdly, the 'colour blind' perspective can quickly lead to an 'assimilationist' position in which members of minority groups are expected to conform to the norms and values of the dominant group (Berry, 1984). Such an outcome, which essentially means that minority group members should give up their distinctive cultural and linguistic identities, may be strenuously resisted by those minority groups, with corresponding negative implications for the success of the school desegregation policy.

An alternative to the 'colour blind' perspective is what Berry (1984) and Schofield (1986) call the 'pluralist' strategy. In this approach, cultural diversity is recognized and different value systems are acknowledged. The aim is to develop teaching methods and curricula which actually capitalize on group differences for the mutual benefit of both majority and minority group students. One way this can be achieved is through the establishment of small ethnically mixed cooperative learning groups in which students are assigned different sub-tasks which are all necessary for the achievement of the overall group goal. So, for example, in a project on nutrition members of different ethnic groups could be asked to research the nutritional basis of their traditional culinary techniques and diets. When these different component parts are put together (much as in a 'jig-saw', Aronson et al., 1978), an overall group project can produced in which all the group members have made a valued and distinctive contribution. As seen in chapter 2, there is a good deal of evidence that such cooperative interdependence has beneficial effects on mutual attraction among group members, and it appears that these benefits also extend to cross-ethnic relations (Slavin, 1985). Of course, such a pluralist approach, based as it is on making some group distinctions more salient, must tread a very delicate path between fostering positive mutual differentiation between groups and avoiding the regression into familiar and destructive patterns of negative stereotyping which so often accompany salient category divisions (Hewstone and Brown, 1986). Nevertheless, as Tajfel (1981) concludes in his discussion of minority groups, 'It may be useful to see in each intergroup situation whether and how it might be possible for each group to achieve, preserve, or defend its vital interests . . . in such a way that the self respect of other groups is not adversely affected at the same time' (Tajfel, 1981, p. 343).

Summary

1 A major determinant of intergroup behaviour is the nature of the goal relationships existing between groups. Where these are conflictual – what one
group gains another loses – intergroup competition and antagonism are
likely to result. Alongside these negative orientations run biases and mis-
perceptions favouring the ingroup.

2 Discriminatory or biased intergroup attitudes may be functional in assist-
ing the group to achieve its objectives. A similar function may underlie
another common consequence of intergroup conflict – increased ingroup
cohesion. Although conflict generates cohesion, there is little evidence that
cohesion in turn intensifies intergroup competition. The outcome of an
intergroup encounter often has important effects on ingroup cohesiveness:
usually winning groups show greater cohesion than losing groups. This
may not happen if group members believe they have voluntarily chosen to
belong to the losing group. In such circumstances failure can result in
raised self-esteem and stronger affiliation to the ingroup.

3 If conflictual goal relationships generate hostility and competition, then
common or superordinate goals should lead to friendliness and cooperation. Much evidence supports this. However, it is important that the outcome of the cooperative endeavours is successful. If the superordinate goal
is not achieved, then there is a danger that the failure may be blamed on the
outgroup, with negative effects on attraction to that outgroup. Furthermore, it is often helpful if groups can make distinctive contributions to
joint ventures so that their identities are not threatened by the blurring
of group boundaries which may occur in the context of superordinate
goals.

4 Contact between groups will lead to friendlier and less-prejudiced intergroup attitudes if it occurs under conditions in which groups of equal
status are cooperating with institutional support. However, controversy
still exists over whether that contact should avoid drawing attention to
group differences, how to maximize the extent to which positive attitude
change will generalize to other outgroup members and the implications of
pursuing 'colour blind' teaching strategies in multiracial schools.

Further reading

Hewstone, M. R. C. and Brown R. J. (eds) (1986) *Contact and Conflict in Intergroup Encounters*. Oxford: Blackwell.

Sherif, M. (1966) *Group Conflict and Cooperation*. London: Routledge and Kegan Paul. Originally published as *In Common Predicament*. Boston, Mass.: Houghton Miffin Company.

Worchel, S. and Austin, W. (eds) (1985) *The Social Psychology of Intergroup Relations*. Chicago: Nelson Hall.

CHAPTER 8

Social Categorization, Social Identification and Intergroup Relations

In chapter 7 we saw how important intergroup goal relationships were in shaping group members' attitudes and behaviour towards both their own group and various outgroups. As noted there, this conclusion sprang from the realistic group conflict approach with its emphasis on the primary determining role played by objective features of the social environment: conflicts over scarce resources and disputes about power were seen *to cause* mutually antagonistic group behaviour, generate heightened ingroup cohesion and lead to biased intergroup perceptions. These social psychological changes are, in the realistic group conflict perspective, functional adaptations of groups to the situations confronting them. In this chapter I want to reverse the emphasis somewhat and ask the question: does the mere fact of belonging to one group have any consequences for our attitudes towards other groups? Does being of one nationality (or religion or ethnicity or class) in and of itself generate predictable orientations towards members of another country (or religion and so on)? As we shall see, there are good grounds for thinking that it does; discriminatory intergroup behaviour arising from simply being assigned to one category rather than another, and independent of any objective relationships between the groups, is remarkably easy to observe.

In seeking to explain this phenomenon I will concentrate particularly on two social psychological processes: social categorization and social identification. The first is concerned with how individuals mentally order their social world. How do we classify other people, why do we do so and what consequences do these social classifications have for our perceptions of and attitudes towards those others? The answers to all these questions have important implications for intergroup behaviour. However, dividing up the world into categories does not only serve the cognitive function of helping us to simplify and make sense of it; it also helps us to define who we are. Not only do we perceive others as members of one group rather than another, we also categorize *ourselves*. Our sense of identity, in other words, derives from our various group memberships. Central to this process of social identification is the importance for individuals of being able to see their group as positively distinct from other groups. How they manage to do this – and what happens when they fail to do so – provides the focus for the second part of this chapter.

Ordering and simplifying the world

Let me begin by recalling from the 'summer camp' studies described in chapter 7 the curious observation of what happened when one of the groups learned that there was another group in the vicinity:

> When the presence of another group was definitely announced, the Rattlers immediately wanted to challenge them, and to be the *first* to challenge. Performance in all activities which might now become competitive (tent pitching, baseball, etc.) was entered into with more zest and also with more efficiency. Since the efforts to help 'all of us' to swim occurred after this, it is possible that even this strictly ingroup activity was influenced by the presence of an out-group and a desire to excel it in all ways. (Sherif et al., 1961, pp. 94–5)

Remember that these indications of intergroup rivalry occurred before the actual intergroup competitions had been announced; just being in one group and becoming aware of a second group seemed to trigger feelings of competitiveness.

This finding was confirmed by Ferguson and Kelley (1964). They found that two laboratory groups, working alongside each other with no suggestion of any competition, nevertheless showed clear favouritism for their own group when evaluating the two groups' products. Such results have been replicated many times since and, indeed, it has even proved possible to observe ingroup bias in situations in which groups are linked explicitly by cooperative goal relationships (Brewer, 1979b; Brown, 1984a). Taken together with Sherif et al.'s (1961) observation these findings strongly suggest that conflictual goal relationships are not actually necessary to elicit ingroup bias in people's judgements. However, they do not conclusively show that mere group membership was the critical variable at work since several other factors were also present; in several of the studies the group members had interacted and worked with one another. What might happen if these factors were removed from the situation and one was left simply with the fact of being a member of one group and not of another?

Mere group membership and intergroup discrimination

Rabbie and Horwitz (1969) were the first to investigate this question. As seen in chapter 2, they found that dividing schoolchildren into two arbitrary groups produced only very slight ingroup favouring biases in their intergroup ratings (Horwitz and Rabbie, 1982). When that group division was accompanied by some interdependence of fate, then those biases became much more evident. However, Tajfel et al. (1971) took this minimal group paradigm one stage further and showed conclusively that mere categorization *was* sufficient to elicit ingroup favouritism. Moreover, this favouritism took the form not of mere bias in pencil and paper judgements but of clear-cut behavioural dicrimination in the allocation of rewards. Like Rabbie and Horwitz, they assigned schoolboys to one of two groups on a very arbitrary basis: their alleged preference for one of two abstract artists Paul Klee and Vassilij Kandinsky. However, in this experiment the children knew only which group they themselves had been assigned to, the identity of their fellow ingroup and outgroup members being kept hidden by use of code numbers. Then, under the general pretext of the experiment ('a study of decision-making'), the children were asked to

Table 8.1 Two sample matrices from minimal group experiment

	Reward numbers												
Matrix 1													
Member 72 of Klee group	18	17	16	15	14	13	12	11	10	9	8	7	6	5
Member 47 of Kandinsky group	5	6	7	8	9	10	11	12	13	14	15	16	17	18
Matrix 2													
Member 74 of Klee group	25	23	21	19	17	15	13	11	9	7	5	3	1	
Member 44 of Kandinsky group	19	18	17	16	15	14	13	12	11	10	9	8	7	

On each page subjects must choose one pair of numbers.

These are two of several different types of matrix used. Matrix 1 was designed to measure general ingroup favouritism, while matrix 2 was designed to measure the tendency to maximize the difference between ingroup and outgroup recipients. In the experiment, these matrices would be presented to each subject at least twice: once as above, and once with the group affiliations of the two recipients reversed.

In the original experiments 1 point = 1/10p. Given that each booklet contained some sixteen pages (each with point values ranging from 1 to 29) the total amount of money which each boy thought he was dispensing was not inconsiderable. In 1970 this probably amounted to about £0.50 which, at today's prices, is probably equivalent to around £3.00.

Source: Tajfel et al. (1971)

allocate money to various recipients using specially prepared booklets of decision matrices (see table 8.1 for examples). The identity of the recipients on each page was unknown but their group affiliation was revealed. To eliminate self-interest as a possible motive in the allocations the children were never able to award mcney to themselves directly.

The results were clear. Although they made some effort to be fair in their allocation, the children showed a persistent tendency to award more money to ingroup recipients than to those whom they believed belonged to the other group. Thus, in matrix 1 in table 8.1 over 70 per cent of the subjects made choices favouring their own group with a mean response from people in the Klee group (say) of between the 14/9 and 13/10 boxes. This was true even when, in absolute terms, the ingrouper might be worse off. For example, in matrix 2 in table 8.1, the mean response from people in the Kandinsky group was somewhere between the 13/13 and 11/12 options. Notice that this choice results in the Kandinsky recipient actually receiving 6 or 7 points *less* than he might otherwise have done but, crucially, he thereby receives more than the Klee recipient. The results are rather surprising when one considers how sparse this social setting really was. The children were allocated to two meaningless groups on a flimsy criterion.[1] They did not interact with members of their own or the other group. The two groups had no current or past relationship with each other. And yet, when asked to allocate sums of money to anonymous others, the children consistently favoured ingroup members over outgroupers. Simply being assigned to a group does, after all, seem to have predictable effects on intergroup behaviour.

Intergroup discrimination in this minimal group situation has proved to be a remarkably robust phenomenon. In more than two dozen independent studies in several different countries using a wide range of experimental participants of both sexes (from young children to adults), essentially the same result has been found: the mere act of allocating people into arbitrary social categories is sufficient to elicit biased judgements and discriminatory behaviour (see Brewer, 1979b; Tajfel, 1982b; Brewer and Kramer, 1985).

Despite this empirical consensus the minimal group paradigm has attracted controversy. This has focused on the interpretation of the observed data as revealing discrimination or fairness (Branthwaite et al. 1979; Turner, 1980, 1983a; Bornstein et al., 1983a), possible demand characteristics associated with the paradigm (Gerard and Hoyt, 1974; Tajfel, 1978a), statistical treatment of the data (Aschenbrenner and Schaefer, 1980; Brown et al., 1980), rival ways of measuring intergroup orientations (Bornstein et al., 1983a, b; Turner, 1983a, b), and doubts about the paradigm's external validity associated with its obviously high degree of artificiality (Aschenbrenner and Schaefer, 1980; Brown et al., 1980).

Space does not permit me to discuss all these issues here. However, it is worth making the following observations on two of the more important issues in question. The first concerns whether or not participants in these experiments are really showing ingroup favouritism or, alternatively, are displaying behaviour better described as some form of 'fairness'. My view is that while it seems clear that people do show a clear propensity towards equalizing ingroup and outgroup outcomes in these situations, it is nevertheless true that they are nearly always more 'fair' to ingroupers than to outgroupers. In other words, although people's choices cluster around the centre or 'fair' point (e.g. 13/13 in matrix 2), when an ingroup member is the recipient on the top line the responses tend to be on the *left* of centre; when an outgrouper is the beneficiary on the same line the responses move to the right of centre. Furthermore, the evidence for this persistent bias is derived not just from particular reward allocation matrices but from a variety of other dependent measures which have also shown that ingroup members or products receive more favourable ratings than equivalent outgroup stimuli (Brewer, 1979b; Brown et al., 1980). Again, this bias is seldom very extreme in its extent but it is both reliable and pervasive. Thus, as Turner (1980) suggests, the intergroup discrimination observed as a result of social categorization represents something of a compromise between ingroup favouritism and 'fairness'.

The second issue concerns the artificiality of the minimal group paradigm which has led some commentators to question its utility since the results may not be generalizable to the 'real world' (Aschenbrenner and Schaefer, 1980).[2] Any attempt to control variables and obtain a measure of precision in observation inevitably involves an element of artifice. Indeed, that artificiality may be an experiment's principal virtue since it permits the investigation of processes or combinations of processes which may not exist naturally uncontaminated by other factors (Henshel, 1980; Turner, 1981b). What these particular experiments show is that mere group membership has predictable consequences in and of itself. What implications these will then have for 'real' groups in the world outside the laboratory depends on the conjunction of those consequences, the consequences of other processes we have already discussed (see chapters 6 and 7) and those which are yet to be considered (see below). Thus, the real point of the minimal group experiments is not that they have

generated a 'finding' which should then simply be extrapolated whole-
sale to all groups everywhere. Rather, they should be seen as a further
step in discovering not just the shape of one of the pieces of the jigsaw,
but how that piece interlocks with all the others.

Categorical differentiation

It is one thing to establish a phenomenon, another to explain it. What
underlies the apparently gratuitous discrimination in these most minimal of groups? One early explanation was in terms of norms (Tajfel et
al., 1971). According to this view, being made aware that one is a
member of a group like 'Klee' or 'Kandinsky' might, in most of the
cultures in which the experiments have been conducted, evoke associations with teams and team games. These associations might make a
competitive norm highly salient. This could then lead to the unequal
allocation of money between the groups in an attempt to 'win'. That
this competitiveness is not full blown might be explained by the
countervailing norm of fairness, another valued attribute in Western
cultures. This form of explanation is supported by the findings from a
cross-cultural study which found variations in the extent of minimal
group discrimination among children of European, Samoan and
Maori origin (Wetherell, 1982). All three groups showed clear ingroup
favouritism, although the latter two showed somewhat less than the
first. These two groups showed more concern with joint outcomes.
One might plausibly surmise that these results reflected the different
cultural norms in the three samples (Wetherell, 1982).

Attractive though such an account may be, it has at least two shortcomings which have inhibited its widespread adoption as an explanation of intergroup discrimination (Turner, 1980). First, such a
normative account needs to be able to predict in advance which of a
number of norms will predominate in any particular situation. After
all, there are a variety of cultural norms that might be relevant: fairness, as we have seen, is one; profit maximization (surely salient in
most Western countries) is another; equity is yet another. Without
some theory of norm salience we are only able to explain 'after the
event' why a particular pattern of discrimination occurred. At present,
such a theory does not exist and so the so-called 'explanation' becomes
little more than a redescription of the experimental findings. A second
and related criticism is that normative accounts are by their nature
rather too general and over-inclusive. They do not really permit one to
predict the systematic variations in response to the minimal group situation which it is possible to observe even *within one culture* (Turner,

1981a). For example, introducing status or changing the nature of the recipients both have reliable effects on levels of discrimination (Commins and Lockwood, 1979; Brown and Deschamps, 1980–1).

A second explanation – in terms of categorization processes (e.g. Doise, 1976) – offers some hope of avoiding these problems. Some earlier work had shown that if a dichotomous classification is imposed on a set of physical stimuli (e.g. lines of different lengths, squares of varying area) then judgements of stimuli falling into different classes will become distorted with the effect that perceived differences *between* the two categories become exaggerated (Tajfel and Wilkes, 1963; Marchand, 1970). A similar phenomenon has been observed with more social stimuli: attitude statements that are categorized as having come from one of two sources may be seen as more polarized than those which have not been so classified (Eiser, 1971).

What underlies these judgemental biases? According to Tajfel (1959, 1981), who pioneered this work, they are a result of a fundamental cognitive process, that of categorical differentiation. Following Bruner (1957), Tajfel argued that social categories are useful to us because they bring order and simplicity to what would otherwise be a too complex and chaotic world. We simply do not have the capacity to respond uniquely to every single person or object we encounter in the course of our daily lives. Indeed, even if we did have that capacity, it would be highly dysfunctional to do so since such stimuli possess many characteristics in common with each other, as well as attributes which mark them out from other stimuli. By assigning them to categories based on these similarities and differences we can deal with them much more economically. To give a simple example: suppose I visit some foreign city. If (as frequently seems to happen on such occasions) I get lost, it is very useful to me to be able to recognize particular categories of people (e.g. police, taxi drivers, local residents) to ask for directions. I will probably find my way to Notre Dame or St Mark's Square much more quickly by using social categories like these than by simply asking the first person I come across, who will probably turn out to be an equally lost fellow tourist! Tajfel suggests that in order for social categories to be useful ordering and simplifying devices like this it is important that they discriminate clearly between class and non-class members. Thus, the function of the differentiation process is to sharpen the distinctions between the categories – and, relatedly, to blur the differences *within* them[3] – so that the recognition of and response to members *and* non-members of those categories is facilitated. In this way our mental and social worlds can be better organized and structured.

If, like Doise (1976), we apply this analysis to the minimal group context it suggests that the situation confronting the experimental participants is sufficiently ill defined for them to latch onto the previously meaningless categories (Klee and Kandinsky) and use them to make sense of it. Once that particular (and only) classification has been adopted the inevitable categorical differentiation occurs, and occurs in the only way possible here, by allocating different amounts to ingroup and outgroup recipients. In fact, Doise suggests that differentiation can occur at any or all of three different levels: the evaluative, the perceptual and the behavioural. The latter, which is manifested in minimal group experiments, is assumed to be the most influential.

The advantage of an approach such as this is that it can make predictions about variations in differentiation/discrimination in particular contexts. Take, for example, the case where two social categories cut across one another (e.g. ethnicity and gender). The categorical differentiation model suggests that in 'criss-cross' situations like this the discrimination observed in terms of any of the original categories will be reduced because the simultaneous processes of between-category differentiation and within-category assimilation effectively cancel one another out (see figure 8.1). Deschamps and Doise (1978) and Vanbeselaere (1987) have found evidence of such reduced differentiation when categories (both real and artificial) are crossed. Similarly, Arcuri (1982) found that memory errors in the recall of a social episode were affected by the presence and arrangement of two different categorizations in a way which supported the categorical differentiation model. Note, however, that if the two crossing categories result in a double ingroup in juxtaposition with a double outgroup (i.e. in figure 8.1, black men v. white women), then there is evidence that this results in enhanced rather than reduced differentiation (Brown and Turner, 1979).

In the criss-cross example just described there were just two categories; in some social situations there may be many more. At an international conference I attended recently I was confronted by more than a hundred people of varying nationality, gender, area of academic specialism, institutional affiliation, language use and skin, eye and hair colour. This raises the important question of category salience: which of the several available dimensions of categorization will actually be used to perceive, understand and respond to situations such as these? Bruner (1957) suggested that the categories most likely to be used in a given situation are those which are most 'accessible' to the person at the time, and those which best 'fit' the stimuli confronting him or her.

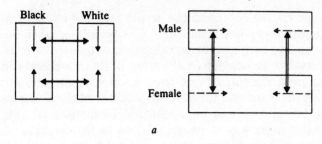

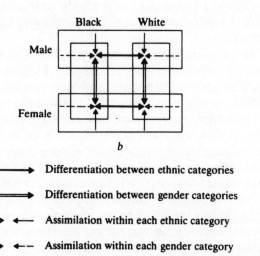

◄────►	Differentiation between ethnic categories
◄═══►	Differentiation between gender categories
→ ◄	Assimilation within each ethnic category
—→ ◄—	Assimilation within each gender category

Figure 8.1 Effect of criss-cross categorizations according to the categorical differentiation model. (a) simple categorization; (b) crossed categorization

Put rather too simply, 'accessibility' refers to attributes of the perceiver, 'fit' to properties of the environment. Thus, what makes a particular category system accessible to a person are such things as values, motives, tasks and goals. These may derive from the culture (or group) to which the person belongs and from immediate situational demands. Thus, for members of a football supporters club the category of 'football team' (ours or theirs) is likely to be particularly accessible on Saturday afternoons during the football season, but somewhat less so whilst sunning themselves on a Mediterranean beach during their summer holiday.

But however disposed a person is to use certain categories rather than others, the categories chosen will not be completely arbitrary but must to some degree represent the actual communalities and differences in the situation; they must 'fit'. I well remember when one of my children went into hospital for an operation at the age of four. Lying in the hospital bed he began to make sense of this novel and somewhat threatening environment. At one point he observed a man in a white coat entering the ward and asked if this was one of the doctors coming to see him. His chosen and highly functional method of simplifying that hospital context was to assign all men to the category 'doctors' and all women to the category 'nurses'. As elsewhere, in this hospital the correlation between gender and occupation was extremely high and hence gender acted as a convenient and highly economical category for subsuming all the different varieties of doctors and nurses he had encountered hitherto.[4]

What are the key determinants of category fit? One, as we have just seen, is a reasonable covariation of the category division with differences and similarities among the people or objects in question (Rosch, 1978; Oakes, 1987). In addition, Campbell (1958) has suggested that such factors as proximity and common fate amongst stimuli will lead them to be categorized together. People who live or work near one another, or who engage in common activities, are more likely to be perceived as belonging to the same group than those who do not. Taylor (1981) has argued that distinctiveness may also act as a cue for category activation. She suggests that the presence of a single woman in a room full of men is more likely to lead to a gender categorization being used than in a sexually heterogeneous situation. Kanter (1977), for example, reports how the presence of a few 'token' women in a traditionally male occupational role (salesperson) in an organization frequently led to the use of the gender categorization (and accompanying stereotypes) by the men.

But the distinctiveness of a member of a category by itself does not always lead to that category being employed, as Oakes and Turner (1986) have shown. They presented subjects with a recording of a mixed-sex discussion group and asked them to form impressions of one of the men in the group. The sex composition of the six-person group was systematically varied so that the target person was either a solo male or one of several men. Half the subjects were asked to focus on the group as a whole, the remainder to concentrate on just the single target individual. Oakes and Turner found that it was mainly under the latter task instructions that the 'distinctiveness' of the target male seemed to lead to sex-stereotyped impressions. When the task was to consider the group as a whole, most evidence of gender categorization was found in the balanced three men–three women group. Oakes and Turner believe that this was because under the 'collective' task instructions the use of gender categories was more appropriate in the three-three arrangement since it provided the most information about the similarities and differences amongst the group members. With the 'individualized' instructions, on the other hand, the task was to identify in what way the target person was special and, under the one-five arrangement, gender was an obvious candidate.

Stereotyping and other cognitive biases

Stemming directly from these categorization phenomena are a number of other cognitive and perceptual biases which have important implications for intergroup relations. People's recall memory, for instance, is affected by the presence of relevant social categories. This was demonstrated clearly by Taylor et al. (1978) when they asked subjects to recall portions of a taped mixed-race or mixed-sex discussion group. Their task was to attribute various statements which had been made during the discussion to the correct speakers. Taylor et al. (1978) found that subjects made more within-category errors than between-category errors. That is, they were more likely to remember correctly the race (or sex) of the speaker who had made a certain remark than they were the precise person. Category-based memory errors like these may also be evaluatively rather selective, as Howard and Rothbart (1980) showed. Like Taylor et al., they asked subjects to recall various statements (about behaviours) which had previously been associated with members of two experimentally created groups. The subjects themselves belonged to one of these two groups also. Some of the behaviours reflected favourably on the speaker, others were clearly unfavourable in tone. Howard and Rothbart found that whilst the subjects were equally accurate at recalling the group origin of the favourable statements, when it came to remembering who had made the *unfavourable* statements they were much better at recalling out-group remarks than ingroup remarks! (see figure 8.2).

Howard and Rothbart's findings suggest that social categories can generate in people's minds certain expectancies about ingroup and outgroup characteristics. This is the phenomenon known more generally as stereotyping: the attribution to all or most members of a category various traits, which may be positive, negative or merely neutral. Stereotyping acts as a kind of mental short-cut so that the perception of a person as belonging to a particular category (e.g. men) carries with it the inference that that person is likely to be 'dominant', 'task orientated', 'aggressive', 'rational' and so on (Ashmore, 1981). Precisely

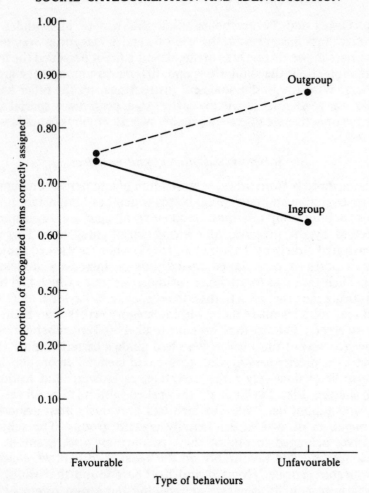

Figure 8.2 Selective recall for unfavourable behaviours associated with ingroup and outgroup members (from Howard and Rothbart, 1980, figure 1. Copyright (1980) by the American Psychological Association. Reprinted by permission of the author)

because stereotypes are short-cuts, they sometimes lead us to make quite incorrect inferences. For example, in our perceptions or memories of confusing or complex situations we will often fall back on stereotypes to fill in the gaps in our minds. Hamilton and Rose (1980) found that people's recall of a number of slides depicting various occupational groups (e.g. stewardess, salesman) associated with different traits (e.g. attractive, talkative) was reliably influenced by common stereotypes of these occupations. Thus, although in the slides which were actually presented there were just as many 'attractive stewardesses' as 'attractive salesmen' (in fact, there were exactly two of each) subjects erroneously remembered more of the former than of the latter, as can be seen in table 8.2. Notice that the frequency estimates along the falling diagonal (where the traits are stereotypic of the occupation) are all well above the true value of 2.0. Hamilton (1981) calls this 'illusory correlation' since subjects are falsely perceiving a correlation between the occupational categories and certain traits when, in fact, there is none.

Table 8.2 Stereotypes as illusory correlations: mean frequency estimates of stereotypic and neutral traits associated with different occupational groups in a recall task

	Traits stereotypic of			
Occupational category	Accountant/ librarian (e.g. perfectionist/ serious)	Doctor/ stewardess (e.g. wealthy/ attractive)	Salesman/ waitress (e.g. talkative/ busy)	Neutral traits
Accountant/librarian	2.7*	2.0	2.2	2.3
Doctor/stewardess	2.2	2.7*	2.4	2.1
Salesman/waitress	1.9	2.1	2.9*	2.3

* Indicates match between stereotypic traits and occupational categories. The true value in all cells should have been 2.0.

Source: Hamilton and Rose (1980), table 1. Copyright (1980) by the American Psychological Association. Reprinted by permission of the author

In a number of studies, Hamilton has explored the origins of such illusory correlational perceptions. One such basis seems to be statistical infrequency or numerical distinctiveness. For example, suppose that one group of persons 'occurs' less often than another (i.e. it is a minority group), and that undesirable behaviours generally occur less frequently than desirable behaviours. This situation is depicted in the upper half of table 8.3. Notice that there is no *actual* correlation between the frequency of desirable behaviours and group membership; the ratio of desirable to undesirable behaviours is the same in each group. However, because of the statistical 'distinctiveness' of the lower right-hand cell, people seem to have a propensity to overestimate its size, that is, they attribute more undesirable behaviour to the smaller group. Hamilton and Gifford (1976) found exactly this using a similar procedure to the Hamilton and Rose (1980) study just described. The attribution of desirable and undesirable behaviours to the two groups is shown in the lower half of table 8.3. It can be seen that, although subjects were relatively accurate in assigning the desirable behaviours to the two groups, they attributed too many of the less frequent negative behaviours to the smaller (and more distinctive) group B and rather too few to group A.[5] Translated into the context of the real world, this suggests that in a predominantly white country people will more readily remember antisocial behaviours (e.g. muggings) by blacks than they will the same acts committed by whites, and hence incorrectly perceive a correlation between criminality and skin colour.

Table 3.3   Statistical infrequency as a source of illusory correlation

	Group	
	A	B
Distribution of behaviours between two groups in the stimuli		
Desirable	18.0 (67%)	9.0 (33%)
Undesirable	8.0 (67%)	4.0 (33%)
Distribution of behaviours between two groups as perceived by subjects		
Desirable	17.5 (65%)	9.5 (35%)
Undesirable	5.8 (48%)	6.2 (52%)

Source: Hamilton and Gifford (1976), table 1

The possession of a stereotype about a group implies that members of that group are seen as similar to one another, at least on that particular dimension. It should be clear, therefore, how stereotypes are a direct offshoot of the categorical differentiation process discussed above. Recall that the process results not only in the perception of exaggerated differences between categories but also of enhanced similarities *within* them. However, this enhancement of within-group homogeneity may not be a symmetrical phenomenon. Jones et al. (1981) asked members of four different university eating clubs to estimate the variability (on a number of traits) of their own and the other clubs. They found that the students consistently perceived the other clubs as being more homogeneous than their own. Similar findings have been reported by Park and Rothbart (1982) with members of three college sororities, and by Wilder (1984a) with artificial laboratory groups. 'They' are all alike but 'we' are distinguishable from one another, it seems.

Wilder (1986) has advanced several arguments to explain this outgroup homogeneity effect. These include such factors as differential amount and quality of interaction with (and hence knowledge of) in- and outgroup members and the need for people to seek individuality within the group (see also Quattrone, 1985). Although some of these explanations undoubtedly have some validity, they cannot be the whole story. To begin with, Jones et al. (1981) reported only very weak or non-existent correlations between people's differential acquaintance with their own and other group members and the degree of relative ingroup–outgroup homogeneity perceived. Furthermore, Wilder (1984a) obtained his results with minimal groups which had had little or no interaction with one another. However, perhaps most damaging of all to the various outgroup homogeneity hypotheses are the results of two studies which actually found greater perceived homogeneity in the *ingroup*. Stephan (1977) observed that children from both segregated and integrated schools in southern USA rated their own ethnic groups as more homogeneous than two outgroups. A colleague of mine noticed that two of the three ethnic groups which Stephan (1977) studied were minority groups (Chicanos and blacks), and also that all other studies reporting the outgroup homogeneity effect had used either majority or equal-sized groups. We speculated, therefore, that a critical variable influencing people's perceptions of intragroup homogeneity might be the majority or minority status of the ingroup. Perhaps a minority, because of its smaller size, might feel a greater need to enhance its cohesion by perceiving the ingroup as internally very homogeneous, and in so doing sustain its identity as a distinctive group. We therefore conducted a minimal group experiment in which the relative size of the groups was varied and in which the subjects were asked to make the usual judgements of ingroup and outgroup variability (Simon and Brown, 1987). As we expected, only those who were not in a minority position showed the usual outgroup homogeneity result; those in the minority showed a reversed *ingroup* homogeneity effect: the outgroup was seen as more variable than the ingroup (see figure 8.3).[6] And in confirmation of our suspicion about the role of social identity processes, these latter subjects showed markedly higher levels of group identification than did the nonminority subjects.

So far we have considered stereotypes as a natural outgrowth of the categorization process, a consequence of the individual's need to simplify and order the world. However, as Tajfel (1981) has pointed out, stereotypes serve another, more social, function: that of helping to explain social events and justify ingroup actions. This ideological aspect of stereotyping has been analysed by Pettigrew (1979), who has pointed to what he calls the 'ultimate attribution error' which often occurs in intergroup settings. Drawing on Ross's (1977) notion of the 'fundamental attribution error' in which people tend to assume internal or dispositional causes for others' behaviours and outcomes but external or situational causes for one's own (unless these happen to be very positive), Pettigrew (1979) suggests that our explanations for

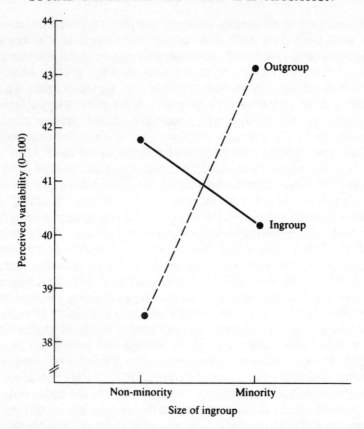

Figure 8.3 Perceived intragroup variability in minority–majority contexts (from Simon and Brown, 1987, derived from table 1)

ingroup–outgroup behaviour may be similarly biased. That is, negative behaviour (for example, some act of violence) by outgroup members will be seen as dispositionally caused ('that's the way they are') while the same behaviour from ingroup members will be 'explained away' as being due to external causes ('we were provoked'). On the other hand, favourable behaviours will tend to be explained in exactly the opposite fashion: positive outgroup actions being attributed to luck ('an exceptional case') or extraordinary effort, whilst the corresponding ingroup actions will be more internally attributed.

Clear evidence of these tendencies was provided by Taylor and Jaggi (1974). They presented Indian (Hindu) office workers with a number of situations in which either a Hindu or a Muslim person behaved in a socially desirable or undesirable manner. For example, one of the vignettes portrayed a shopkeeper who was either generous to or cheated a customer. The subjects' job in each case was to attribute the person's behaviour to some internal cause (e.g. 'Hindu shopkeepers are generous/unreasonable people') or to some external factors (e.g. 'he was compelled by social rules to act as he did'). The Hindu subjects consistently displayed Pettigrew's 'ultimate error': when Hindus behaved positively it was mainly attributed internally; the same behaviour by the Muslim outgroup was attributed to external causes (proportion of internal attributions: Hindus, 58 per cent; Muslims, 2 per cent). For the negative behaviours the reverse occurred (Hindus 2 per cent; Muslims 32 per cent) These biased attributions were accompanied by unfavourable stereotypes of Muslims as being less generous, hospitable, friendly and honest than Hindus.

Although Taylor and Jaggi's (1974) results provided unequivocal evidence of attributions favouring the ingroup, a subsequent study in Malaysia established that this was by no means a universal phenomenon. Hewstone and Ward (1985) replicated Taylor and Jaggi's experiment with Malaysian and Chinese subjects, each making judgements about hypothetical Malaysian and Chinese characters. Although the Malaysians made somewhat similar intergroup attributions to the Hindus in Taylor and Jaggi's study, the Chinese subjects showed no such bias favouring the ingroup. Hewstone and Ward point out that the Malay subjects, like Indian Hindus, were actually a high-status majority group in their society. The Chinese, on the other hand, are a minority discriminated against in Malaysia. Hewstone and Ward speculate that these status differences may well have been important in determining the nature of the two groups' intergroup attitudes. As we shall see in a later section, this is consistent with other findings from stratified intergroup situations.

These two studies were concerned with groups' explanations for everyday events. Another area where people commonly look for and attribute causes are the achievements of different groups in society. Here, too, we find evidence of group-serving attributions. Hewstone et al. (1982) examined the mutual achievement attributions of students attending state and private schools in Britain. The students were asked to make causal attributions about the exam performance (good or bad) of some fictitious students from the two types of school. Perhaps not surprisingly, the state and private school students differed in their explanations. Private school students explained one of their own member's 'success' as due mainly to his superior ability, but the 'successful' state student was seen mainly to have tried hard. On the other hand, a poorly performing private schoolboy was thought not to have tried hard enough, whilst the equivalent state student was thought not to have sufficient ability. As Hewstone et al. (1982, p. 256) put it, it was almost as if the members of these elite schools were saying 'they fail because they're stupid, we fail because we don't try'. A rather different set of explanations was forthcoming from the state school students, however. For them, although successful students (of both types of school) were thought to have ability and tried hard, they believed that luck played a bigger part in the private school student's success.

Similarly discrepant explanations can be found for the causes of unemployment given by those in a job and by those out of work, as Furnham (1982) found. Employed respondents in his study were most likely to believe that unemployed people do not try hard enough to get jobs or are unwilling to move to find work. For them, the unemployed were seen as being (internally) responsible for their plight, a view to be found often enough in the editorial columns of some popular newspapers in Britain. In contrast, unemployed respondents were much more likely to blame external factors for their failure to find work (e.g. 'an influx of immigrants' or 'weak trade unions'). The one internal factor they did cite more often than employed people was, interestingly, sickness and physical handicap. Although these are internal causes in the sense of being located with the person, they are still factors largely outside personal control and in that sense can be considered as psychologically external. Once again, we see that people on different sides of a socially important category division possess very different – and often conflicting – cognitions about the world they inhabit.

The social categorization approach offers a simple and powerful explanation of discriminatory intergroup behaviour in terms of a cognitive process which has been shown to be operative in a number of other psychological domains (e.g. Bartlett, 1932; Piaget, 1942; Bruner et al., 1956). This close connection underlines the point that the origins of phenomena such as stereotyping and other associated biases lie in the workings of normal human cognition and are not, as some theorists have claimed, the product of an aberrant personality type (see chapter 6). Despite these advantages, however, there is one important limitation to such a purely cognitive explanation: it cannot readily account for the assymmetry which is such a pervasive feature of intergroup differentiation. Why is it, in other words, the ingroup (and not the outgroup) which comes off best in intergroup perceptions, judgements, attributions and resource allocations? The categorization approach can account for the fact that groups are made more distinctive from one another, but it cannot explain why that distinctiveness is so often valued positively for the ingroup and negatively for the outgroup. To understand what underlies that *positive* distinctiveness, we must return to a concept which has cropped up several times already in this book – that of social identity.

The search for group distinctiveness

Dividing the world into a manageable number of categories does not just help us to simplify and make sense of it; it also serves one other very important function, it helps us to define who we are. Not only do we classify others as members of this or that group, but we also locate ourselves in relation to those same groups. Our sense of identity, in other words, is closely bound up with our various group memberships (see chapter 2).

A theory of social identity

This idea that social identity derives from group membership has a long history (e.g. Mead, 1934), but it was not until more recently that it was realized that social identity processes might have implications for intergroup behaviour (Tajfel, 1978a; Tajfel and Turner, 1979). This can happen if we assume, with Tajfel and Turner (1979), that by and large people prefer to have a positive self-concept rather than a negative one. Since part of our self-concept (or identity) is defined in terms of group affiliations, it follows that there will also be a preference to view those ingroups positively rather than negatively. But how do we arrive at such an evaluation? Tajfel and Turner (1979) extend Festinger's (1954) social comparison theory (discussed in chapters 3 and 4) and suggest that our *group* evaluations are also essentially relative in nature; we assess our own group's worth or prestige by comparing it to other groups. The outcome of these intergroup comparisons is critical for us because indirectly it contributes to our own self-esteem. If our own group can be perceived as clearly superior on some dimension of value (like skill or sociability) then we, too, can bask in that reflected glory. Cialdini et al. (1976) found evidence of exactly this phenomenon amongst college football supporters. On the days following a victory by their side, college scarves and other insignia – all indicating heightened pride in college membership – were much more in evidence than on days following the defeat. Because of our presumed need for a positive self-concept, it follows that there will be a bias in these comparisons to look for ways in which the ingroup can, indeed, be distinguished favourably from outgroups. Tajfel calls this 'the establishment of positive distinctiveness' (Tajfel, 1978a, p. 83). Note that here again is a further parallel with Festinger's (1954) theory, for Festinger suggested that ability comparisons within the group would be subject to a 'unidirectional drive upwards' (Festinger, 1954, p. 124). However, Festinger believed that the kind of comparisons we are discussing here are rarely made (Festinger, 1954, p. 136).

How can this theory (social identity theory as it is known) help to explain the persistent tendency for people to display intergroup discrimination, even in as barren a context as the minimal group paradigm? Consider again the situation facing the experimental subjects: they have been allocated to one of two equally meaningless groups. Indeed, so meaningless are they that there is literally nothing to differentiate them except the group labels and the fact that they themselves are in one group and not the other. They are referred to by code numbers thus leading to feelings of anonymity. Given this anonymity the only possible source of identity, primitive though it may be, is their ingroup. However, that group is initially indistinguishable from the other group and hence, according to the theory, contributes little positive to its members' self-esteem. Accordingly, the pressures for distinctiveness come into play and the members of both groups seek to differentiate their own group positively from the other by the only means which the experimenters have provided: by allocating more money to fellow ingroupers than to outgroupers. Recall, also, that they will often do this even at the cost of some absolute gain to the ingroup (the maximizing difference strategy).

The presumed link between intergroup discrimination and self-esteem was demonstrated by Oakes and Turner (1980). They found that subjects in a minimal group experiment who were not given the usual opportunity to make intergroup reward allocations showed lower self-esteem than those who were. In a follow-up experiment, Lemyre and Smith (1985) confirmed this result and established that it was indeed the opportunity to display *intergroup* discrimination which elevated self-esteem. Control subjects who, although having been categorized, could only distribute rewards between two ingroupers or two outgroupers, or who could not distribute rewards at all, all showed lower self-esteem than those able to make *inter*group decisions.

Social identity theory, then, seems to provide a plausible account of people's readiness to favour these most minimal of ingroups. But its applicability is not limited to these rather contrived experimental situations; part of its attraction has been its ability to make sense of a wide range of phenomena in natural contexts. I shall describe just three examples; for others see Tajfel (1982a) and Brown (1984b).

The first example is the well-known tendency for groups of workers in industrialized countries to be concerned about the size of wage relativities *vis à vis* other groups of workers. This was particularly prevalent in the British engineering industry in the 1970s but, historically, examples of disputes centering on differentials go back at least as far as the early nineteenth century. For instance, 150 years ago, shoemakers in Wellingborough were campaigning for parity with other areas:

> The humble petition of the Journeymen Cordwainers, of the said town, sheweth, that your petitioners are under the necessity of applying to their masters for an advance in wages, owing to the great rise in the price of provisions at the present time. They beg leave also to state, that they have for a number of years past been receiving considerably less, as wages, than their brother mechanics at Northampton, Daventry, Towcester, Brackley, and Kettering; and also that the advance which they humbly solicit of their masters would only render their wages equal to the wages which their fellow mechanics have been receiving at the above mentioned places. (From a handbill dated 1825, found in William Horner's Memorandum Book and quoted in the *Sunday Times*, 24 April 1977)

What is interesting about these industrial conflicts is that they may have little 'realistic' basis in the sense that there is rarely an explicit conflict of interest between the groups concerned. Often, indeed, the workers may have different employers and may work in a completely different industry. The other important aspect of differentials disputes is – as the words imply – that they are about the *difference* between groups rather than about their levels of wages in absolute terms. These two points were borne out very clearly in a study of an aircraft engineering factory which I conducted some years ago (Brown, 1978).

In this factory there were three main groups of workers: production, development and the toolroom. The latter consisted of the most highly skilled workers and were generally regarded as having the highest status in the factory. The production and development departments were more on a par with each other, although their relative standing was a source of some dispute between them. For many years these three groups – who, incidentally, belonged to the same trade unions – cooperated well together presenting a united and often highly militant front in their negotiations with management. However, a few years before the study this unity had largely disappeared resulting, as I was to discover, in a fairly tense network of intergroup relations. I interviewed a number of shop stewards from each of these departments, quizzing them at some length about their intergroup attitudes. One of my questions asked them to suggest new wage levels for the groups. I found that although existing wage structure was generally maintained (toolroom, then development, then production), each group sought to modify it so that its own position relative to the other groups was improved. The toolroom respondents were particularly notable in desiring a differential over the nearest group which was over three times larger than the existing gap. And it was clear that it was the difference which mattered as much as the absolute wage level. I was able to establish this using some matrices adapted from the minimal group experiments. An example is shown in table 8.4. Respondents had to choose one of the five pairs of options. When presented with this array of wage relativities, members of the toolroom were virtually unanimous in choosing the extreme right-hand pair. Notice that this meant a sacrifice of as much as £2 per week in absolute terms in order to establish a £1 differential over the other groups. That this intergroup differentiation cut across the groups' 'real' interests was realized by one of the stewards: 'Your sectarian point of view is going to cost *you* money and *save* the company money' (Brown, 1978, p. 423). But, as one of his colleagues commented: 'The purchasing power of the money, you see, very often doesn't come into it. It's a question of status – I suppose we're all snobs at heart, or whatever – but honour and status does seem to come into it' (Brown, 1978, p. 419). Observations such as these – and others from the same study described in the chapter 7 – seem much more explicable by social identity theory than the realistic group conflict theory discussed in chapter 7.

As a second illustration of social identity processes, we can turn to the attempts by various ethnic and national groups maintain the integrity of their language (Giles, 1977). Examples abound. Just in Europe one thinks immediately of the Flemings and Walloons in Belgium, the Catalans in Spain, Bretons in France, and Welsh Nationalists in

Table 8.4 Matrix used to measure intergroup differentiation in wage comparisons

	Wages				
Toolroom group	£69.30	£68.80	£68.30	£67.80	£67.30
Production and Development groups	£70.30	£69.30	£68.30	£67.30	£66.30

Source: Brown (1978)

Britain. In all these cases, we see attempts by groups to make themselves distinct from other groups in one of the most fundamental ways of all – language. It is fundamental in two ways. First, because our membership of ethnic/national groups is intimately connected with the use of language or dialect. It is part of our cultural heritage and indeed may even be a defining attribute for group membership. In other words, our social identities may be directly expressed through language. But language is important to intergroup relations in another way: it is also the prime means of communication with outgroups. Depending on the language, dialect or accent we choose to use, we can communicate more or less effectively with members of the outgroup: attempt to integrate or cut ourselves off. So language is both an expression of and a mediator of intergroup behaviour. These considerations have led Giles and his colleagues to explain the behaviour of ethnolinguistic groups in terms of social identity processes (Giles and Johnson, 1981). Giles has suggested that where identity is threatened, efforts to establish distinctiveness may take the form of linguistic divergence, and two experimental studies have found exactly that (Bourhis and Giles, 1977; Bourhis et al., 1978). Both were set in the context of a language laboratory and in both the language students were confronted with a speaker who threatened their linguistic identities. Clear evidence of language divergence by the students was found, either by broadening their accent or by switching languages altogether. This differentiation is particularly significant since, as some earlier work of Giles had established, in most inter*personal* contexts people tend to converge in their language use (Giles and Powesland, 1975). That in intergroup contexts the opposite can happen is indicative that different (identity) processes may be at work (see chapter 1).

As a third example, we consider another occupational group: nurses, people who are more usually associated with caring and self-sacrifice than with group favouritism and animosity. Indeed, this cooperative ethos is enshrined in some codes of nursing ethics (e.g. UKCC, 1984). And yet there is evidence that nurses too are quite ready to display ingroup bias, particularly in relation to their nursing colleagues. For example, in Skevington's (1981) study of a British hospital it was found that higher-status Registered nurses considered themselves as generally superior on a wide range of task-related attributes (e.g. intelligence, confidence, responsibility), whilst the lower-status Enrolled nurses regarded themselves (and were regarded) as superior on more socio-emotional dimensions (e.g. cheerful, thoughtful). A similar phenomenon was observed by van Knippenberg and van Oers

(1984) in their study of academic and psychiatric nurses in The Netherlands. Like Skevington (1981), they found clear evidence of ingroup bias on attributes specific to each group, e.g. theoretical insight v. interpersonal relations (see table 8.5). As can be seen, there was some agreement between the groups as to their respective merits on these attributes: the Baccalaureate nurses (BN) are generally regarded as having superior theoretical insight, whilst the social psychiatric nurses (SPN) are seen as having better interpersonal skills. However, the ratings also convincingly showed that the concession that an outgroup might be superior on one set of dimensions was considerably outweighed by the claim to *ingroup* superiority on the other set. The degree of positive differentiation favouring the ingroup on the latter was generally twice as high as the amount of negative differentiation on the other attributes. Moreover, van Knippenberg and van Oers (1984) also found that the dimension on which each group showed the most ingroup bias (i.e. theoretical insight for the BN group and interpersonal relations for the SPN group) was also the aspect of nursing which each group regarded as most important. This selectivity in making positive intergroup comparisons has been found in other studies also (e.g. Mummendey and Schreiber, 1984), and reminds us that the pursuit of positive distinctiveness is not an unthinking or generalized group response but is always relative to the particular intergroup context in which people find themselves.

In both of these studies the source of the intergroup differentiation seemed traceable to efforts by the nurses to maintain their professional identity. However, a study by Oaker and Brown (1986) of relations between specialist nurses (e.g. intensive care, operating theatre staff) and general nurses on the wards raised some questions about this interpretation. Whilst finding clear evidence of ingroup favouritism (both groups regarded their own group as friendlier than the other) and some evidence of discord between the groups, we failed to establish a positive correlation between that ingroup bias and

Table 8.5 Ingroup bias in intergroup perceptions of Dutch nurses

	Theoretical insight		Interpersonal relations	
Respondents	BN	SPN	BN	SPN
Baccalaureate nurses (BN)	+ 0.9	− 0.6	− 0.2	+ 0.5
Social psychiatric nurses (SPN)	+ 0.1	− 0.6	− 0.8	+ 0.4

The higher the score, the higher the evaluation.

Source: van Knippenberg and van Oers (1984), table 2

strength of ingroup identification. In fact, quite contrary to what social identity theory would predict, the observed association was *negative*. There is thus some doubt about the exact nature of the presumed link between intergroup differentiation and social identity.

These doubts are reinforced by two further studies in which the predicted positive association between identification and differentiation was examined in some detail (Brown and Williams, 1984; Brown et al., 1986). Both were carried out in industrial settings: one a bakery, the other a paper mill. In both, the ingroups of interest were the respondents' own workgroup and the outgroups were other workgroups in the factory and the management. On a variety of indices, clear positive differentiation was observed (see table 7.1 in chapter 7). The identification with the ingroup was also predominantly positive. And yet, within each group, the relationship between the strength of this identification and the indices of differentiation was very variable, ranging in different groups from positive (as predicted), through non-existent to negative. A much more powerful and reliable predictor of intergroup differentiation in both studies was perceived conflict with the outgroup, a finding more in keeping with the Sherif approach considered in chapter 7.

How may these findings be understood? One possibility is that the notion of social identity as merely a cognitive self-definition or a sense of belonging to a group is too narrow. Perhaps we need to think of group memberships not just as contributions to self-concept and self-esteem, as proposed by social identity theory, but also as providing a variety of social interpretations or ideologies for the individual. For instance, membership of a trade union could have a number of meanings (self-interest, political, moral), all of which could result in an equally strong sense of attachment or identification. But the kind of intergroup attitudes and behaviour displayed to any given outgroup (management, say) will depend crucially on which of these meanings predominates in the individual or group (Brown et al., 1986).

Responses to status inequality

The three examples I chose to illustrate social identity processes all had one other feature in common, a feature characteristic of nearly all intergroup relationships in the real world: they all featured groups of unequal status. The three groups in the aircraft engine factory formed a clear hierarchy among themselves and, of course, all enjoyed much less power and status than their employers (Brown, 1978). Minority group languages or dialects are nearly always devalued by the dominant linguistic group (Giles and Powesland, 1975). In each of the nursing studies there was an identifiable 'inferior' group. These are just three (fairly mild) instances of status disparity. To list the numerous other examples of inequality and oppression around the world would take up the rest of this chapter, if not the book. Instead, let us consider what happens when people belong to a group of dominant or subordinate status.

Let us consider the case of the high-status group first. For members of such groups there are few immediate identity problems. On a whole host of comparative criteria, their group emerges as superior to other groups in society. Obvious examples of such high-status groups are those in managerial executive positions in business or those working in the professions (e.g. medicine, law). Not only do they get paid considerably better than the vast majority of society but they are consensually accorded prestige and respect. From the point of view of social identity, therefore, their self-concept (derived from their group's high standing in relation to other groups) is both secure and positive. Thus, their answers to questions about the comparative worth of their own and other groups are likely to reflect this (to them) self-evident superiority. They are, in other words, likely to show clear signs of positive intergroup differentiation. Experimental studies of intergroup behaviour in hierarchical situations confirm that this generally happens (van Knippenberg, 1984). Sachdev and Bourhis (1987), for example, modified the minimal group paradigm devised by Tajfel et al. (1971) so that the groups created seemed to be of equal or unequal ability on some creativity measure. The subjects in the experiment were then asked to evaluate the creativity of ingroup and outgroup members on some other task. As is clear from figure 8.4, both the high- and equal-status groups showed distinct ingroup favouritism in their evaluations, whilst the lower-status groups tended to favour the outgroup.

The fact that the equal-status groups in this study showed almost as much bias as the high-status groups suggests that the intergroup differentiation (or bias) revealed by these two groups may be serving rather different functions. For the high-status groups it may be merely to maintain their already secure dominance; for equal-status groups, on the other hand, it may be to *achieve* some distinctiveness, as I suggested earlier in putting forward the social identity explanation of discrimination in the minimal group situation. Indeed, it could be argued that it is precisely in circumstances of status equality that one might expect the greatest intergroup rivalry (and hence discrimination) since it is there that groups have the least positive distinctiveness (Brown, 1984c). A needle match between two teams adjacent in a league is

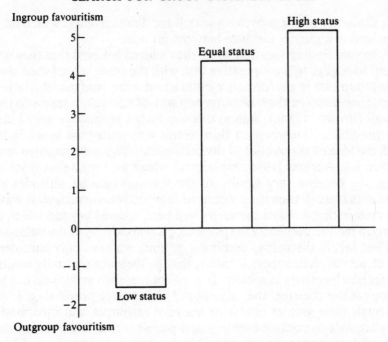

Figure 8.4 The effects of status position on ingroup bias (from Sachdev and Bourhis, 1987, derived from the three favouritism measures in table 1)

likely to elicit much more competitiveness than a game between two teams at opposite ends of the table.

It was this idea that formed the basis of a series of experiments I conducted on the effects of intergroup similarity (Brown, 1984a; Brown and Abrams, 1986). In these experiments schoolchildren believed that they were undertaking a task in conjunction with members of another school. That school was described as being variously rather similar to them in status (they were alleged to be about as good as them at various academic disciplines) or was better or was worse than them. In addition, the prevailing attitudes towards those school disciplines at the other school were depicted as either similar or different. We found three main results. The first was that when the children believed that the other school held similar attitudes to them they thought they would like them better than when the outgroup attitudes were different (Brown, 1984a; Brown and Abrams, 1986). This parallels similar findings obtained at the interpersonal level and is predictable from Festinger's (1954) social comparison theory (Byrne, 1971; see chapter 4). It was also rather against the social identity hypothesis that similarity might provoke a search for distinctiveness which might then lead to a greater distance between groups.

A second finding was that when the children believed that they were about to engage in a cooperative task with the other school their levels of ingroup bias in performance evaluations were *moderated* relatively when they believed that the outgroup was of equivalent status to their school (Brown, 1984a). Again, this was rather against the social identity prediction. However, a third result was somewhat more in line with the idea of the pursuit of distinctiveness. This was obtained in the Brown and Abrams (1986) experiment where we found that when the outgroup became very similar to the ingroup (similar attitudes *and* similar in status), then the amount of ingroup bias *increased*. It was as if a certain threshold of similarity had been crossed beyond which the ingroup felt threatened by the psychological proximity of the outgroup.

Thus far, in discussing dominant groups, we have only considered the effects of their superior *status*, that is, their consensually positive evaluation by others in society. But, of course, such groups do not just enjoy greater prestige, they also usually have more *power* (Ng, 1980). Through their greater access to material resources and information they are able to control events – and people – to a larger extent than subordinate groups. In a factory it is the managers who, by and large, determine production targets, line speeds and the like; it is the workers who have to implement them. How do members of high-power groups treat those with less power? Common observation suggests not very well. History is replete with instances of those in positions of power wielding that power for their own ends to the detriment of those below them.

Curiously, however, social psychologists interested in intergroup relations have rather neglected this important topic. One of the few experiments to examine the effects of power differentials is by Sachdev and Bourhis (1985) (see also Ng, 1980, 1982 for other work in this area). Once again, they employed the minimal group paradigm in which subjects were required to make decisions about the allocation of course credits between ingroup and outgroup members. However, depending on experimental condition, they believed that their group's allocations would be variously completely, only partly or not at all instrumental in deciding the actual distribution of the course credits. In fact, the degree of influence that they believed their decisions would have was varied from 100 per cent (absolute power), through 75 per cent (high but not complete power), 50 per cent (equal power), 25 per cent (low power) to 0 per cent (no power). Figure 8.5 shows the amount of ingroup favouritism which was displayed in each of these five conditions. Note that the groups became steadily more discriminatory as their power increased, with the exception that those with absolute power appeared to moderate their bias slightly. Sachdev and Bourhis (1985) suggest that the 'absolute power' groups were so secure in their position that they could affort to exhibit a form of 'noblesse oblige' *vis à vis* their powerless counterparts. The slightly less secure 'high-power' groups, on the other hand, were clearly fully intent on consolidating their superiority still further. As we shall see shortly, these may not be the only circumstances when dominant groups seek to take advantage of their advantages.

Now let us turn our attention to the groups at the other end of the spectrum. What are the consequences of belonging to a group of subordinate status? At first glance these seem negative. Members of

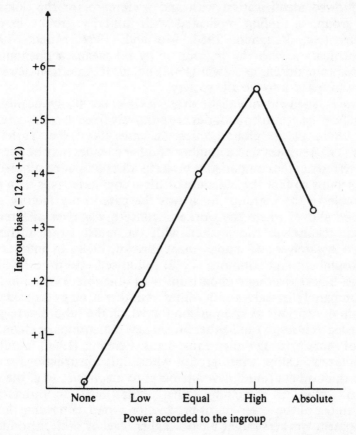

Figure 8.5 The effect of power on intergroup discrimination (from Sachdev and Bourhis, 1985, averaging across three favouritism measures in table 1)

such groups will frequently discover that they have lower wages (if they have a job at all), poorer housing, fewer educational qualifications and are consensually regarded as being inferior on a number of criteria. Thus, not only are they worse off in a direct material sense but psychologically too they may well be disadvantaged. If identity is indeed maintained through intergroup comparisons, as social identity theory suggests, then the outcome of the available comparisons is unremittingly negative for their self-esteem.

One reaction to this state of affairs is simply to try to leave the group, as Tajfel (1978a) has suggested. Examples of members of 'inferior' groups distancing themselves physically or psychologically from their group are not hard to find. In their classic studies of ethnic identification, Clark and Clark (1947) found that black children in the USA showed identification with and preference for the dominant white group, a finding replicated with minority groups in other countries (e.g. Vaughan, 1964; Morland, 1969; Milner, 1975).[7] Disidentification with the ingroup is by no means a phenomenon restricted to children, as Lewin (1948) noted of American Jews who attempt to 'pass' into Gentile society.

However, such individualistic strategies may not always be possible, especially if the group boundaries are relatively fixed as is the case with many ethnic and religious groups. In cases like these, Tajfel and Turner (1979) suggest that a number of other avenues may be pursued. One is to restrict the comparisons made to other similar or subordinate status groups so that the outcome of these comparisons is then more favourable to the ingroup. Such was the case in my factory study described above, where the workers' concern was over differentials amongst themselves rather than with the much larger difference between themselves and management (Brown, 1978). In another context, Rosenberg and Simmons (1972) found self-esteem to be higher amongst blacks making comparisons with other blacks than in those who compared themselves with whites. Another strategy is to side-step the main dimensions of comparison (on which the subordinate group is regarded as inferior) and either invent new dimensions or change the value of those existing dimensions. Thus, Lemaine (1966) found that in a children's camp, those groups whose hut constructions seemed poorer than others found new attributes to emphasize (e.g. the hut's garden). I observed something rather similar in the aircraft factory. One member of the lower-status production group, conceding that the development workers might have a higher level of skill, introduced a new argument in production's favour: the extra responsibility of producing airworthy engines:

because it was Development, you could leave several bolts out here and there, you know, it was a gash set up. That is why *we* claim as Production workers that *we* build an engine that goes upstairs in the plane. When *they* build one it goes over the test bed, and all that can do is ruin the test bed. If it goes up there – well that's the end of it if it falls out of the sky. Concorde? You can forget it if *it* falls out the sky; that's the end of it. The Yanks would love that! . . . That adds strength to the fact that the Production side are as good as Development. (Brown, 1978, p. 416)

The lifestyles of subcultural groups like the 'punks' of the 1980s or the 'hippies' of the 1970s, which were characterized by a complete negation of the dominant society's values in fashion, music and morality, may be another example of the same phenomenon. Still a third route is to confront directly the dominant group's superiority by agitating for social and economic change. Such were the goals of the Black Movement in the USA in the 1960s and the revolution in Spain in 1937, and such are currently the demands of feminist groups in many industrialized societies.

Which of these tactics will be chosen may well depend on the prevailing social climate. If it is such that no real alternative to the status quo may be conceived, then the first two options seem more likely; without some sense that the status and power relations are not fixed it is difficult for subordinate groups openly to challenge the existing order (the third strategy). Tajfel and Turner (1979) have proposed that for such 'cognitive alternatives' to exist, some perception of instability and illegitimacy are necessary. The system must be seen to be changing and to be based on arbitrary principles of justice. Experimental studies support this idea.

One of these was conducted by Caddick (1982) and involved school students in two small face-to-face groups. On the pretext of an interest in group productivity, he gave the groups two tasks to perform (drawing a map of the school grounds; 'spot the ball' football quiz). On the second of these he manufactured a status difference between the groups by announcing that one group had done very much better than the other. For half the sessions this status difference seemed quite fair and above board and this legitimacy was reinforced in a third task in which the same group appeared to win. However, in the remaining sessions an element of illegitimacy was introduced by the experimenter drawing the children's attention to the fact that the winning group had in fact had a slightly easier task. This unfairness was compounded in the third task when the winning group was made to seem unwilling to give the other group a chance with the easier task.[8] The students were then asked to evaluate the two groups' performance on the earlier map-drawing task. The levels of ingroup bias are shown in table 8.6. Notice that, as usual, the higher-status groups display more bias than the losing groups. However, both high- and low-status groups increase their intergroup differentiation sharply under the conditions where the status difference is rendered illegitimate. The subordinate group now sees the possibility of achieving a positive identity after all (since the contest was so manifestly loaded against them) and forcibly assert the superiority of their group. The dominant group's response in the 'illegitimate' conditions, on the other hand, may have been motivated more by a desire to defend their now fragile superiority.

Table 8.6 Reactions to 'legitimate' and 'illegitimate' status relations: levels of ingroup bias in group performance evaluations

	Status difference	
	Legitimate	Illegitimate
High-status groups (winners)	+ 9.6	+ 27.4
Low-status groups (losers)	+ 2.2	+ 21.3

A positive score indicates ingroup bias.

Source: Caddick (1982), table 1

Such reactions to insecure status relationships by low-status groups have been observed in other studies also. Laboratory experiments by Turner and Brown (1978) and Brown and Ross (1982) confirm that perceptions of illegitimacy and instability are associated with enhanced ingroup bias and a reversal of the usual trend for subordinate groups to show deferential favouritism towards the outgroup. And Vaughan (1978), in a sociohistorical analysis, has convincingly demonstrated a connection between the ethnic preferences amongst Maori children and changes in New Zealand society, particularly the growth of urbanization and the rise of Maori consciousness. In the 1960s amongst rural Maori groups, whose relationship to the dominant Pakeha (white) group was somewhat serf-like, there was a strong tendency for Maori children to identify with white doll figures and to hold outgroup favouring (and ingroup denigrating) stereotypes. In contrast, a decade later, after the worldwide socioeconomic upheavals of the 1960s and in urban areas in New Zealand (where such changes were most in evidence), Maori children were showing clear ingroup preference in both their ethnic indentifications and their intergroup stereotypes. It seems, then, that where groups coexist in stable and justifiable status relations subordinate groups show little sign of throwing off their 'inferiority'; if, however, the hierarchical relationships appear to be undergoing change or are seen to be based on illegitimate assumptions, then such groups may start to assert themselves by displaying ingroup favouritism and a rejection of the dominant group's 'superiority'.

These effects of status inequalities on social identity processes, though still imperfectly understood, fit rather well with some of the consequences of relative deprivation discussed in chapter 6. There, it will be remembered, we concluded that people's feelings of deprivation were primarily generated by a sense of injustice about the position of one's own group in relation to another. Whether that comparison led to feelings of deprivation or gratification depended crucially, as we saw, on which outgroup was chosen. Relative deprivation theorists stress the importance of similarity as a basic for choice and, indeed, as some of the work described earlier in this section indicated, outgroup similarity does sometimes seem to lead to comparability. However, the research on the effects of instability and illegitimacy suggests that even apparently very disparate groups can become comparable if the basis for the difference between them becomes undermined by structural change or a new ideology. Thus, to return to the example of South Africa with which we ended chapter 6: our analysis suggests that the upsurge in anti-government protest over the past decade and the corresponding tightening of the screw by the forces of the state are both fuelled, in part at least, by a realization by both sides that the old order is no longer immutable. That realization, in turn, is surely not unrelated to the deepening crisis in the South African economy and the now worldwide condemnation of the system of apartheid.

A few last words

Before concluding this chapter – and this book – a few last comments are necessary. It will probably not have escaped attention that I have liberally sprinkled this book with examples of group phenomena from the real world. Some of these, particularly in the last three chapters, have concerned quite large groups or wide-scale social change. I have done this in the belief that the processes I have been discussing are not mere theoretical abstractions but have real and very concrete social implications. However, in providing these illustrations I do not want for one moment to imply that social psychology – even a thoroughgoing group psychology – can provide all, or even most, of the explanation for these phenomena. Such an explanation will never be complete without a proper understanding and analysis of the historical, political and economic factors at work in each context, and I believe that social psychologists would do well to be more modest about the extent and explanatory power of their theories.

Nevertheless, it must also be recognized that, in the last analysis, group behaviour does still involve the actions of individuals. It was dividual citizens and policemen involved in that Bristol 'riot' which I described in chapter 1; it was individual shop stewards (I still remember some of their names) who talked of their concern over eroded differentials in the aircraft engine factory in this final chapter. Thus, however important sociostructural forces undoubtedly were in all the situations described in these pages, it is still important to know how these forces were perceived by, reacted to and reshaped by the groups of individuals concerned. This, for me, is ultimately what the social psychology of group processes is all about.

Summary

1 Conflicts of interest between groups are not necessary for the arousal of biases favouring the ingroup. This is shown by studies involving 'minimal groups' in which the mere fact of group membership was enough to trigger intergroup discrimination in the allocation of rewards.

2 One explanation for this apparently gratuitious discrimination is in terms of categorical differentiation, a cognitive process in which the differences between groups are exaggerated and the similarities within them are enhanced. This categorization process is highly functional in helping to simplify and systematize the individual's social world.

3 A number of cognitive biases stem form this categorization process: stereotyping (the attribution of traits to all or most members of a group even when there is no basis for such an inference); memory distortions such that unfavourable and stereotypical attributes of outgroups are remembered more easily than favourable or counter-stereotypical characteristics; illusory correlation (the false perception of an association between trait frequency and group membership, sometimes based on statistically 'distinctive' infrequent co-occurrences); differential perception of homogeneity within the ingroup and the outgroup, usually such that the outgroup is seen as more homogeneous, except when the ingroup is a small minority, when the reverse occurs; and attributional errors such that causal explanations for intergroup events consistently favour the ingroup.

4 The categorization approach can explain the enhanced differentiation between groups, but not the fact that the differentiation is asymmetrical,

consistently biased towards the ingroup. To explain that positivity bias, a theory of social identity has been proposed. In this theory people's sense of self-worth partly derives from their group memberships and the evaluation of those groups compared to other groups. It is assumed that people prefer a positive self-concept which then leads them to seek out some positive distinctiveness for their ingroup(s) in the form of biased perceptions and discriminatory behaviour. However, the link between identification and positive intergroup differentiation cannot be a simple one since observed correlations between the two variables are not consistently strong.

5 Most intergroup situations involve status and power differences. Dominant groups generally show more ingroup favouritism than subordinate groups, except when the status differences are seen to be illegitimate or unstable. In such circumstances subordinate groups may challenge the 'superiority' of dominant groups.

Further reading

Doise, W. (1976) *L'articulation psychosociologique et les relations entre groupes*. Brussels: A. de Boeck. English translation: *Groups and Individuals*. Cambridge: Cambridge University Press, 1978.

Hamilton, D.L. (ed.) (1981) *Cognitive Processes in Stereotyping and Intergroup Behaviour*. New York: Lawrence Erlbaum.

Tajfel, H. (1981) *Human Groups and Social Categories*. London: Cambridge University Press.

Turner, J.C. and Giles, H. (eds) (1981) *Intergroup Behaviour*. Oxford: Blackwell.

Worchel, S. and Austin, W. (eds) (1985) *The Social Psychology of Intergroup Relations*, 2nd edn. Chicago: Nelson Hall.

Notes

Chapter 1 The Reality of Groups

1   For a more detailed discussion of the issues covered in this and the following section, see Brown and Turner (1981).
2   Note that in suggesting that we may need other kinds of theories I am not proposing here that those need to be pitched at a different level of explanation. Indeed, with Allport, I believe that a social psychology of group processes should be concerned with the behaviour of individuals. The difference is that I am concerned with individuals as group members and not with individuals as individuals. See also Taylor and Brown (1979) and Moscovici (1979) for a spirited debate over this question of levels of explanation.
3   I am indebted to my colleague Stephen Reicher for this example and also for much of the analysis which follows (see Reicher, 1982, 1984a).
4   In fact, of course, no shocks were actually administered.
5   Actually, Diener is somewhat ambiguous on this question of loss of identity since he does allow that groups can occasionally provide people with a social identity (see Diener, 1980, pp. 234–5). This is much closer to the position taken here.
6   A similar pattern did not hold for social scientists, a result which Reicher attributes to a methodological factor (there were far fewer social scientists taking part in the study, which affected the potency of the deindividuation manipulation for them).

Chapter 2 Elementary Process in Groups

1   Aronson and Mills, however, did not formally check with the subjects that this was the case.
2   The authors do not reveal what voltage these shocks were and neither do they discuss the questionable ethics of this manipulation.
3   See, for example, Schlenker (1975) for an alternative explanation of the severity–attraction relationship.
4   Note that although the group members were positively interdependent

in relation to each other, their group was *negatively* interdependent in relation to other groups. See Julian and Perry (1967) for a later experiment which attempted to remove this confounding.

5 We shall come back to this work in chapter 4 in our discussions of social influence.

6 The Centre for Group Dynamics – the base for Lewin and his colleagues – was at the Massachusetts Institute of Technology in the late 1940s. Bales himself was at Harvard, not many miles away. Although Bales actually worked at the Centre, curiously he does not include a reference to Lewin in his first book (Bales, 1950), although several of Lewin's associates are mentioned, including Deutsch. In later publications he has made explicit the influence which Lewin's ideas had in the development of his work (Bales and Cohen, 1979; Bales, 1984).

7 In this he is clearly adopting a functionalist perspective, a point underlined by his close association with Parsons, a leading figure in functionalist sociology (e.g. Parsons et al., 1953).

8 One of the virtues of Bales's system is that it can be both a research tool and a useful pedagogic device. I have found that the inclusion of an observation exercise based on Bales's system into an undergraduate course provides a valuable experiential introduction for both observers and participants into some of the regularities and complexities of intragroup process (see Foot, 1982).

9 In practice this reduces to twenty-six since the central area (neutral on all three dimensions) is seldom used.

10 Similar concepts have been developed in other areas of social psychology: for example, the 'rules of the situation' discussed by Argyle et al. (1981) in the context of interpersonal interactions, and the 'subjective norm' variable in Fishbein and Ajzen's (1975) theory of reasoned action.

11 The illusion has long been known to astronomers and navigators used to observing stars at night. The experience of movement is compelling and persists even when one is fully aware that the light does not move. The subjects in the experiment, however, were not actually told that the movement was illusory, merely that 'after a short time the light will start to move' (Sherif, 1936, p. 95).

12 Remember that the autokinetic illusion depends for its effect on having total darkness, so dark that one cannot even see one's hand in front of one's face. This is, in fact, quite an unusual situation for may people. Even at night there is usually some residual ambient light which, after one's eyes have dark-adapted, permits a fair degree of vision.

Chapter 3 Structural Aspects of Groups

1 This also is consistent with Bales's idea of an equilibrium between the two orientations (see chapter 2).

2 O'Rourke's (1963) study underlines the importance of combining both field and laboratory techniques in social psychological research. His data suggest that some of the extrapolations which have been made from the prototypical Bales-type of laboratory group may not be warranted once one examines the behaviour of naturally formed groups. The value of pursuing such a two-pronged methodological strategy was established long ago by Lewin (1947) and Katz (1953) but is sometimes overlooked by current group researchers (cf., for example, Turner, 1981b).

3 Here we shall only be concerned with ability evaluation; validation of opinions is dealt with in chapter 4.

4 Although, admittedly, in an archival study such as this Simonton (1980) could hardly have obtained data on other more psychological attributes of the generals!

5 Note that Fiedler, like Bales, assumes the task and socio-emotional orientations to be bipolar opposites.

6 Meta-analysis is a statistical technique for combining the results of several independent studies. The increased sample size resulting from this aggregation permits a more powerful test of a hypothesis than the studies considered separately (Rosenthal, 1978).

Chapter 4 Social Influence in Groups

1 One study which claimed to have done so was that of Perrin and Spencer (1981). They conducted a replication of Asch's experiment amongst British engineering students in 1980 and found no conformity to the incorrect majority. From this they concluded that the conformity which Asch had observed was specific to the cultural and historical conditions of the USA in the early 1950s and is not a general effect. However, as they admit, their use of science students who are well socialized into making objective physical judgements may help to account for their results. In any case, a study since then, also partly conducted in a British university, has confirmed that significant levels of conformity *can* still be obtained in the Asch paradigm (Nicholson et al., 1985).

2 The authors do not say, though, whether this was done rigidly or flexibly.

3 Intriguingly, the minority influence subjects also excelled the control subjects (exposed to no influence) in both quantity and originality. This result has important implications for theories of group productivity, as we shall see in chapter 5.

4 An after-image is the visual sensation one gets when one stares at a bright light for a few seconds and looks away at a blank wall or white piece of paper. By its nature it is a subjective phenomenon and hence not publicly accessible.

5 Written mathematically, this relationship is a power function: $I = sN^t$, where I is impact, N the number of stimuli and t has a value < 1; s is a constant which varies between situations and tasks.

Chapter 5 Individuals versus Groups

1 The problem is as follows: 'Someone buys a horse for £60 and sells it for £70. Then he/she buys it back for £80 and sells it again for £90. How much money did the horse-trader make?' This problem is interesting because although it has a logically correct answer (£20), such a solution is sometimes difficult to demonstrate to those who believe the answer is £10 or some other plausible but incorrect figure.

2 Actually, Steiner (1972, p. 20) erroneously computes this figure to be 0.596, and does not mention the values for the other two tasks. As we shall see, this mistake and omission has important implications for his theory of process loss.

3 Of course, figure 5.1 appears to be the exact inverse of the hypothetical curve shown in figure 4.8. This is because it plots average output per person along the ordinate instead of total group output. It is easy to verify, however, that re-plotting the graph for total output against size would show the typical negatively accelerating shape.

4 This result confirms the conclusion from studies of *intra*group goal relations which is unambiguously that cooperative task structures facilitate group performance and educational achievement (Johnson et al., 1981; Slavin, 1983; see chapter 2).

Chapter 6 Prejudice and Discontent

1 As with any correlational analysis causality is difficult to establish here. Furthermore, the relationship is open to a number of interpretations that have little to do with displaced aggression (see Konecni, 1979).

2 The 'long hot summer' explanation of riots can surely only be a partial one, however. Although several of the outbreaks of urban unrest in Britain in recent years *have* occurred in the summer months, only the most chauvinistic defender of the British climate would describe those summers as overly long or hot!

Chapter 7 Intergroup Conflict and Cooperation

1 This last stage was not included in the two earlier experiments and will not be described here but will be discussed in a later section. There were also some differences in the group formation phase which will be noted presently.

2 These friendships had formed in the first few days of the camp.

3 Stagner and Eflal (1982) believe that this weak effect for cohesion may have been due to the wording of their cohesion measures which referred to 'fellow workers' rather than fellow union members. If the strike in the

Ford plants was not 100 per cent then such a wording would have included the strike breakers in the target of evaluation, with an obvious effect on the cohesiveness ratings.

4　These correlations were not actually reported by Taylor et al. (1983) but can be derived from the data they present in their paper.

5　In the event the situation proved to be more real than hypothetical. In the decade since I conducted the study, this particular company has implemented several job-cutting programmes on a much wider scale than I outlined in my 'imaginary situation'.

Chapter 8　Social Categorization, Social Identification and Intergroup Relations

1　In a later experiment this was made still more tenuous by tossing a coin to determine group membership. Similar results were found (Billig and Tajfel, 1973; see chapter 6).

2　Of course, this criticism is also applicable to laboratory experiments in any discipline, not just to the particular paradigm we are concerned with here.

3　In fact, in the original experiments just referred to, evidence for this process of category assimilation was *not* found (Tajfel and Wilkes 1963; Eiser, 1971). However, other experiments *have* found such evidence (e.g. Doise et al., 1978; McGarty and Penny, 1988).

4　The fact that on this occasion the person happened to be a male nurse understandably caused him some consternation!

5　That this effect was due to "distinctiveness" rather than to some feature of undesirable traits was shown by a later experiment by Hamilton and Gifford (1976) in which the 'desirable' behaviours in group B were the least frequent co-occurrence. A similar overestimation of this distinctive cell frequency was found.

6　In a recent meta-analysis of several group homogeneity experiments Mullen and Hu (1987) have confirmed the reality of this reversal under minority group conditions.

7　That this is not a universal or necessary consequence is revealed by studies in different historical contexts which failed to find such misidentification (Hraba and Grant, 1970; Vaughan, 1978). We return to this point shortly.

8　I assisted Caddick in the running of this experiment and remember the highly angry and vocal reactions of the losing group to this patently unjustifiable usurpation of power by the high-status group!

References

Abeles, R. P. (1976) Relative deprivation, rising expectations and black militancy. *Journal of Social Issues*, 32, 119–37.

Adorno, T. W., Frenkel-Brunswick, E., Levinson, D. J. and Sanford, R. N. (1950) *The Authoritarian Personality*. New York: Harper.

Allen, V. L. (1965) Situational factors in conformity, in Berkowitz, L. (ed.) *Advances in Experimental Social Psychology*, vol. 2. New York: Academic Press.

Allen, V. L. (1975) Social support for nonconformity, in Berkowitz, L. (ed.) *Advances in Experimental Social Psychology*, vol. 8. New York: Academic Press.

Allen, V. L. and Wilder, D. A. (1975) Categorization, belief similarity, and group discrimination. *Journal of Personality and Social Psychology*, 32, 971–7.

Allen, V. L. and Wilder, D. A. (1980) Impact of group consensus and social support on stimulus meaning: mediation of conformity by cognitive restructuring. *Journal of Personality and Social Psychology*, 39, 1116–24.

Allport, F. H. (1924) *Social Psychology*. New York: Houghton Mifflin.

Allport, F. H. (1962) A structuronomic conception of behaviour: individual and collective. *Journal of Abnormal and Social Psychology*, 64, 3–30.

Allport, G. W. (1954) *The Nature of Prejudice*. Reading, Mass.: Addison-Wesley.

Amir, Y. (1976) The role of intergroup contact in change of prejudice and ethnic relations, in Katz, P. A. (ed.) *Towards the Elimination of Racism*. New York: Pergamon.

Arcuri, L. (1982) Three patterns of social categorization in attribution memory. *European Journal of Social Psychology*, 12, 271–82.

Argyle, M., Furnham, A. and Graham, J. (1981) *Social Situations*. London: Cambridge University Press.

Argyle, M. and Little, B. R. (1972) Do personality traits apply to social behaviour?, in Endler, N. S. and Magnusson, D. (eds) *Interactional Psychology and Personality*. New York: Wiley.

Aronson, E., Blaney, N., Stephan, C., Sikes, J. and Snapp, M. (1978) *The Jig-Saw Classroom*. London: Sage.

Aronson, E. and Mills, J. (1959) The effect of severity of initiation on liking for a group. *Journal of Abnormal and Social Psychology*, 59, 177–81.

Asch, S.E. (1951) Effects of group pressure upon the modification and distortion of judgements, in Guetzkow, M. (ed.) *Groups, Leadership, and Men*. Pittsburgh: Carnegie Press.

Asch, S.E. (1952) *Social Psychology*. New Jersey: Prentice Hall.

Asch, S.E. (1955) Opinions and social pressure. *Scientific American*, 193, 31–55.

Asch, S.E. (1956) Studies of independence and conformity: I. A minority of one against a unanimous majority. *Psychological Monographs*, 70(a), 1–70.

Aschenbrenner, K.M. and Schaefer, R.E. (1980) Minimal group situations: comments on a mathematical model and on the research paradigm. *European Journal of Social Psychology*, 10, 389–98.

Ashmore, R.D. (1981) Sex stereotypes and implicit personality theory, in Hamilton, D.L. (ed.) *Cognitive Processes in Stereotyping and Intergroup Behaviour*. New York: Lawrence Erlbaum.

Association of University Teachers (1985) *Rules of the Association*. London: Centurian Press.

Bagley, C. and Verma, G. (1979) *Racial Prejudice, the Individual and Society*. Farnborough: Saxon House.

Bales, R.F. (1950) *Interaction Process Analysis: a Method for the Study of Small Groups*. Chicago: University of Chicago Press.

Bales, R.F. (1953) The equilibrium problem in small groups, in Parsons, T., Bales, R.F. and Shils, E.A. (eds) *Working Papers in the Theory of Action*. New York: The Free Press.

Bales, R.F. (1970) *Personality and Interpersonal Behaviour*. New York: Holt Rinehart and Winston.

Bales, R.F. (1984) The integration of social psychology. *Social Psychology Quarterly*, 47, 98–101.

Bales, R.F. (1985) The new field theory in social psychology. *International Journal of Small Group Research*, 1, 1–18.

Bales, R.F. and Cohen, S.P. (1979) *SYMLOG: a System for the Multiple Level Observation of Groups*. New York: Free Press.

Bandura, A (1973) *Aggression: a Social Learning Analysis*. Englewood Cliffs, NJ: Prentice Hall.

Baron, R.A. and Ransberger, V.M. (1978) Ambient temperature and the occurrence of collective violence: the 'long, hot summer' revisted. *Journal of Personality and Social Psychology*, 36, 351–60.

Baron, R.S. and Roper, G. (1976) Reaffirmation of social comparison views of choice shifts: averaging and extremity effects in an autokinetic situation. *Journal of Personality and Social Psychology*, 33, 521–30.

Bartlett, F.C. (1932) *Remembering: a Study in Experimental and Social Psychology*. Cambridge: Cambridge University Press.

Bartlett, J. (1962) *Familiar Quotations*. London: Macmillan.

Bartol, K.M. and Martin, D.C. (1986) Women and men in task groups, in

Ashmore, R.D. and Del Boca, F.K. (eds) *The Social Psychology of Female–Male Relations*. New York: Academic Press.

Bavelas, A. (1969) Communications patterns in task-oriented groups, in Cartwright, D. and Zander, A. (eds) *Group Dynamics: Research and Theory*, 3rd edn. New York: Harper and Row.

Berkowitz, L. (1962) *Aggression: a Social Psychological Analysis*. New York: McGraw Hill.

Berkowitz, L. (1974) Some determinants of impulsive aggression: role of mediated associations with reinforcements for aggression. *Psychological Review*, 81, 165–76.

Berry, J.W. (1967) Independence and conformity in subsistence level societies. *Journal of Personality and Social Psychology*, 7, 415–18.

Berry, J.W. (1984) Cultural relations in plural societies: alternatives to segregation and their sociopsychological implications, in Miller, N. and Brewer, M.B. (eds) *Groups in Contact: the Psychology of Desegregation*. New York: Academic Press.

Berry, J.W., Kalin, R. and Taylor, D.M. (1977) *Multiculturalism and Ethnic Attitudes in Canada*. Ottawa: Supply and Services Canada.

Billig, M.G. (1976) *Social Psychology and Intergroup Relations*. London: Academic Press.

Billig, M.G. and Cochrane, R. (1979) Values of political extremists and potential extremists: a discriminant analysis. *European Journal of Social Psychology*, 9, 205–22.

Billig, M.G. and Tajfel, H. (1973) Social categorization and similarity in intergroup behaviour. *European Journal of Social Psychology*, 3, 27–52.

Blake, R.R. and Mouton, J.S. (1962) Overevaluation of own group's product in intergroup competition. *Journal of Abnormal and Social Psychology*, 64, 237–8.

Blake, R.R., Shepard, H.A. and Mouton, J.S. (1964) *Managing Intergroup Conflict in Industry*. Texas: Gulf Publishing Company.

Blascovich, J., Ginsburg, G.P. and Howe, R.C. (1975) Blackjack and the risky shift. II: monetary stakes. *Journal of Experimental Social Psychology*, 11, 224–32.

Blascovich, J., Ginsburg, G.P. and Howe, R.C. (1976) Blackjack, choice shifts in the field. *Sociometry*, 39, 274–6.

Blascovich, J., Veach, T.L. and Ginsburg, G.P. (1973) Blackjack and the risky shift. *Sociometry*, 36, 42–55.

Borgatta, E.F. and Bales, R.F. (1953) The consistency of subject behaviour and the reliability of scoring in interaction process analysis. *American Sociological Review*, 18, 566–9.

Bornstein, F., Crum, L., Wittenbraker, J., Harring, K., Insko, C.A. and Thibaut, J. (1983a) On the measurement of social orientations in the Minimal Group Paradiam. *European Journal Social Psychology*, 13, 321–50.

Bornstein, F., Crum, L., Wittenbraker, J., Harring, K., Insko, C.A. and Thibaut, J. (1983b) Reply to Turner's comments. *European Journal of Social Psychology*, 13, 369–81.

Bourhis, R.Y. and Giles, K. (1977) The language of intergroup distinctiveness, in Giles, H. (ed.) *Language, Ethnicity and Intergroup Relations*. London: Academic Press.

Bourhis, R.Y., Giles, H., Leyens, J.P. and Tajfel, H. (1978) Psycholinguistic distinctiveness: language divergence in Belgium, in Giles, H. and St Clair, R. (eds) *Language and Social Psychology*. Oxford: Blackwell.

Boyanowsky, E.O. and Allen, V.L. (1973) Ingroup norms and self-identity as determinants of discriminatory behaviour. *Journal of Personality and Social Psychology*, 25, 408–18.

Brandstätter, H., Davis, J.H. and Stocher-Kreichganer, G. (eds) (1982) *Contemporary Problems in Group Decision Making*. New York: Academic Press.

Branthwaite, A., Doyle, S. and Lightbown, N. (1979) The balance between fairness and discrimination. *European Journal of Social Psychology*, 9, 149–63.

Bray, R.M., Johnson, D. and Chilstrom, J.T. (1982) Social influence by group members with minority opinions: a comparison of Hollander and Moscovici. *Journal of Personality and Social Psychology*, 43, 78–88.

Bray, R.M. and Noble, A.M. (1978) Authoritarianism and decisions of mock juries: evidence of jury bias and group polarization. *Journal of Personality and Social Psychology*, 36, 1424–30.

Brewer, M.B. (1979a) The role of ethnocentrism in intergroup conflict, in Austin, W. and Worchel, S. (eds) *The Social Psychology of Intergroup Relations*. Monterey: Brooks/Cole.

Brewer, M.B. (1979b) In-group bias in the minimal intergroup situation: a cognitive-motivational analysis. *Psychological Bulletin*, 86, 307–24.

Brewer, M.B. and Campbell, D.T. (1976) *Ethnocentrism and Intergroup Attitudes: East African Evidence*. New York: Sage.

Brewer, M.B. and Kramer, R.M. (1985) The psychology of intergroup attitudes and behaviour. *Annual Review of Psychology*, 36, 219–43.

Brickner, M.A., Harkins, S.G. and Ostrom, T.M. (1986) Effects of personal involvement: thought provoking implications for social loafing. *Journal of Personality and Social Psychology*, 51, 763–9.

Bronfenbrenner, U. (1970) *Two Worlds of Childhood: US and USSR*. New York: Russell Sage.

Brown, Roger (1965) *Social Psychology*. New York: Macmillan.

Brown, Roger (1986) *Social Psychology*, 2nd edn. New York: The Free Press.

Brown, R.J. (1978) Divided we fall: an analysis of relations between sections of a factory work-force, in Tajfel, H. (ed.) *Differentiation between Social Groups: Studies in the Social Psychology of Intergroup Relations*. London: Academic Press.

Brown, R.J. (1984a) The effects of intergroup similarity and cooperative vs. competitive orientation on intergroup discrimination. *British Journal of Social Psychology*, 23, 21–33.

Brown, R. J. (ed.) (1984b) Intergroup processes. *British Journal of Social Psychology*, 23, no.4 (whole issue).

Brown, R. J. (1984c) The role of similarity in intergroup relations, in Tajfel, H. (ed.) *The Social Dimension: European Developments in Social Psychology*. Cambridge: Cambridge University Press.

Brown, R. J. and Abrams, D. (1986) The effects of intergroup similarity and goal interdependence on intergroup attitudes and task performance. *Journal of Experimental Social Psychology*, 22, 78–92.

Brown, R. J., Condor, S., Mathews, A., Wade, G. and Williams, J. A. (1986) Explaining intergroup differentiation in an industrial organisation. *Journal of Occupational Psychology*, 59, 273–86.

Brown, R. J. and Deschamps, J-C. (1980-1) Discrimination entre individus et entre groupes. *Bulletin de Psychologie*, 34, 185–95.

Brown, R. J. and Ross, G. F. (1982) The battle for acceptance: an exploration into the dynamics of intergroup behaviour, in Tajfel, H. (ed.) *Social Identity and Intergroup Relations*. Cambridge: Cambridge University Press.

Brown, R. J., Tajfel, H. and Turner, J. C. (1980) Minimal group situations and intergroup discrimination: comments on the paper by Aschenbrenner and Schaefer. *European Journal of Social Psychology*, 10, 399–414.

Brown, R. J. and Turner, J. C. (1979) The criss-cross categorization effect in intergroup discrimination. *British Journal of Social and Clinical Psychology*, 18, 371–83.

Brown, R. J. and Turner, J. C. (1981) Interpersonal and intergroup behaviour, in Turner, J. C. and Giles, H. (eds) *Intergroup Behaviour*. Oxford: Blackwell.

Brown, R. J. and Wade, G. S. (1987) Superordinate goals and intergroup behaviour: the effects of role ambiguity and status on intergroup attitudes and task performance. *European Journal of Social Psychology*, 17, 131–42.

Brown, R. J. and Williams, J. A. (1984) Group identification: the same thing to all people? *Human Relations*, 37, 447–564.

Bruner, J. S. (1957) On perceptual readiness. *Psychological Review*, 64, 123–51.

Bruner, J. S., Goodnow, J. J. and Austin, G. A. (1956) *A Study of Thinking*. New York: Wiley.

Burnstein, E. and McRae, A. V. (1962) Some effects of shared threat and prejudice in racially mixed groups. *Journal of Abnormal and Social Psychology*, 64, 257–63.

Burnstein, E. and Vinokur, A. (1973) Testing two classes of theories about group-induced shifts in individual choice. *Journal of Experimental Social Psychology*, 9, 123–37.

Burnstein, E. and Vinokur, A. (1977) Persuasive argumentation and social comparison as determinants of attitude polarization. *Journal of Experimental Social Psychology*, 13, 315–32.

Buys, C. J. (1978) Humans would do better without groups. *Personality and Social Psychology Bulletin*, 4, 123–5.

Byrne, D. (1971) *The Attraction Paradigm*. New York: Academic Press.

Byrne D. and Wong, T.J. (1962) Racial prejudice, interpersonal attraction and assumed dissimilarity of attitudes. *Journal of Abnormal and Social Psychology*, 65, 246–53.

Caddick, B. (1982) Perceived illegitimacy and intergroup relations, in Tajfel, H. (ed.) *Social Identity and Intergroup Relations*. Cambridge: Cambridge University Press.

Cairns, E. (1982) Intergroup conflict in Northern Ireland, in Tajfel, H. (ed.) *Social Identity and Intergroup Relations*. Cambridge: Cambridge University Press.

Campbell, D.T. (1958) Common fate, similarity, and other indices of the status of aggregates of persons as social entities. *Behavioural Science*, 3, 14–25.

Campbell, D.T. (1965) Ethnocentric and other altruistic motives, in Levine, D. (ed.) *Nebraska Symposium on Motivation*. Lincoln, Nebraska: University of Nebraska Press, pp. 283–311.

Cantril, H. (1965) *The Pattern of Human Concerns*. New York: Rutgers University Press.

Caplan, N. (1970) The new ghetto man: a review of recent empirical studies. *Journal of Social Issues*, 26, 59–73.

Carlsmith, J.M. and Anderson, C.A. (1979) Ambient temperature and the occurrence of collective violence: a new analysis. *Journal of Personality and Social Psychology*, 37, 337–44.

Carlson, R. (1971) Sex differences in ego functioning: exploratory studies of agency and communion. *Journal of Consulting and Clinical Psychology*, 37, 267–77.

Carlyle, T. (1841) *On Heroes, Hero-worship, and the Heroic*. London: Fraser.

Carter, L.F. and Nixon, M. (1949) An investigation of the relationship between four criteria of leadership ability for three different tasks. *The Journal of Psychology*, 27, 245–61.

Cartwright, D. and Zander, A. (eds) (1969) *Group Dynamics: Research and Theory*, 3rd edn. New York: Harper and Row.

Chemers, M.M., Hays, R.B., Rhodewalt, F. and Wysocki, J. (1985) A person–environment analysis of job stress: a contingency model explanation. *Journal of Personality and Social Psychology*, 49, 628–35.

Chemers, M.M., Rice, R.W., Sundstorm, E. and Butler, W.M. (1975) Leader esteem for the least preferred co-worker score, training and effectiveness: an experimental examination. *Journal of Personality and Social Psychology*, 31, 401–9.

Christie, R. and Jahoda, M. (eds) (1954) *Studies in the Scope and Method of 'The Authoritarian Personality'*. New York: The Free Press.

Cialdini, R.B., Borden, R.J., Thorne, A., Walker, M.R., Freeman, S. and Sloan, L.R. (1976) Basking in reflected glory: three (football) field studies. *Journal of Personality and Social Psychology*, 34, 366–74.

Clark, K.B. and Clark, M.P. (1947) Racial identification and preference in

Negro children, in Newcomb, T.M. and Hartley, E.L. (eds) *Readings in Social Psychology*. New York: Holt, Rinehart and Winston.

Clement, D.E. and Sullivan, D.W. (1970) No risky shift effect with real groups and real risks. *Psychonomic Science*, 18, 243–5.

Clore, G.L., Bray, R.M., Itkin, S.M. and O'Murphy, P. (1978) Inter-racial attitudes and behaviour at a summer camp. *Journal of Personality and Social Psychology*, 36, 107–16.

Coch, L. and French, J.R.P. (1948) Overcoming resistance to change. *Human Relations*, 11, 512–32.

Codol, J-P. (1975) On the so called 'superior conformity of the self' behaviour: twenty experimental investigations. *European Journal of Social Psychology*, 5, 457–501.

Commins, B. and Lockwood, J. (1979) The effects of status differences, favoured treatment and equity on intergroup comparisons. *European Journal of Social Psychology*, 9, 281–9.

Cook, S.W. (1978) Interpersonal and attitudinal outcomes in cooperating interracial groups. *Journal of Research and Development in Education*, 12, 97–113.

Cook, S.W. (1979) Social science and school desegregation: did we mislead the Supreme Court? *Personality and Social Psychology Bulletin*, 5, 420–37.

Cottrell, N. (1972) Social facilitation, in McClintock, C. (ed.) *Experimental Social Psychology*. New York: Holt, Rinehart and Winston.

Cowen, E.L., Landes, J. and Schaet, D.E. (1958) The effects of mild frustration on the expression of prejudiced attitudes. *Journal of Abnormal and Social Psychology*, 58, 33–8.

Crawford, T.J. and Naditch, M. (1970) Relative deprivation, powerlessness, and militancy: the psychology of social protest. *Psychiatry*, 33, 208–23.

Davey, A. (1983) *Learning To Be Prejudiced*. London: Edward Arnold.

Davies, J.C. (1969) The J-curve of rising and declining satisfactions as a cause of some great revolutions and a contained rebellion, in Graham, H.D. and Gurr, T.R. (eds) *The History of Violence in America: Historical and Comparative Perspectives*. New York: Praeger.

Davis, J.H. (1969) *Group Performance*. New York: Addison Wesley.

Davis, J.H. (1973) Group decision and social interaction: a theory of social decision schemes. *Psychological Review*, 80, 97–125.

Davis J.H., Kerr, N.L., Atkin, R.S., Holt, R. and Meek, D. (1975) The decision process of 6- and 12-person juries assigned unanimous and two-thirds majority rules. *Journal of Personality and Social Psychology*, 32, 1–14.

Davis, J.H., Kerr, N.L., Sussman, M. and Rissman, A.K. (1974) Social decision schemes under risk. *Journal of Personality and Social Psychology*, 30, 248–71.

Davis, J.H. and Restle, F. (1963) The analysis of problems and prediction of group problem solving. *Journal of Abnormal and Social Psychology*, 66, 103–16.

Deschamps, J-C. and Brown, R.J. (1983) Superordinate goals and intergroup conflict. *British Journal of Social Psychology*, 22, 189–95.

Deschamps, J-C. and Doise, W. (1978) Crossed category membership in intergroup relations, in Tajfel, H. (ed.) *Differentiation between Social Groups. Studies in the Social Psychology of Intergroup Relations.* London: Academic Press.

Deutsch, M. (1949a) A theory of cooperation and competition. *Human Relations*, 2, 129–52.

Deutsch, M. (1949b) An experimental study of the effects of cooperation and competition upon group process. *Human Relations*, 2, 199–231.

Deutsch, M. (1968) Field theory, in Lindzey, G. and Aronson, E. (eds) *Handbook of Social Psychology*. Reading, Mass: Addison Wesley.

Deutsch, M. and Gerard, H.B. (1955) A study of normative and informational social influence upon individual judgement. *Journal of Abnormal and Social Psychology*, 51, 629–36.

Diener, E. (1976) Effects of prior destructive behavior, anonymity, and group presence on deindividuation and aggression. *Journal of Personality and Social Psychology*, 33, 497–507.

Diener, E. (1979) Deindividuation, self-awareness, and disinhibition. *Journal of Personality and Social Psychology*, 37, 1160–71.

Diener, E. (1980) Deindividuation: the absence of self-awareness and self-regulation in group members, in Paulus, P. (ed.) *The Psychology of Group Influence*. Hillsdale, NJ: Lawrence Erlbaum.

Dion, K.L. (1973) Cohesiveness as a determinant of ingroup–outgroup bias. *Journal of Personality and Social Psychology*, 28, 163–71.

Doise, W. (1969) Intergroup relations and polarization of individual and collective judgements. *Journal of Personality and Social Psychology*, 12, 136–43.

Doise, W. (1976) *L'articulation psychosociologique et les relations entre groupes*. Brussels: A. de Boeck. English translation: *Groups and Individuals*. Cambridge: Cambridge University Press, 1978.

Doise, W., Deschamps, J-C. and Meyer, G. (1978) The accentuation of intra-category similarities, in Tajfel, H. (ed.) *Differentiation between Social Groups: Studies in the Social Psychology of Intergroup Relations.* London: Academic Press.

Dollard, J., Doob, L.W., Miller, N.E., Mowrer, O.H. and Sears, R.R. (192?) *Frustration and Aggression*. New Haven: Yale University Press.

Doms, M. and van Avermaet, E. (1980) Majority influence, minority influence, and conversion behaviour: a replication. *Journal of Experimental Social Psychology*, 16, 283–92.

Dornbusch, S.M. (1955) The military academy as an assimilating institution. *Social Forces*, 33, 316–21.

Duval, S. and Wicklund, R.A. (1972) *A Theory of Objective Self Awareness*. New York: Academic Press.

Ebbesen, E.B. and Bowers, R.J. (1974) Proportion of risky to conservative arguments in a group discussion and choice shifts. *Journal of Personality and Social Psychology*, 29, 316–27.

Egerbladh, T. (1981) A social decision scheme approach on group size, task difficulty and ability level. *European Journal of Social Psychology*, 11, 161–71.

Eiser, J.R. (1971) Enhancement of contrast in the absolute judgement of attitude statements. *Journal of Personality and Social Psychology*, 17, 1–10.

Farrell, J.G. (1975) *The Siege of Krishnapur*. Harmondsworth: Penguin.

Fassheber, P. and Terjung, B. (1985) SYMLOG rating data and their relationship to performance and behaviour beyond the group situation. *International Journal of Small Group Research*, 1, 97–108.

Faust, W.L. (1959) Group versus individual problem solving. *Journal of Abnormal and Social Psychology*, 59, 68–72.

Feldbaum, C.L., Christenson, T.E. and O'Neal, E.C. (1980) An observational study of the assimilation of the newcomer to the preschool. *Child Development*, 51, 497–507.

Ferguson, C.K. and Kelley, H.H. (1964) Significant factors in over-evaluation of own group's product. *Journal of Abnormal and Social Psychology*, 69, 223–8.

Festinger, L. (1950) Informal social communication. *Psychological Review*, 57, 271–82.

Festinger, L. (1953) An analysis of compliant behaviour, in Sherif, M. and Wilson, M.O. (eds) *Group Relations at the Crossroads*. New York: Harper and Row.

Festinger, L. (1954) A theory of social comparison processes. *Human Relations*, 7, 117–40.

Festinger, L. (1957) *A Theory of Cognitive Dissonance*. Evanston, Ill: Row, Peterson & Co.

Festinger, L., Schachter, S. and Back, K. (1950) *Social Pressures in Informal Groups*. New York: Harper.

Fiedler, F.E. (1965) A contingency model of leadership effectiveness, in Berkowitz, L. (ed.) *Advances in Experimental Social Psychology*, vol. 1. New York: Academic Press. Reprinted 1978 in Berkowitz, L. (ed.) *Group Processes*. New York: Academic Press.

Fiedler, F.E. (1978) Recent developments in research on the contingency model, in Berkowitz, L. (ed.) *Group Processes*. New York: Academic Press.

Fiedler, F.E., Chemers, M.M. and Makar, L. (1976) *Improving Leadership Effectiveness: the Leader Match Concept*. New York: Wiley.

Fischhoff, B. and Beyth-Marom, R. (1976) Failure has many fathers. *Policy Sciences*, 7, 388–93.

Fishbein, M. and Ajzen, I. (1975) *Beliefs, Attitudes, Intention and Behaviour: an Introduction to Theory and Research*. Reading, Mass: Addison-Wesley.

Fleishman, E.A. (1973) Twenty years of consideration and structure, in

Fleishman, E. A. and Hunt, J. F. (eds) *Current Developments in the Study of Leadership*. Carbondale: Soult Illinois University Press.

Flowers, M. L. (1977) A laboratory test of some implications of Janis' groupthink hypothesis. *Journal of Personality and Social Psychology*, 35, 888–96.

Fogelson, R. M. (1970) Violence and grievances: reflections on the 1960s riots. *Journal of Social Issues*, 26, 141–63.

Foot, H. C. (1982) Interactional analysis: the observation of individuals in a group setting, in Breakwell, G. M., Foot, H. and Gilmour, R. (eds) *Social Psychology: a Practical Manual*. London: The British Psychological Society.

Fraser, C. (1974) Determinants of individual and group decisions involving risks. Final Report to the Social Science Research Council. London: SSRC.

Fraser, C., Gouge, C. and Billig, M. (1971) Risky shifts, cautious shifts, and group polarization. *European Journal of Social Psychology*, 1, 7–30.

Freud, S. (1932) *Group Psychology and the Analysis of the Ego*. London: Hogarth Press.

Frey, K. S. and Ruble, D. N. (1985) What children say when the teacher is not around: conflicting goals in social comparison and performance assessment in the classroom. *Journal of Personality and Social Psychology*, 48, 550–62.

Furnham, A. (1982) Explanations for unemployment in Britain. *European Journal of Social Psychology*, 12, 335–52.

Gaskell, G. and Smith, P. (1984) Relative deprivation in black and white youth: an empirical investigation. *British Journal of Social Psychology*, 23, 121–31.

Gerard, H. B. and Hoyt, M. F. (1974) Distinctiveness of social categorization and attitude toward ingroup members. *Journal of Personality and Social Psychology*, 29, 836–42.

Gerard, H. B. and Mathewson, G. C. (1966) The effects of severity of initiation on liking for a group: a replication. *Journal of Experimental Social Psychology*, 2, 278–87.

Gerard, H. B., Wilhelmy, R. A. and Conolley, E. S. (1968) Conformity and group size. *Journal of Personality and Social Psychology*, 8, 79–82.

Gergen, K. J. (1971) *The Concept of Self*. New York: Holt, Rinehart and Winston.

Gibson, J. J. (1966) *The Senses Considered as Perceptual Systems*. Boston: Houghton Mifflin.

Giles, H. (ed.) (1977) *Language, Ethnicity and Intergroup Relations*. London: Academic Press.

Giles, H. and Johnson, P. (1981) Language in ethnic group relations, in Turner, J. C. and Giles, H. (eds) *Intergroup Behaviour*. Oxford: Blackwell.

Giles, H. and Powesland P. F. (1975) *Speech Style and Social Evaluation*. London: Academic Press.

Goethals, G. R. and Darley, J. M. (1977) Social comparison theory: an attributional approach, in Suls, J. and Miller, R. L. (eds) *Social Comparison Processes: Theoretical and Empirical Perspectives*. Washington: Hemisphere.

Goethals, G. R. and Zanna, M. P. (1979) The role of social comparison in choice shifts. *Journal of Personality and Social Psychology*, 37, 1469–76.

Gruder, C. L. (1971) Determinants of social comparison choices. *Journal of Experimental Social Psychology*, 7, 473–89.

Guimond, S. and Dubé-Simard, L. (1983) Relative deprivation theory and the Quebec Nationalist Movement: the cognition–emotion distinction and the personal–group deprivation issue. *Journal of Personality and Social Psychology*, 44, 526–35.

Gurr, T. R. (1970) *Why Men Rebel*. Princeton, NJ: Princeton University Press.

Hackman, J. R. and Morris, C. G. (1975) Group tasks, group interaction process, and group performance effectiveness: a review and proposed integration, in Berkowitz, L. (ed.) *Advances in Experimental Social Psychology*, vol. 8. New York: Academic Press.

Hackman, J. R. and Morris, C. G. (1978) Group process and group effectiveness: a reappraisal, in Berkowitz, L. (ed.) *Group Processes*. New York: Academic Press.

Hamilton, D. L. (1981) Illusory correlation as a basis for stereotyping, in Hamilton, D. L. (ed.) *Cognitive Processes in Stereotyping and Intergroup Behaviour*. New York: Lawrence Erlbaum.

Hamilton, D. L. and Gifford, R. K. (1976) Illusory correlation in interpersonal perception: a cognitive basis of stereotypic judgements. *Journal of Experimental Social Psychology*, 12, 392–407.

Hamilton, D. L. and Rose, T. L. (1980) Illusory correlation and the maintenance of stereotypic beliefs. *Journal of Personality and Social Psychology*, 39, 832–45.

Harding, J. and Hogrefe, R. (1952) Attitudes of white department store employees toward negro co-workers. *Journal of Social Issues*, 8, 18–28.

Hare, A. P. (1976) *Handbook of Small Group Research*, 2nd edn. New York: The Free Press.

Hare, A. P. (1985) Creativity and conformity during Egypt–Israel negotiations. *International Journal of Small Group Research*, 1, 122–30.

Hare, A. P. and Naveh, D. (1985) Creative problem solving: Camp David Summit, 1978. *Small Group Behaviour*, 16, 123–36.

Harkins, S. G. (1987) Social loafing and social facilitation. *Journal of Experimental Social Psychology*, 23, 1–18.

Harkins, S. G. and Petty, R. E. (1982) Effects of task difficulty and task uniqueness on social loafing. *Journal of Personality and Social Psychology*, 43, 1214–29.

Harris, R. (1985) Myth and reality in Northern Ireland: an anthropological study, in McWhirter, L. and Trew, K. (eds) *The Northern Ireland Conflict: Myth and Reality*. Unpublished MS, Queens University, Belfast.

Hartley, J., Kelly, J. and Nicholson, N. (1983) *Steel Strike: a Case Study in Industrial Relations*. London: Batsford.

Harvey, J.H. and Smith, W.P. (1977) *Social Psychology: an Attributional Approach*. St Louis: Mosby.

Harvey, O.J. (1953) An experimental approach to the study of status relations in informal groups. *American Sociological Review*, 18, 357-67.

Hastie, R., Penrod, S.D. and Pennington, N. (1983) *Inside the Jury*. Cambridge, Mass: Harvard University Press.

Heinicke, C. and Bales, R.F. (1953) Developmental trends in the structure of small groups. *Sociometry*, 16, 7-38.

Hendrick, C., Bixenstine, V.E. and Hawkins, G. (1971) Race vs. belief similarities as determinants of attraction: a search for a fair test. *Journal of Personality and Social Psychology*, 17, 250-8.

Hennessy, P. (1986) *Cabinet*. Oxford: Blackwell.

Henshel, R.C. (1980) The purposes of laboratory experimentation and the virtues of deliberate artificiality. *Journal of Experimental Social Psychology*, 16, 466-78.

Hewstone, M.R.C. and Brown, R.J. (1986) Contact is not enough: an intergroup perspective on the contact hypothesis, in Hewstone, M.R.C. and Brown, R.J. (eds) *Contact and Conflict in Intergroup Encounters*. Oxford: Blackwell.

Hewstone, M.R.C., Jaspers, J. and Lalljee, M. (1982) Social representations, social attribution and social identity: the intergroup images of 'public' and 'comprehensive' schoolboys. *European Journal of Social Psychology*, 12, 241-69.

Hewstone, M.R.C. and Ward, C. (1985) Ethnocentrism and causal attribution in Southeast Asia. *Journal of Personality and Social Psychology*, 48, 614-23.

Hill, G.W. (1982) Group versus individual performance: are n + 1 heads better than one? *Psychological Bulletin*, 91, 517-39.

Hogg, M.A. and Turner, J.C. (1987) Social identity and conformity: a theory of referent informational influence, in Doise, W. and Moscovici, S. (eds) *Current Issues in European Social Psychology*, vol. 2. Cambridge: Cambridge University Press.

Hollander, E.P. (1958) Conformity, status, and idiosyncrasy credit. *Psychological Review*, 65, 117-27.

Hollander, E.P. (1960) Competence and conformity in the acceptance of influence. *Journal of Abnormal and Social Psychology*, 61, 361-5.

Hollander, E.P. (1978) *Leadership Dynamics: a Practical Guide to Effective Relationships*. New York: Free Press.

Hollander, E.P. (1982) *Principles and Methods of Social Psychology*, 4th edn. New York: Oxford University Press.

Hollander, E.P. and Julian, J.W. (1970) Studies in leader legitimacy, influence, and innovation, in Berkowitz, L. (ed.) *Advances in Experimental Social Psychology*, vol. 5. New York: Academic Press.

Holt, J.H. (1987) The social labouring effect: a study of the effect of social identity on group productivity in real and notional groups using Ringelmann's methods. Unpublished manuscript, University of Kent.

Homans, G. C. (1950) *The Human Group*. New York: Harcourt, Brace and World.

Hoppe, R. A. (1962) Memorizing by individuals and groups: a test of the pooling-of-ability model. *Journal of Abnormal and Social Psychology*, 65, 64–7.

Horowitz, D. L. (1973) Direct, displaced and cumulative ethnic aggression. *Comparative Politics*, 6, 1–16.

Horwitz, M. and Rabbie, J. M. (1982) Individuality and membership in the intergroup system, in Tajfel, H. (ed.) *Social Identity and Intergroup Relations*. Cambridge: Cambridge University Press.

Hosking, D. (1981) A critical evaluation of Fiedler's contingency hypothesis, in Stephenson, G. M. and Davis, J. (eds) *Progress in Applied Social Psychology*, vol. 1. Chichester: Wiley.

Hovland, C. and Sears, R. R. (1940) Minor studies in aggression: VI. Correlation of lynchings with economic indices. *Journal of Psychology*, 9, 301–10.

Howard, J. W. and Rothbart, M. (1980) Social categorization and memory for ingroup and outgroup behaviour. *Journal of Personality and Social Psychology*, 38, 301–10.

Hraba, J. and Grant, G. (1970) Black is beautiful: a re-examination of racial preference and identification. *Journal of Personality and Social Psychology*, 16, 398–402.

Ingham, A. G., Levinger, G., Graves, J. and Peckham, V. (1974) The Ringlemann effect: studies of group size and group performance. *Journal of Experimental Social Psychology*, 10, 371–84.

Insko, C. A., Nacoste, R. W. and Moe, J. L. (1983) Belief congruence and racial discrimination: review of the evidence and critical evaluation. *European Journal of Social Psychology*, 13, 153–74.

Isenberg, D. J. (1986) Group polarization: a critical review and meta-analysis. *Journal of Personality and Social Psychology*, 50, 1141–51.

Isenberg, D. J. and Ennis, J. G. (1981) Perceiving group members: a comparison of derived and imposed dimensions. *Journal of Personality and Social Psychology*, 42, 293–305.

Jackson, J. M. and Williams, K. D. (1985) Social loafing on difficult tasks: working collectively can improve performance. *Journal of Personality and Social Psychology*, 49, 937–42.

Jacobs, R. and Campbell, D. T. (1961) The perpetuation of an arbitrary tradition through several generations of a laboratory microculture. *Journal of Abnormal and Social Psychology*, 62, 649–58.

Jacobson, S. R. (1973) Individual and group responses to confinement in a skyjacked plane. *American Journal of Orthopsychiatry*, 43, 459–69.

Jaffe, Y. and Yinon, Y. (1979) Retaliatory aggression in individuals and groups. *European Journal of Social Psychology*, 9, 177–86.

Janis, I. L. (1972) *Victims of Groupthink*. Boston: Houghton Mifflin.

Janis, I.L. and Mann, L. (1977) *Decision Making* New York: The Free Press.

Johnson, D.W., Maruyama, G., Johnson, R., Nelson, D. and Skon, L. (1981) Effects of cooperative, competitive, and individualistic goal structures on achievement: a meta-analysis. *Psychological Bulletin*, 89, 47–62.

Johnson, R.D. and Downing, L.L. (1979) Deindividuation and valence of cues: effects on prosocial and antisocial behaviour. *Journal of Personality and Social Psychology*, 37, 1532–8.

Jones, E. (1964) *The Life and Work of Sigmund Freud* (Abridged). Harmondsworth: Penguin.

Jones, E.E., Wood, G.C. and Quattrone, G.A. (1981) Perceived variability of personal characteristics in ingroups and outgroups: the role of knowledge and evaluation. *Personality and Social Psychology Bulletin*, 7, 523–8.

Julian, J.W., Bishop, D.W. and Fiedler, F.E. (1966) Quasi-therapeutic effects of intergroup competition. *Journal of Personality and Social Psychology*, 3, 321–7.

Julian, J.W. and Perry, F.A. (1967) Cooperation contrasted with intra-group and inter-group competition. *Sociometry*, 30, 79–90.

Kahn, A. and Ryen, A.H. (1972) Factors influencing the bias towards one's own group. *International Journal of Group Tensions*, 2, 33–50.

Kanter, R.M. (1977) Some effects of proportions on group life: skewed sex ratios and responses to token women. *American Journal of Sociology*, 82, 965–90.

Katz, D. (1953) Field studies, in Festinger, L. and Katz, D. (eds) *Research Methods in the Behavioural Sciences*. London: Staples Press.

Katz, D. and Kahn, R.L. (1978) *The Social Psychology of Organizations*, 2nd edn. New York: Wiley.

Kelley, H.H. (1967) Attribution theory in social psychology, in Levine, D. (ed.) *Nebraska Symposium on Motivation*. Lincolin: University of Nebraska Press.

Kerr, N. and Bruun, S. (1981) Ringlemann revisited: alternative explanations for the social loafing effect. *Personality and Social Psychology Bulletin*, 7, 224–31.

Kirkhart, R.O. (1963) Minority group identification and group leadership. *Journal of Social Psychology*, 59, 111–17.

Konecni, V.J. (1979) The role of aversive events in the development of intergroup conflict, in Austin, W.G. and Worchel, S. (eds) *The Social Psychology of Intergroup Relations*. Monterey: Brooks/Cole.

Kravitz, D.A. and Martin, B. (1986) Ringlemann rediscovered: the original article. *Journal of Personality and Social Psychology*, 50, 936–41.

Kuhn, M.H. and McPartland, T.S. (1954) An empirical investigation of self attitudes. *American Sociological Review*, 19, 68–76.

Lamm, H. and Trommsdorff, G. (1973) Group versus individual performance on tasks requiring ideational proficiency: a review. *European Journal of Social Psychology*, 3, 361–88.

Latane, B. (1981) The psychology of social impact. *American Psychologist*, 36, 343–56.

Latane, B., Williams, K. and Harkins, S. (1979) Many hands make light the work: the causes and consequences of social loafing. *Journal of Personality and Social Psychology*, 37, 822–32.

Latane, B. and Wolf, S. (1981) The social impact of majorities and minorities. *Psychological Review*, 88, 438–53.

Lauderdale, P., Smith-Cunnien, P., Parker, J. and Inverarity, J. (1984) External threat and the definition of deviance. *Journal of Personality and Social Psychology*, 46, 1058–68.

Laughlin, P. R. (1980) Social combination processes of cooperative problem-solving groups on verbal intellective tasks, in Fishbein, M. (ed.) *Progress in Social Psychology*, vol. 1. Hillsdale, NJ: Erlbaum.

Laughlin, P. R. and Early, P. C. (1982) Social combination models, persuasive arguments theory, social comparison theory, and choice shift. *Journal of Personality and Social Psychology*, 42, 273–80.

Leavitt, H. J. (1951) Some effects of certain communication patterns on group performance. *Journal of Abnormal and Social Psychology*, 46, 38–50.

Le Bon, G. (1896) *The Crowd: a Study of the Popular Mind*. London: T. Fisher Unwin.

Leik, R. K. (1963) Instrumentality and emotionality in family interaction. *Sociometry*, 26, 131–45.

Lemaine, G. (1966) Inegalité, comparison et incomparabilité: esquisse d'une theorie de l'originalité sociale. *Bulletin de Psychologie*, 20, 1–9.

Lemyre, L. and Smith, P. M. (1985) Intergroup discrimination and self esteem in the Minimal Group Paradigm. *Journal of Personality and Social Psychology*, 49, 660–70.

Lewicki, R. D. (1981) Organizational seduction: building commitment to organizations. *Organizational Dynamics*, 10, 5–21.

Lewin, K. (1947) Frontiers in group dynamics. *Human Relations*, 1, 5–42.

Lewin, K. (1948) *Resolving Social Conflicts*. New York: Harper and Row.

Lewin, K. (1952) *Field Theory in Social Science*. New York: Harper and Row.

Lewin, K. (1965) Group decision and social change, in Proshansky, H. and Seidenberg, B. (eds) *Basic Studies in Social Psychology*. New York: Holt Rinehart and Winston.

Lippitt, R. and White, R. (1943) The 'social climate' of children's groups, in Barker, R. G., Kounin, J. and Wright, H. (eds) *Child Behaviour and Development*. New York: McGraw Hill.

Lodge, D. (1962) *Ginger You're Barmy*. Harmondsworth: Penguin.

Lorge, I., Fox, D., Davitz, J. and Brenner, M. (1958) A survey of studies contrasting the quality of group performance and individual performance. *Psychological Bulletin*, 55, 337–72.

Lorge, I. and Solomon, H. (1955) Two models of group behaviour in the solution of eureka-type problems. *Psychometrika*, 20, 139–48.

Lott, A. J. and Lott, B. E. (1961) Group cohesiveness, communication level, and conformity. *Journal of Abnormal and Social Psychology*, 62, 408-12.

Maass, A. and Clark, R. D. (1983) Internalization versus compliance: differential processes underlying minority influence and conformity. *European Journal of Social Psychology*, 13, 197-215.

Maass, A. and Clark, R. D. (1984) Hidden impact of minorities: fifteen years of minority influence research. *Psychological Bulletin*, 95, 428-50.

Maass, A. and Clark, R. D. (1986) Conversion theory and simultaneous majority/minority influence: can reactance offer an alternative explanation? *European Journal of Social Psychology*, 16, 305-9.

Maass, A., Clark, R. D. and Haberkorn, G. (1982) The effects of differential ascribed category membership and norms on minority influence. *European Journal of Social Psychology*, 12, 89-104.

McCarthy, M. (1979) *Missionaries and Cannibals*. New York: Hodder and Stoughton.

McDougall, W. (1920) *The Group Mind*. Cambridge: Cambridge University Press.

McGarty, C. and Penny, R. E. C. (1988) Categorization, accentuation and social judgement. *British Journal of Social Psychology* (in press).

McGrath, J. E. (1984) *Groups: Interaction and Performance*. New York: Prentice Hall.

McGrew, W. J. (1972) Aspects of social development in nursery school children, with emphasis on introduction to the group, in Blurton-Jones, N. (ed.) *Ethological Studies of Child Development*. London: Cambridge University Press.

McGuire, W. J., McGuire, C. V., Child, P. and Fujioka, T. (1978) Salience of ethnicity in the spontaneous self-concept as a function of one's ethnic distinctiveness in the social environment. *Journal of Personality and Social Psychology*, 36, 511-20.

McGuire, W. J., McGuire, C. V. and Winton, W. (1979) Effects of household sex composition on the salience of one's gender in the spontaneous self concept. *Journal of Experimental and Social Psychology*, 15, 77-90.

Mackie, D. M. (1986) Social identification effects in group polarization. *Journal of Personality and Social Psychology*, 50, 720-8.

Mackie, D. and Cooper, J. (1984) Attitude polarization: effects of group membership. *Journal of Personality and Social Psychology*, 46, 575-85.

MacNeil, M. K. and Sherif, M. (1976) Norm change over subject generations as a function of arbitrariness of prescribed norms. *Journal of Personality and Social Psychology*, 34, 762-73.

Maier, N. R. F. and Solem, A. R. (1952) The contribution of a discussion leader to the quality of group thinking: the effective use of minority opinions. *Human Relations*, 5, 277-88.

Mann, L. (1980) Cross-cultural studies of small groups, in Triandis, H. C. and Brislin, R. W. (eds) *Handbook of Cross-Cultural Psychology*, vol. 5. New York: Allyn & Bacon.

Mann, R. D. (1961) Dimensions of individual performance in small groups under task and social-emotional conditions. *Journal of Abnormal and Social Psychology*, 62, 674–82.

Marchand, B. (1970) Auswirkung einer emotional wertrollen und einer emotional neutralen klassifikation auf die Schatzung einer Stimulus-Serie. *Zeitschrift fur Soziale Psychologie*, 1, 264–74.

Marquart, D. I. (1955) Group problem solving. *Journal of Social Psychology*, 41, 102–13.

Martin, R. (1987) Influence minorité et relations entre groupe, in Moscovici, S. and Mugny, G. (eds) *Psychologie de la Conversion*. Paris: Cossett de Val.

Mead, G. H. (1934) *On Social Psychology*. Chicago: University of Chicago Press.

Mead, M. (1935) *Sex and Temperament in Three Primitive Societies*. New York: Morrow.

Merei, F. (1949) Group leadership and institutionalization. *Human Relations*, 2, 23–39.

Merton, R. K. (1957) *Social Theory and Social Structure*. New York: The Free Press.

Mettee, D. R. and Smith, G. (1977) Social comparison and interpersonal attraction, in Suls, J. and Miller, R. L. (eds) *Social Comparison Processes: Theoretical and Empirical Perspectives*. Washington: Hemisphere.

Milgram, S., Bickman, L. and Berkowitz, L. (1969) Note on the drawing power of crowds of different size. *Journal of Personality and Social Psychology*, 13, 79–82.

Milgram, S. and Toch, H. (1969) Collective behaviour: crowds and social movements, in Lindzey, G. and Aronson, E. (eds) *Handbook of Social Psychology*, 2nd edn, vol. 4. Reading, Mass: Addison-Wesley.

Miller, C. E., Jackson, P., Mueller, J. and Schersching, C. (1987) Some social psychological effects of group decision rules. *Journal of Personality and Social Psychology*, 52, 325–32.

Miller, N. and Brewer, M. B. (eds) (1984) *Groups in Contact: the Psychology of Desegregation*. New York: Academic Press.

Miller, N., Brewer, M. B. and Edwards, K. (1985) Cooperative interaction in desegregated settings: a laboratory analogue. *Journal of Social Issues*, 41, 63–79.

Miller, N. E. (1948) Theory and experiment relating psychoanalytic displacement to stimulus-response generalization. *Journal of Abnormal and Social Psychology*, 43, 155–78.

Miller, N. E. and Bugelski, R. (1948) Minor studies in aggression: the influence of frustrations imposed by the ingroup on attitudes toward outgroups. *Journal of Psychology*, 25, 437–42.

Milner, D. (1975) *Children and Race*. Harmondsworth: Penguin.

Minard, R. D. (1952) Race relationships in the Pocahontas coal field. *Journal of Social Issues*, 8, 29–44.

Minuchin, S. (1974) *Families and Family Therapy*. Cambridge, Mass: Harvard University Press.

Mischel, W. (1968) *Personality and Assessment*. New York: Wiley.

Moreland, R.L. (1985) Social categorization and the assimilation of 'new' group members. *Journal of Personality and Social Psychology*, 48, 1173-90.

Moreland, R.L. and Levine, J.M. (1982) Socialization in small groups: temporal changes in individual–group relations, in Berkowitz, L. (ed.) *Advances in Experimental Social Psychology*, vol. 15. New York: Academic Press.

Morland, J.K. (1969) Race awareness among American and Hong Kong Chinese children. *American Journal of Sociology*, 75, 360-74.

Morley, I.E. and Stephenson, G.M. (1977) *The Social Psychology of Bargaining*. London: Allen & Unwin.

Moscovici, S. (1976) *Social Influence and Social Change*. London: Academic Press.

Moscovici, S. (1979) A rejoinder. *British Journal of Social Psychology*, 18, 181.

Moscovici, S. and Lage, E. (1976) Studies in social influence: III. Majority vs minority influence in a group. *European Journal of Social Psychology*, 6, 149-74.

Moscovici, S., Lage, E. and Naffrechoux, M. (1969) Influence of a consistent minority on the responses of a majority in a colour perception task. *Sociometry*, 32, 365-79.

Moscovici, S., Mugny, G. and van Avermaet, E. (eds) (1985) *Perspectives on Minority Influence*. Cambridge: Cambridge University Press.

Moscovici, S. and Personnaz, B. (1980) Studies in social influence: V. Minority influence and conversion behaviour in a perceptual task. *Journal of Experimental Social Psychology*, 16, 270-82.

Moscovici, S. and Personnaz, B. (1986) Studies on latent influence by the spectrometer method: I. The impact of psychologization in the case of conversion by a minority or a majority. *European Journal of Social Psychology*, 16, 345-360.

Moscovici, S. and Zavalloni, M. (1969) The group as a polarizer of attitudes. *Journal of Personality and Social Psychology*, 12, 125-35.

Mugny, G. (1982) *The Power of Minorities*. London: Academic Press.

Mugny, G. and Papastamou, S. (1975-6) A propos du 'credit idiosynchrasique' chez Hollander: conformisme initial ou négociation? *Bulletin de Psychologie*, 29, 970-6.

Mullen, B. (1983) Operationalizing the effect of the group on the individual: a self-attention perspective. *Journal of Experimental Social Psychology*, 19, 295-322.

Mullen, B. and Hu, L. (1987) Perceptions of ingroup and outgroup variability: a meta-analytic integration. Unpublished manuscript, Syracuse University.

Mummendey, A. and Schreiber, H.-J. (1984) 'Different' just means 'better':

some obvious and some hidden pathways to in-group favouritism. *British Journal of Social Psychology*, 23, 363-7.

Myers, A. (1962) Team competition, success, and the adjustment of group members. *Journal of Abnormal and Social Psychology*, 65, 325-32.

Myers, D.G. (1978) Polarizing effects of social comparison. *Journal of Experimental Social Psychology*, 14, 554-63.

Myers, D.G. and Lamm, H. (1976) The group polarization phenomenon. *Psychological Bulletin*, 83, 602-27.

Nadler, A., Goldberg, M. and Jaffe, Y. (1982) Effect of self-differentiation and anonymity in group on deindividuation. *Journal of Personality and Social Psychology*, 42, 1127-36.

Nemeth, C.J. and Kwan, J.L. (1985) Originality of word associations as a function of majority vs minority influence. *Social Psychology Quarterly*, 48, 277-82.

Nemeth, C.J. and Wachtler, J. (1983) Creative problem solving as a result of majority vs minority influence. *European Journal of Social Psychology*, 13, 45-55.

Newcomb, T.M. (1965) Attitude development as a function of reference groups: the Bennington study, in Proshansky, H. and Seidenberg, B. (eds) *Basic Studies in Social Psychology*. New York: Holt, Rinehart and Winston.

Newcomb, T.M., Koenig, K.E., Flacks, R. and Warwick, D.P. (1967) *Persistence and Change: Bennington College and its Students after 25 years*. New York: Wiley.

Ng, S.H. (1980) *The Social Psychology of Power*. London: Academic Press.

Ng, S.H. (1982) Power and intergroup discrimination, in Tajfel, H. (ed.) *Social Identity and Intergroup Relations*. Cambridge: Cambridge University Press.

Nicholson, N., Cole, S.G. and Rocklin, T. (1985) Conformity in the Asch situation: a comparison between contemporary British and US university students. *British Journal of Social Psychology*, 24, 59-63.

Nosanchuk, T.A. and Erickson, B.H. (1985) How high is up? Calibrating social comparison in the real world. *Journal of Personality and Social Psychology*, 48, 624-34.

Oaker, G. and Brown, R.J. (1986) Intergroup relations in a hospital setting: a further test of Social Identity Theory. *Human Relations*, 39, 767-78.

Oakes, P.J. (1987) The salience of social categories, in Turner, J.C., Hogg, M.A., Oakes, P.J., Reicher, S.D. and Wetherell, M.S. *Rediscovering the Social Group: a Self-Categorization Theory*. Oxford: Blackwell.

Oakes, P.J. and Turner, J.C. (1980) Social categorization and intergroup behaviour: does minimal intergroup discrimination make social identity more positive? *European Journal of Social Psychology*, 10, 295-302.

Oakes, P.J. and Turner, J.C. (1986) Distinctiveness and the salience of social category membership: is there an automatic perceptual bias towards novelty? *European Journal of Social Psychology*, 16, 325-44.

O'Rourke, J. (1963) Field and laboratory: the decision making behaviours of family groups in two experimental conditions. *Sociometry*, 26, 422–35.

Orwell, G. (1962) *The Road to Wigan Pier*. Harmondsworth: Penguin.

Osborn, A. F. (1957) *Applied Imagination*. New York: Scribner.

Pandey, J. (1976) Effects of leadership style, personality characteristics and method of leader selection on members' and leaders' behaviour. *European Journal of Social Psychology*, 6, 475–89.

Park, B. and Rothbart, M. (1982) Perception of outgroup homogeneity and levels of social categorization: memory for the subordinate attributes of ingroup and outgroup members. *Journal of Personality and Social Psychology*, 42, 1051–68.

Parsons, T. and Bales, R. F. (1956) *Family: Socialization and Interaction Process*. Glencoe: Free Press.

Parsons, T., Bales, R. F. and Shils, E. A. (eds) (1953) *Working Papers in the Theory of Action*. New York: The Free Press.

Pastore, N. (1952) The role of arbitrariness in the frustration–aggression hypothesis. *Journal of Abnormal and Social Psychology*, 47, 728–31.

Perlmutter, H. V. and de Montmollin, G. (1952) Group learning of nonsense syllables. *Journal of Abnormal and Social Psychology*, 47, 762–9.

Perrin, S. and Spencer, C. (1981) Independence or conformity in the Asch experiment as a reflection of cultural and situational factors. *British Journal of Social Psychology*, 20, 205–9.

Personnaz, B. (1981) Study in social influence using the spectrometer method: dynamics of the phenomena of conversion and covertness in perceptual responses. *European Journal of Social Psychology*, 11, 431–8.

Peters, L. H., Hartke, D. D. and Pohlmann, J. T. (1985) Fiedler's contingency theory of leadership: and application of the meta-analysis procedures of Schmidt and Hunter. *Psychological Bulletin*, 97, 274–85.

Pettigrew, T. F. (1958) Personality and sociocultural factors in intergroup attitudes: a cross-national comparison. *Journal of Conflict Resolution*, 2, 29–42.

Pettigrew, T. F. (1971) *Racially Separate or Together?* New York: McGraw Hill.

Pettigrew, T. F. (1979) The ultimate attribution error: extending Allport's cognitive analysis of prejudice. *Personality and Social Psychology Bulletin*, 5, 461–76.

Pettigrew, T. F. (in press) *Modern Racism: American Black–White Relations since the 1960s*. Cambridge, Mass.: Harvard University Press.

Phillips, E. L., Shenker, S. and Revitz, P. (1951) The assimilation of the new child into the group. *Psychiatry*, 14, 319–25.

Piaget, J. (1942) *Classes, relations et nombres: essai sur les 'groupements' de la logistique et la reversibilité de la pensée*. Paris: Vrin.

Prentice-Dunn, S. and Rogers, R. W. (1982) Effects of public and private self-awareness on deindividuation and aggression. *Journal of Personality and Social Psychology*, 43, 503–13.

Putallaz, M. and Gottman, J. M. (1981) An interactional model of children's entry into peer groups. *Child Development*, 52, 986–94.

Quattrone, G.A. (1985) On the perception of a group's variability, in Worchel, S. and Austin, W. (eds) *The Social Psychology of Intergroup Relations*, 2nd edn. Chicago: Nelson Hall.

Rabbie, J.M. and Bekkers, F. (1978) Threatened leadership and intergroup competition. *European Journal of Social Psychology*, 8, 9-20.

Rabbie, J.M., Benoist, F., Oosterbaan, H. and Visser, L. (1974) Differential power and effects of expected competitive and cooperative intergroup interaction upon intra- and outgroup attitudes. *Journal of Personality and Social Psychology*, 30, 46-56.

Rabbie, J.M. and Horwitz, M. (1969) Arousal of ingroup–outgroup bias by a chance win or loss. *Journal of Personality and Social Psychology*, 13, 269-77.

Radloff, R. (1966) Social comparison and ability evaluation. *Journal of Experimental Social Psychology Supplement*, 1, 6-26.

Rapoport, A. and Chammah, A.M. (1965) *Prisoners' Dilemma: a Study in Conflict and Cooperation*. Ann Arbor: The University of Michigan Press.

Reicher, S.D. (1982) The determination of collective behaviour, in Tajfel, H. (ed.) *Social Identity and Intergroup Relations* Cambridge: Cambridge University Press.

Reicher, S.D. (1984a) The St Pauls riot: an explanation of the limits of crowd action in terms of a social identity model. *European Journal of Social Psychology*, 14, 1-21.

Reicher, S.D. (1984b) Social influence in the crowd: attitudinal and behavioural effects of deindividuation in conditions of high and low group salience. *British Journal of Social Psychology*, 23, 341-50.

Reicher, S. and Potter, J. (1985) Psychological theory as intergroup perspective: a comparative analysis of 'scientific' and 'lay' accounts of crowd events. *Human Relations*, 38, 167-89.

Reid, F.J.M. and Sumiga, L. (1984) Attitudinal politics in intergroup behaviour: interpersonal vs. intergroup determinants of attitude change. *British Journal of Social Psychology*, 23, 335-40.

Rice, R.W. (1978) Construct validity of the least preferred co-worker score. *Psychological Bulletin*, 85, 1199-237.

Rijsman, J.B. (1974) Factors in social comparison of performance influencing actual performance. *European Journal of Social Psychology*, 4, 279-311.

Ringelmann, M. (1913) Recherches sur les moteurs animes: travail de l'homme. *Annales de l'Institut National Agronomique*, 2nd series, 12, 1-40.

Rokeach, M. (1948) Generalized mental rigidity as a factor in ethnocentrism. *Journal of Abnormal and Social Psychology*, 43, 259-78.

Rokeach, M. (ed.) (1960) *The Open and Closed Mind*. New York: Basic Books.

Rokeach, M. and Mezei, L. (1966) Race and shared belief factors in social choice. *Science*, 151, 167-72.

Rokeach, M., Smith, P.W. and Evans, R.I. (1960) Two kinds of prejudice or one?, in Rokeach, M. (ed.) *The Open and Closed Mind*. New York: Basic Books.

Rosch, E. (1978) Principles of categorization, in Rosch, E. and Lloyd, B. (eds) *Cognition and Categorization*. Hillsdale, NJ: Lawrence Erlbaum.

Rosenbaum, M.E. (1986) The repulsion hypothesis: on the nondevelopment of relationships. *Journal of Personality and Social Psychology*, 51, 1156–66.

Rosenbaum, M.E., Moore, D.L., Cotton, J.L., Cook, M.S., Hieser, R.A., Shover, M.N. and Gray, M.J. (1980) Group productivity and process: pure and mixed reward structures and task interdependence. *Journal of Personality and Social Psychology*, 39, 626–42.

Rosenberg, M. and Simmons, R.G. (1972) *Black and White Self-esteem: the Urban School Child*. Washington DC: American Sociological Association.

Rosenthal, R. (1966) *Experimenter Effects in Behavioural Research*. New York: Appleton.

Rosenthal, R. (1978) Combining the results of independent studies. *Psychological Bulletin*, 85, 185–93.

Ross, L.D. (1977) The intuitive psychologist and his shortcomings: distortions in the attribution process, in Berkowitz, L. (ed.) *Advances in Experimental Social Psychology*, vol. 10. New York: Academic Press.

Rothbart, M. and John, O.P. (1985) Social categorization and behavioural episodes: a cognitive analysis of the effects of intergroup contact. *Journal of Social Issues*, 41, 81–104.

Runciman, W.G. (1966) *Relative Deprivation and Social Justice*. London: Routledge and Kegan Paul.

Ryen, A.H. and Kahn, A. (1975) Effects of intergroup orientation on group attitudes and proxemic behaviour. *Journal of Personal and Social Psychology*, 31, 302–10.

Sachdev, I. and Bourhis, R.Y. (1985) Social categorization and power differentials in group relations. *European Journal of Social Psychology*, 15, 415–34.

Sachdev, I. and Bourhis, R.Y. (1987) Status differentials and intergroup behaviour. *European Journal of Social Psychology*, 17, 277–93.

Sanders, G.S. and Baron, R.S. (1977) Is social comparison irrelevant for producing choice shifts? *Journal of Experimental Social Psychology*, 13, 303–14.

Schachter, S. (1951) Deviation, rejection and communication. *Journal of Abnormal and Social Psychology*, 46, 190–207.

Schachter, S., Elletson, N., McBride, D. and Gregory, D. (1951) An experimental study of cohesiveness and productivity. *Human Relations*, 4, 229–38.

Schachter, S., Nuttin, J., de Monchaux, C., Maucorps, D.H., Osmer, D., Duijker, J., Rommetveit, R. and Israel, J. (1954) Cross-cultural experiments on threat and rejection. *Human Relations*, 7, 403–39.

Schlenker, B.R. (1975) Liking for a group following an initiation: impression management or dissonance reduction. *Sociometry*, 38, 99-118.

Schofield, J.W. (1986) Black-White contact in desegregated schools, in Hewstone, M.R.C. and Brown, R.J. (eds) *Contact and Conflict in Intergroup Encounters*. Oxford: Blackwell.

Scott, W.A. and Scott, R. (1981) Intercorrelations among structural properties of primary groups. *Journal of Personality and Social Psychology*, 41, 279-92.

Semin, G. and Glendon, A.I. (1973) Polarization and the established group. *British Journal of Social and Clinical Psychology*, 12, 113-21.

Shaw, Marjorie E. (1932) A comparison of individuals and small groups in the rational solution of complex problems. *American Journal of Psychology*, 44, 491-504.

Shaw, Marvin E. (1964) Communication networks, in Berkowitz, L. (ed.) *Advances in Experimental Social Psychology*, vol. 1. New York: Academic Press.

Shaw, Marvin E. (1976) *Group Dynamics*, 2nd edn. New York: McGraw Hill.

Shaw, Marvin E. and Ashton, N. (1976) Do assembly bonus effects occur on disjunctive tasks? A test of Steiner's theory. *Bulletin of the Psychonomic Society*, 8, 469-71.

Sherif, C.W. (1971) Review of 'Personality and Interpersonal Behaviour'. *American Sociological Review*, 36, 115-19.

Sherif, C.W., Kelly, M., Rodgers, H.L., Sarup, G. and Tittler, B.I. (1973) Personal involvement, social judgement and action. *Journal of Personality and Social Psychology*, 27, 311-28.

Sherif, M. (1936) *The Psychology of Social Norms*. New York: Harper and Row.

Sherif, M. (1966) *Group Conflict and Cooperation*. London: Routledge and Kegan Paul. Originally published as *In Common Predicament*. Boston, Mass.: Houghton Miffin.

Sherif, M., Harvey, O.J., White, B.J., Hood, W.R. and Sherif, C.W. (1961) *Intergroup Conflict and Cooperation. The Robber's Cave Experiment*. Norman: University of Oklahoma.

Sherif, M. and Sherif, C.W. (1953) *Groups in Harmony and Tension: an Integration of Studies on Intergroup Relations*. New York: Octagon Books.

Sherif, M. and Sherif, C.W. (1964) *Reference Groups*. New York: Harper and Row.

Sherif, M. and Sherif, C.W. (1967) The adolescent in his group in its setting, in Sherif, M. (ed.) *Social Interaction*. Chicago: Aldine.

Sherif, M. and Sherif, C.W. (1969) *Social Psychology*. New York: Harper and Row.

Sherif, M., White, B.J. and Harvey, O.J. (1955) Status in experimentally produced groups. *American Journal of Sociology*, 60, 370-9.

Shouval, R., Venaki, S., Bronfenbrenner, U., Devreux, E.C. and Kiely, E. (1975) Anomalous reactions to social pressure of Israeli and Soviet children raised in family versus collective settings. *Journal of Personality and Social Psychology*, 32, 477–89.

Siegel, A. E. and Siegel, S. (1957) Reference groups, membership groups, and attitude change. *Journal of Abnormal and Social Psychology*, 55, 360–4.

Simon, B. and Brown, R. J. (1987) Perceived intragroup homogeneity in minority–majority contexts. *Journal of Personality and Social Psychology*, 53, 703–11.

Simonton, D. K. (1980) Land battles, generals and armies: individual and situational determinants of victory and casualties. *Journal of Personality and Social Psychology*, 38, 110–19.

Singh, R., Bohra, K. A. and Dalal, A. K. (1979) Favourableness of leadership situations studies with information integration theory. *European Journal of Social Psychology*, 9, 253–64.

Skevington, S. (1981) Intergroup relations and nursing. *European Journal of Social Psychology*, 11, 43–59.

Slater, P. E. (1955) Role differentiation in small groups. *American Sociological Review*, 20, 300–10.

Slater, P. E. (1961) Parental role differentiation. *American Journal of Sociology*, 67, 296–311.

Slavin, R. E. (1983) When does cooperative learning increase student achievement? *Psychological Bulletin*, 94, 429–45.

Slavin, R. E. (1985) Cooperative learning: applying contact theory in desegregated schools. *Journal of Social Issues*, 41, 45–62.

Sorrentino, R. M. and Field, N. (1986) Emergent leadership over time: the functional value of positive motivation. *Journal of Personality and Social Psychology*, 50, 1091–9.

Sorrentino, R. M., King, G. and Leo, G. (1980) The influence of the minority on perception: a note on a possible alternative explanation. *Journal of Experimental Social Psychology*, 16, 293–301.

Spence, J. T. and Helmreich, R. L. (1978) *Masculinity and Femininity: their Psychological Dimensions, Correlates and Antecedents*. Austin and London: University of Texas Press.

Stagner, R. and Congdon, C. S. (1955) Another failure to demonstrate displacement of aggression. *Journal of Abnormal and Social Psychology*, 51, 695–6.

Stagner, R. and Eflal, B. (1982) Internal union dynamics during a strike: a quasi-experimental study. *Journal of Applied Psychology*, 67, 37–44.

Stasser, G., Kerr, N. and Davis, J. H. (1980) Influence processes in decision making groups: a modeling approach, in Paulus, P. (ed.) *Psychology of Group Influence*. Hillsdale, NJ: Lawrence Erlbaum.

Stein, D. D., Hardyck, J. A. and Smith, M. B. (1965) Race and belief: an open and shut case. *Journal of Personality and Social Psychology*, 1, 281–9.

Steiner, I. D. (1972) *Group Process and Productivity*. New York: Academic Press.

Steiner, I. D. (1974) Whatever happened to the group in social psychology? *Journal of Experimental Social Psychology*, 10, 94–108.

Steiner, I.D. (1982) Heuristic models of groupthink, in Brandstätter, H., Davis, J.H. and Stocher-Kreichganer, G. (eds) *Contemporary Problems in Group Decision Making*. New York: Academic Press.

Steiner, I.D. (1986) Paradigms and groups, in Berkowitz, L. (ed.) *Advances in Experimental Social Psychology*, vol. 19. London: Academic Press.

Stephan, W.G. (1977) Cognitive differentiation in intergroup perception. *Sociometry*, 40, 50-8.

Stephan, W.G. and Rosenfield, D. (1978) Effects of desegregation on racial attitudes. *Journal of Personality and Social Psychology*, 36, 795-804.

Stephan, W.G. and Stephan, C.W. (1984) The role of ignorance in intergroup relations, in Miller, N. and Brewer, M.B. (eds) *Groups in Contact: the Psychology of Desegregation*. New York: Academic Press.

Stephenson, G.M., Brandstätter, H. and Wagner, W. (1983) An experimental study of social performance and delay on the testimonial validity of story recall. *European Journal of Social Psychology*, 13, 175-91.

Stephenson, G.M. and Brotherton, C.J. (1975) Social progression and polarization: a study of discussion and negotiation in groups of mining supervisors. *British Journal of Social and Clinical Psychology*, 14, 241-52.

Stephenson, G.M., Clark, N.K. and Wade, G.S. (1986) Meetings make evidence? An experimental study of collaborative and individual recall of a simulated police interrogation. *Journal of Personality and Social Psychology*, 50, 1113-1122.

Stevens, S.S. (1957) On the psychophysical law. *Psychological Review*, 64, 153-81.

Stiles, W.B. (1980) Comparison of dimensions derived from rating versus coding of dialogue. *Journal of Personality and Social Psychology*, 38, 359-74.

Stogdill, R.M. (1974) *Handbook of Leadership*. New York: The Free Press.

Stoner, J.A.F. (1961) A comparison of individual and group decisions including risk. Unpublished thesis, Massachusetts Institute of Technology, School of Management.

Stoner, J.A.F. (1968) Risky and cautious shifts in group decisions: the influence of widely held values. *Journal of Experimental Social Psychology*, 4, 442-59.

Strube, M.J. and Garcia, J.E. (1981) A meta-analytic investigation of Fiedler's contingency model of leadership effectiveness. *Psychological Bulletin*, 90, 307-21.

Suls, J. and Miller, R.L. (eds) (1977) *Social Comparison Processes: Theoretical and Empirical Perspectives*. Washington: Hemisphere.

Summer, W.G. (1906) *Folkways*. New York: Ginn.

Tajfel, H. (1959) The anchoring effects of value in a scale of judgements. *British Journal of Psychology*, 50, 294-304.

Tajfel, H. (1972) Experiments in a vacuum, in Israel, J. and Tajfel, H. (eds) *The Context of Social Psychology*. London: Academic Press.

Tajfel, H. (ed.) (1978a) *Differentiation between Social Groups: Studies in the Social Psychology of Intergroup Relations*. London: Academic Press.

Tajfel, H. (1978b) Intergroup behaviour: I. Individualistic perspectives, in Tajfel, H. and Fraser, C. (eds) *Introducing Social Psychology*. Harmondsworth: Penguin.

Tajfel, H. (1979) Individuals and groups in social psychology. *British Journal of Social and Clinical Psychology*, 18, 183–90.

Tajfel, H. (1981) *Human Groups and Social Categories*. Cambridge: Cambridge University Press.

Tajfel, H. (ed.) (1982a) *Social Identity and Intergroup Relations*. Cambridge: Cambridge University Press.

Tajfel, H. (1982b) Social psychology of intergroup relations. *Annual Review of Psychology*, 33, 1–30.

Tajfel, H., Flament, C., Billig, M.G. and Bundy, R.P. (1971) Social categorization and intergroup behaviour. *European Journal of Social Psychology*, 1, 149–78.

Tajfel, H. and Turner, J.C. (1979) An integrative theory of social conflict, reprinted in Austin, W. and Worchel, S. (eds) *The Social Psychology of Intergroup Relations*, 2nd edn, 1985. Chicago: Nelson Hall.

Tajfel, H. and Wilkes, A.L. (1963) Classification and quantitative judgement. *British Journal of Psychology*, 54, 101–14.

Tanford, S. and Penrod, S. (1984) Social influence model: a formal integration of research on majority and minority influence processes. *Psychological Bulletin*, 95, 189–225.

Tanter, R. (1966) Dimension of conflict behaviour within and between nations, 1958–1960. *Journal of Conflict Resolution*, 10, 41–64.

Tanter, R. (1969) International war and domestic turmoil: some contemporary evidence, in Graham, H.D. and Gurr, T.R. (eds) *Violence in America*. New York: Bantam Books.

Taylor, D.M. and Brown, R.J. (1979) Towards a more social social psychology? *British Journal of Social and Clinical Psychology*, 18, 173–80.

Taylor, D.M., Doria, J. and Tyler, J.K. (1983) Group performance and cohesiveness: an attributional analysis. *Journal of Social Psychology*, 119, 187–98.

Taylor, D.M. and Guimond, S. (1978) The belief theory of prejudice in an intergroup context. *Journal of Social Psychology*, 105, 11–25.

Taylor, D.M. and Jaggi, V. (1974) Ethnocentrism and causal attribution in a South Indian context. *Journal of Cross-Cultural Psychology*, 5, 162–71.

Taylor, D.W., Berry, P.C. and Block, C.H. (1958) Does group participation when using brainstorming facilitate or inhibit creative thinking? *Administrative Science Quarterly*, 3, 23–47.

Taylor, D.W. and Faust, W.I. (1952) Twenty questions: efficiency in problem solving as a function of size of group. *Journal of Experimental Psychology*, 44, 360–8.

Taylor, M.C. (1982) Improved conditions, rising expectations, and dissatisfaction: a test of the past/present relative deprivation hypothesis. *Social Psychology Quarterly*, 45, 24–33.

Taylor, S.E. (1981) A categorization approach for stereotyping, in Hamilton, D.L. (ed.) *Cognitive Processes in Stereotyping and Intergroup Behaviour*. New York: Lawrence Erlbaum.

Taylor, S.E., Fiske, S.T., Etcoff, N.L. and Ruderman, A.J. (1978) Categorical and contextual bases of person memory and stereotyping. *Journal of Personality and Social Psychology*, 36, 778-93.

Teger, A.I. and Pruitt, D.G. (1967) Components of group risk taking. *Journal of Experimental Social Psychology*, 3, 189-205.

Tetlock, P.E. (1981) Personality and isolationism: context analysis of senatorial speeches. *Journal of Personality and Social Psychology*, 41, 737-43.

Tetlock, P.E. (1983) Cognitive style and political ideology. *Journal of Personality and Social Psychology*, 45, 118-26.

Tetlock, P.E. (1984) Cognitive style and political belief systems in the British House of Commons. *Journal of Personality and Social Psychology*, 46, 365-75.

Tetlock, P.E., Hannum, K.A. and Micheletti, P.M. (1984) Stability and change in the complexity of senatorial debate: testing the cognitive versus rhetorical style hypothesis. *Journal of Personality and Social Psychology*, 46, 979-90.

Titus, H.E. and Hollander, E.P. (1957) The California F scale in psychological research (1950-1955). *Psychological Bulletin*, 54, 47-74.

Tolstoy, L. (1986) *War and Peace*. Harmondsworth: Penguin.

Trew, K. (1981a) A sense of national identity: fact or artefact? *Irish Journal of Psychology*, 6, no. 1, 28-36.

Trew, K. (1981b) Group identification in a divided society, in Harbinson, J. (ed.) *Children of the Troubles: Children in Northern Ireland*. Belfast: Stranmillis College.

Trew, K. (1986) Catholic-Protestant contact in Northern Ireland, in Hewstone, M.R.C. and Brown, R.J. (eds) *Contact and Conflict in Intergroup Encounters*. Oxford: Blackwell.

Triandis, H.C., and Davis, E.G. (1965) Race and belief as shared determinants of behaviour intentions. *Journal of Personality and Social Psychology*, 2, 715-25.

Triplett, N. (1898) The dynamogenic factors in pacemaking and competition. *American Journal of Psychology*, 9, 507-33.

Turner, J.C. (1980) Fairness or discrimination in intergroup behaviour? A reply to Branthwaite, Doyle and Lightbown. *European Journal of Social Psychology*, 10, 131-47.

Turner, J.C. (1981a) The experimental social psychology of intergroup behaviour, in Turner, J.C. and Giles, H. (eds) *Intergroup Behaviour*. Oxford: Blackwell.

Turner, J.C. (1981b) Some considerations in generalizing experimental social psychology, in Stephenson, G.M. and Davis, J. (eds) *Progress in Applied Social Psychology*, vol. 1. Chichester: Wiley.

Turner, J.C. (1982) Towards a cognitive redefinition of the social group, in

Tajfel, H. (ed.) *Social Identity and Intergroup Relations*. Cambridge: Cambridge University Press.

Turner, J.C. (1983a) Some comments on . . . 'the measurement of social orientations in the minimal group paradigm'. *European Journal of Social Psychology*, 13, 351–67.

Turner, J.C. (1983b) A second reply to Bornstein, Crum, Wittenbraker, Harring, Insko and Thibaut on the measurement of social orientations. *European Journal of Social Psychology*, 13, 383–7.

Turner, J.C. (1987) The analysis of social influence, in Turner, J.C., Hogg, M.A., Oakes, P.J., Reicher, S.D. and Wetherell, M.S. *Rediscovering the Social Group: a Self-Categorization Theory*. Oxford: Blackwell.

Turner, J.C. and Brown, R.J. (1978) Social status, cognitive alternatives, and intergroup relations, in Tajfel, H. (ed.) *Differentiation between Social Groups: Studies in the Social Psychology of Intergroup Relations*. London: Academic Press.

Turner, J.C. and Giles, H. (eds) (1981) *Intergroup Behaviour*. Oxford: Blackwell.

Turner, J.C., Hogg, M.A., Oakes, P.J., Reicher, S.D. and Wetherell, M.S. (1987) *Rediscovering the Social Group: a Self-categorization Theory*. Oxford: Blackwell.

Turner, J.C., Hogg, M.A., Turner, P.J. and Smith, P.M. (1984) Failure and defeat as determinants of group cohesiveness. *British Journal of Social Psychology*, 23, 97–111.

Turner, R.H. and Killian, L. (1957) *Collective Behaviour*. Englewood Cliffs, NJ: Prentice Hall.

United Kingdom Central Council for Nursing, Midwifery and Health Visiting (1984) *Code of Professional Conduct*, 2nd edn. London: UKCC.

Vanbeselaere, N. (1987) The effects of dichotomous and crossed social categorizations upon intergroup discrimination. *European Journal of Social Psychology*, 17, 143–56.

van Gennep, A. (1960) *The Rites of Passage*. Chicago: University of Chicago Press.

van Knippenberg, A.F.M. (1984) Intergroup differences in group perceptions, in Tajfel, H. (ed.) *The Social Dimension*. London: Cambridge University Press.

van Knippenberg, A. and van Oers, H. (1984) Social identity and equity concerns in intergroup perceptions. *British Journal of Social Psychology*, 23, 351–61.

van Maanen, J. (1976) Breaking in: socialization to work, in Dubin, R. (ed.) *Handbook of Work, Organization and Society*. Chicago: Rand McNally.

Vanneman, R.D. and Pettigrew, T.F. (1972) Race and relative deprivation in the urban United States. *Race*, 13, 461–86.

van Sell, M., Brief, A.P. and Schuler, R.S. (1981) Role conflict and role ambiguity: integration of the literature and directions for future research. *Human Relations*, 34, 43–71.

Vaughan, G.M. (1964) Ethnic awareness in relation to minority-group membership. *Journal of Genetic Psychology*, 105, 119-30.

Vaughan, G.M. (1978) Social change and intergroup preferences in New Zealand. *European Journal of Social Psychology*, 8, 297-314.

Vaught, C. and Smith, D.L. (1980) Incorporation and mechanical solidarity in an underground coal mine. *Sociology of Work and Occupations*, 7, 159-87.

Vecchio, R.P. (1983) Assessing the validity of Fiedler's contingency model of leadership effectiveness: a closer look at Strube and Garcia. *Psychological Bulletin*, 93, 404-8.

Vinokur, A. and Burnstein, E. (1974) Effects of partially shared persuasive arguments on group-induced shifts: a group problem solving approach. *Journal of Personality and Social Psychology*, 29, 305-15.

Vinokur, A., Burnstein, E., Sechrest, L. and Wortman, P.M. (1985) Group decision making by experts: field study of panels evaluating medical technologies. *Journal of Personality and Social Psychology*, 49, 70-84.

Walker, I. and Mann, L. (1987) Unemployment, relative deprivation, and social protest. *Personality and Social Psychology Bulletin*, 13, 275-83.

Walker, I. and Pettigrew, T.F. (1984) Relative deprivation theory: an overview and conceptual critique. *British Journal of Social Psychology*, 23, 301-10.

Walker, T.G. and Main, E.C. (1973) Choice shifts in political decision making: federal judges and civil liberties cases. *Journal of Applied Social Psychology*, 3, 39-48.

Wallach, M.A., Kogan, N. and Bem, D.J. (1962) Group influence on individual risk taking. *Journal of Abnormal and Social Psychology*, 65, 75-86.

Watson, R.I. (1973) Investigation in deindividuation using a cross-cultural survey technique. *Journal of Personality and Social Psychology*, 25, 342-5.

Waxler, N.E. and Mishler, E.G. (1970) Experimental studies of families, in Berkowitz, L. (ed.) *Advances in Experimental Social Psychology*, vol. 5. New York: Academic Press.

Weber, R. and Crocker, J. (1983) Cognitive processes in the revision of stereotypic beliefs. *Journal of Personality and Social Psychology*, 45, 961-77.

Welsh Campaign for Civil Liberties (1984) *Striking Back*. Cardiff: Welsh Campaign for Civil Liberties.

Wetherell, M. (1982) Cross-cultural studies of minimal groups: implications for the social identity theory of intergroup relations, in Tajfel, H. (ed.) *Social Identity and Intergroup Relations*. Cambridge: Cambridge University Press.

Wetherell, M. (1987) Social identity and group polarization, in Turner, J.C., Hogg, M.A., Oakes, P.J., Reicher, S.D. and Wetherell, M.S. *Rediscovering the Social Group: a Self-Categorization Theory*. Oxford: Blackwell.

Wheeler, L. (1966) Motivation as a determinant of upward comparison. *Journal of Experimental Social Psychology*, 1, 27-31.

Wheeler, L., Koestner, R. and Diver, R.E. (1982) Related attributes in the choice of comparison others: it's there, but it isn't all there is. *Journal of Experimental Social Psychology*, 18, 489-500.

Wheeler, L., Shaver, K.G., Jones, R.A., Goethals, G.R. and Cooper, J. (1969) Factors determining choice of a comparison other. *Journal of Experimental Social Psychology*, 5, 219-32.

Whyte, W.F. (1943) *Street Corner Society*, 2nd edn. Chicago: University of Chicago Press.

Whyte, W.H. (1956) *The Organisation Man*. New York: Simon and Schuster.

Wilder, D.A. (1984a) Predictions of belief homogeneity and similarity following social categorization. *British Journal of Social Psychology*, 23, 323-33.

Wilder, D.A. (1984b) Intergroup contact: the typical member and the exception to the rule. *Journal of Experimental Social Psychology*, 20, 177-94.

Wilder, D.A. (1986) Social categorization: implications for creation and reduction of intergroup bias, in Berkowitz, L. (ed.) *Advances in Experimental Social Psychology*, vol. 19. New York: Academic Press.

Wolf, S. (1979) Behavioural style and group cohesiveness as sources of minority influence. *European Journal of Social Psychology*, 9, 381-95.

Wolf, S. (1985) Manifest and latent influence of majorities and minorities. *Journal of Personality and Social Psychology*, 48, 899-908.

Worchel, S. (1979) Intergroup cooperation, in Austin, W. and Worchel, S. (eds) *The Social Psychology of Intergroup Relations*. Monterey: Brooks/Cole.

Worchel, S., Andreoli, V.A. and Folger, R. (1977) Intergroup cooperation and intergroup attraction: the effect of previous interaction and outcome of combined effort. *Journal of Experimental Social Psychology*, 13, 131-40.

Worchel, S. and Austin, W. (eds) (1985) *The Social Psychology of Intergroup Relations*, 2nd edn. Chicago: Nelson Hall.

Worchel, S., Lind, E.A. and Kaufman, K.H. (1975) Evaluations of group products as a function of expectations of group longevity, outcome of competition and publicity of evaluations. *Journal of Personality and Social Psychology*, 31, 1089-97.

Worchel, S. and Norvell, N. (1980) Effect of perceived environmental conditions during cooperation on intergroup attraction. *Journal of Personality and Social Psychology*, 38, 764-72.

Yuker, H.E. (1955) Group atmosphere and memory. *Journal of Abnormal Social Psychology*, 51, 17-23.

Zajonc, R.B. (1980) Compresence, in Paulus, P.B. (ed.) *Psychology of Group Influence*. New York: Lawrence Erlbaum.

Zander, A. (1972) The purposes of national associations. *Journal of Voluntary Associations*, 1, 20-9.

Zander, A., Stotland, E. and Wolfe, D. (1960) Unity of group, identification with group, and self esteem of members. *Journal of Personality*, 28, 463-78.

Zanna, M.P., Goethals, G.R. and Hill, J.F. (1975) Evaluating a sex related ability: social comparison with similar others and standard setters. *Journal of Experimental Social Psychology*, 11, 86–93.

Zelditch, M. (1956) Role differentiation in the nuclear family, in Parsons, T. and Bales, R.F. (eds) *Family: Socialization and Interaction Process.* Glencoe: Free Press.

Zimbardo, P. (1969) The human choice: individuation, reason and order versus deindividuation, impulse and chaos, in Arnold, W.J. and Levine, D. (eds) *Nebraska Symposium on Motivation*, vol. 17. Lincoln: University of Nebraska Press.

Name Index

Subject Index